John Singleton Copley in England

John Singleton Copley in England

EMILY BALLEW NEFF

with an essay by
WILLIAM L. PRESSLY

MERRELL HOLBERTON
PUBLISHERS LONDON

Published on the occasion of the exhibition *John Singleton Copley in England*,
organized by the National Gallery of Art, Washington, D.C.
and the Museum of Fine Arts, Houston

The exhibition is made possible in Washington by
Republic National Bank of New York, Safra Republic Holdings, S.A.,
and Banco Safra, S.A., Brazil.

In Houston, funding has been provided by the
National Endowment for the Arts, a federal agency.

This exhibition is supported by an indemnity loan from the
Federal Council on the Arts and the Humanities.

National Gallery of Art
Washington, D.C.
October 11, 1995–January 7, 1996

The Museum of Fine Arts, Houston
Houston, Texas
February 4– April 28, 1996

First published in 1995 by Merrell Holberton Publishers Ltd,
Axe and Bottle Court, 70 Newcomen Street, London SE1 1YT

ISBN 0 89090 070 1 (paperback)
ISBN 1 85894 023 0 (hardback)

Produced by Merrell Holberton Publishers Ltd in association with
The Museum of Fine Arts, Houston

Designed by Roger Davies
Typeset in Monotype Baskerville by SX Composing, Rayleigh, England
Printed and bound by Graphicom, Vicenza, Italy

Front and back of jacket
Details of cat. 18, *The Death of Major Peirson*
Half title
Cat. 17, *John Singleton Copley*
Frontispiece
Detail of cat. 1, *The Copley Family*

Photographic materials

Photographic materials have been graciously supplied by the owners of works
except as listed here: fig. 7: courtesy of the Library, National Gallery of Art,
Washington, D.C.; fig. 23: Art Resource, NY; fig. 30: courtesy of Courtauld Institute
of Art, London; fig. 63: Alinari/Art Resource, NY; fig. 72: photograph by Hickey &
Robertson; infrared reflectogram (cat. 9): John Twilley, Los Angeles County

Contents

Directors' Foreword

"As Copley walks up the gangplank of a square-rigged ship in June, 1774, our curtain falls behind him, bringing to an end the first act of American art," wrote James Thomas Flexner nearly fifty years ago. The dean of historians of American art was not the first to see Copley's departure for England and the Continent on the eve of Revolution as a turning point in our nation's cultural past; but his assessment of Copley's English career as a diminished, decadent finish to the splendid promise of the painter's years in the American colonies is one that has abided in scholarship and in public opinion to the present day.

To reassess Copley's work in England, to see it fairly and on its own terms, is the goal of this exhibition. Planned to coincide with the extraordinary exhibition *John Singleton Copley in America*, organized by our colleagues at the Metropolitan Museum of Art and the Museum of Fine Arts, Boston, *John Singleton Copley in England* brings together forty paintings and drawings, many of which have not been seen in the United States in more than a generation. We thus hope to measure the genius and the ambition of Copley, our first great painter, in the last half of his career.

It is appropriate that this exhibition should premiere at the National Gallery of Art, which holds the greatest collection of Copley's English paintings. Copley scholar Emily Ballew Neff, Assistant Curator of American Painting and Sculpture at the Museum of Fine Arts, Houston, has organized the exhibition in cooperation with Nicolai Cikovsky and Franklin W. Kelly, Curators of American and British Paintings at the National Gallery of Art, with the participation of George T. M. Shackelford, Houston's Curator of European Painting and Sculpture. We are grateful to them and to the staffs of our institutions for bringing this project to such a handsome conclusion. We would also like cite the important contributions that Professor William L. Pressly and Dr. Ellen G. Miles have made to the exhibition's catalogue.

The National Gallery offers special thanks to Republic National Bank of New York, Safra Republic Holdings, S.A., Banco Safra, Brazil, and Walter H. Welner, Chairman of Republic National Bank of New York, for so generously supporting the exhibition in Washington. *John Singleton Copley in England* marks Republic National Bank's seventh sponsorship at the National Gallery. The Museum of Fine Arts, Houston gratefully acknowledges the support of the National Endowment for the Arts. The exhibiting institutions would also like to thank the Federal Council on the Arts and the Humanities, which has supported the exhibition through an indemnity.

Above all, we are grateful to the museums and collectors in the United States and Great Britain who have agreed to lend their paintings and drawings to this historic exhibition. In particular, we owe a great debt to the Tate Gallery, London, and its director, Nick Serota, who agreed to send Copley's English masterpiece, *The Death of Major Peirson*, to our shores once again, so that American audiences might fully appreciate the brilliance of John Singleton Copley in England.

Earl A. Powell III
Director
NATIONAL GALLERY OF ART

Peter C. Marzio
Director
THE MUSEUM OF FINE ARTS,
HOUSTON

Lenders to the Exhibition

(Alphabetical by institution)

Addison Gallery of American Art, Phillips Academy, Andover, Massachusetts

Museum of Fine Arts, Boston

Courtauld Institute Galleries, London

The Detroit Institute of Arts

Fogg Art Museum, Harvard University Art Museums

Hirschl & Adler Galleries, New York

Henry E. Huntington Library and Art Gallery

Los Angeles County Museum of Art

Mead Art Museum, Amherst College

The Metropolitan Museum of Art

National Gallery of Art, Washington

National Maritime Museum, Greenwich

National Portrait Gallery, Smithsonian Institution, Washington, D.C.

North Carolina Museum of Art

The Art Museum, Princeton University

Royal Academy of Arts, London

The Royal Collection, Her Majesty Queen Elizabeth II

Tate Gallery, London

Wadsworth Atheneum, Hartford, Connecticut

Yale Center for British Art

Yale University Art Gallery

Acknowledgments

When John Singleton Copley arrived in London during the summer of 1774, he expressed pleasant surprise to "find so much Civility in this place." During the course of my research on Copley over the past several years, I have found myself in similar congenial circumstances, and I wish to recognize the many generous people who have helped to make the realization of this project possible.

Earl A. Powell III, Director of the National Gallery of Art, enthusiastically supported this project from the very beginning. For his encouragement, unfailing support, and sage advice at every stage of the project, I thank Peter C. Marzio, Director of the Museum of Fine Arts, Houston. At the museum, I have been blessed to have George T.M. Shackelford, Curator of European Painting and Sculpture, as my mentor, critical advisor, and, not least, friend, for which – in each and every capacity – I am grateful beyond words. It has also been a great pleasure to work with (and learn from) my senior curatorial colleagues at the National Gallery: Nicolai Cikovsky, Jr., Curator of American and British Paintings and Deputy Senior Curator; and Franklin Kelly, Curator of American and British Paintings. Bill Pressly deserves special thanks for his thoughtful essay, as does Ellen G. Miles for her catalogue entry on Copley's s *Watson and the Shark*. Ellen also generously shared her comprehensive entries on the National Gallery's collection of Copley paintings for its systematic catalogue.

For the generous loan of their works of art, and for their patience in answering numerous requests during the preparation of the catalogue, I wish to thank Jock Reynolds and Susan Faxon at the Addison Gallery of American Art, Phillips Academy, Andover, Massachusetts; Malcolm Rogers, Theodore E. Stebbins, Jr., Carol Troyen, Erica E. Hirshler, Janet Comey, Clifford Ackley, Sue Reed, Barbara Shapiro, Jim Wright, Roy Perkinson, Rhona MacBeth, Alison Luxner and Mary Sluskonis at the Museum of Fine Arts, Boston; John Murdoch and David Solkin at the Courtauld Institute Galleries, London; Samuel Sachs II, Nancy Rivard Shaw, Jim Tottis, and Ryan Wieber, at the Detroit Institute of Arts; James Cuno, Ivan Gaskell, and Timothy Burgard at the Fogg Art Museum, Harvard University Art Museums; Stuart Feld, Debra Wieder, and Susan Filosa at Hirschl & Adler Galleries, New York; Edward Nygren, Shelley Bennett, and Amy Meyers, Henry E. Huntington Library and Art Gallery; Ronald Bratton, Ilene Susan Fort, Joe Fronek, Shelley Svoboda, and John Twilley at the Los Angeles County Museum of Art; Martha A. Sandweiss at the Mead Art Museum, Amherst College; Philippe de Montebello, John K. Howat, Peter M. Kenny, Carrie Rebora, and Dorothy Mahon at the Metropolitan Museum of Art, New York; Richard Ormond, Sarah McCormick, Mrs. P.M. Plackett Barber at the National Maritime Museum, Greenwich; Alan Fern, Ellen G. Miles, and Claire Kelly at the National Portrait Gallery, Smithsonian Institution, Washington, D.C.; Lawrence Wheeler, John Coffey, and David Steel at the North Carolina Museum of Art; Allen Rosenbaum and Maureen McCormick at The Art Museum, Princeton University; Sir Philip Dowson, Helen Valentine, and Patricia Eaton at the Royal Academy of Arts, London; Christopher Lloyd, Charles Noble, and The Honourable Cazzy Neville at The Royal Collection of Her Majesty Queen Elizabeth II; Nicholas Serota, Andrew Wilton, Elizabeth Einberg, Robin Hamlyn, Viscount Alexander Dunluce, Ruth Rattenbury, and Carlotta Gelmetti at the Tate Gallery, London; Patrick McCaughey, Elizabeth M. Kornhauser, and Gene Gaddis at the Wadsworth Atheneum, Hartford, Connecticut; Duncan Robinson, Susan Casteras, Kim Kneeland, Jean Winthrop Buck, and Jane D. Crowley at the Yale Center for British Art; and Susan M. Vogel, Helen Cooper, Richard Field, and Robin J. Frank at the Yale University Art Gallery.

Any sensitive reader of this catalogue will recognize (through repeated citations) the enormous debt I owe to Jules David Prown, whose 1966 catalogue raisonné on Copley remains a model for the field. I sincerely thank and salute my 'doktormutter', Susan Rather at the University of Texas at Austin, for providing the best kind of criticism, enthusiasm, and encouragement. The Metropolitan Museum of Art provided financial and intellectual support through, first, a graduate internship, followed by a Jane and Morgan Whitney fellowship in the American Wing. To John K. Howat, H. Barbara Weinberg, and

Carrie Rebora in American Art, and to Marian Burleigh-Motley in the Education Department, I am truly grateful. I especially thank Carrie, who generously shared her copies of Copley letters from the Public Records Office, London, and Paul Staiti, former senior fellow in the American Wing. Diane Dillon at Rice University has been unfailingly generous with sound advice and thoughtful criticism. I also have benefited enormously from the following curators, professors, collectors, librarians, dealers, and individuals: Brian Allen, Jeffrey Barnouw, Doreen Bolger, Patricia C. Burnham, John Clarke, Martin Clayton, Helen Dorey, Joan Dormer, Peter Drummey, Stephen Gallagher, Ira Gruber, John Ingamells, Vivien Knight, Angela Miller, Barbara Milner, Tim Moreton, Theresa-Mary Morton, David Posnett, Pierre Rosenberg, M. Xavier Salmon, Richard Saunders, Richard Shiff, Sir Reresby and Lady Sitwell, Virginia H. Smith, The Earl Spencer, Celia Stern, Jan van der Wateren, Janice Williams, Clara Young, and Kai-Kin Young.

The National Gallery, Washington, D.C., graciously offered to take the administrative lead and assumed the monumental task of coordinating loans. Charles Brock, Exhibitions Assistant, American and British Paintings, in particular, cheerfully handled a number of queries, for which I sincerely thank him. In the Exhibitions Department, I have been greatly aided by Dodge Thompson, Ann B. Robertson, and Jennifer Fletcher, and, in Exhibition Programs, Susan Arensberg and Isabelle Dervaux. Sally Freitag and Michelle Fondas ably handled registrarial affairs. Gaillard Ravenel, Mark Leithauser, Gordon Anson, and Barbara Keyes are responsible for the exhibition's sensitive design. I also thank Marilyn Tebor Shaw, Elizabeth A.C. Perry, and Nancy Yeide, and I owe a special debt of gratitude to Gregory P.J. Most.

At the Museum of Fine Arts, Houston, I am indebted to A. Thereza Crowe for her expert research and organizational skills, and to G. Clifford Edwards, curatorial secretary. I thank Ann Coleman, who contributed her costume expertise, and other curatorial colleagues. Special thanks go to Gwendolyn H. Goffe, David Warren, Frances Marzio, Margaret C. Skidmore, Beth B. Schneider, Alison Eckman, Diane Lovejoy, and Barbara Michels. Jack Eby expertly designed the exhibition in Houston, and Hope Namken headed the Graphics team. Karen Bremer Vetter, Charles Carroll, Tommy Chingos, and Kathleen Crain, and the efficient preparations staff handled administrative and registrarial affairs at the Houston venue. Others who deserve a special note of thanks are: Thomas R. DuBrock, Marcia K. Stein, Tracy Stephenson, Jeannette Dixon, Virginia McFarland, and Jacqui Allen, Margaret Ford, and the Hirsch Library staff, Michael Brown, Kathleen O'Connor, Wynne Phelan, Harlow Tighe, Margaret Mims, and Lisa Reed.

Several interns and docent staff cheerfully and expertly handled various aspects of catalogue research and of checking citations. Special thanks go to Jenny Mayfield Carson, Laura K. Griffis, Eleanor R. Hero, Janet Anderson, Lois Brazda, Marie Blain, Jeanne Cunningham, Martha Erwin, France Heyne, Kate Kirkland, Polly La Duc, and Cecilia Mazzola.

Finally, but not least, I am grateful to Christine Waller Manca for her skillful editing and good humor, and to Hugh Merrell and Paul Holberton of Merrell Holberton Publishers and to Roger Davies for the the sensitive editing and handsome design of the catalogue, and, of course, for their patience. For the work that I have done on this catalogue and exhibition, I dedicate to my loving parents and family.

Emily Ballew Neff
Assistant Curator, American Painting and Sculpture
THE MUSEUM OF FINE ARTS, HOUSTON

Introduction

*Copley's
"Native" Realism
and his English
"Improvement"*

EMILY BALLEW NEFF

John Singleton Copley (1738–1815), through his portrayals of such American icons as Paul Revere (fig. 1), John Adams, and John Hancock, captured an image of the pre-Revolutionary period in American history that has endured to this day. It is recognized, too, that after he had moved from the American colonies to England in 1774, he made significant contributions in the field of contemporary history painting, fashioning himself as an impresario of the popular spectacle and reorienting this genre. However, it is above all the convincing realism of his colonial portraits that subsequent historians have appreciated – his attention to the minutiae of patterned lace, his polished wood and metal surfaces, brilliant fabrics, and lustrous pearls, rendered with the precision of a master carver, tailor, or jeweller (fig. 2). In Copley's complaint of *ca.* 1767, that the colonists considered painting like "any other usefull trade ... like that of a Carpenter tailor or shew maker, not as one of the most noble Arts in the World,"[1] there is more than a little irony, for Copley's American portraits completely disguised the hand of the

Fig. 1 John Singleton Copley
Paul Revere, 1768
Oil on canvas, 35 × 28½ in. (88.9 × 72.3 cm)
Museum of Fine Arts, Boston, Gift of Joseph W. Revere,
William B. Revere, and Edward H.R. Revere,

1. Copley to Benjamin West or Captain R.G. Bruce(?), 1767(?), in *Letters of Copley and Pelham* 1914/1972, pp. 65–6.

Fig. 2 John Singleton Copley
Mrs. George Watson, 1765

Oil on canvas, 50 × 40 in. (127 × 101.6 cm)
National Museum of American Art, partial gift of
Henderson Inches, Jr., in honor of his parents, Mr. and
Mrs. Inches, and museum purchase (made possible in part
by Mr. and Mrs. R. Crosby Kemper through the Crosby
Kemper Foundations; the American Art Forum; and the
Luisita L. and Franz H. Denghausen Endowment

artist, as if their elements were indeed turned, sewed, hammered, or welded with the tools of a master artisan rather than painted with the brush.

This statement to an unknown correspondent in the late 1760s is relevant not only to Copley's American career but also to his reception and development on the other side of the Atlantic. Most views of Copley tend to define his art nationalistically. He was, the story goes, an essentially American artist who reflects the realism, pragmatism, and materialism of the colonial period. Once abroad, he evolves into an essentially British artist who has lost these 'American' characteristics and succumbed to decadent aristocratic fashion. Although its nationalist implications have their own interest, such a limited view discredits the artist and diminishes our understanding of his motivation and achievement in his own time and milieu. But through a better appreciation of the nature of Copley's realism, as defined by himself, his patrons, and his contemporaries, as well as by later historians, a more complex, astute artist with a keen eye both for his colonial and for his English market emerges.

The literature on Copley abounds with tales of the artist's realism. Like the ancient Greek painter Zeuxis whose convincing image of grapes caused credulous birds to swoop down on the luscious-looking fruit, Copley painted portraits of such astonishing verism that they supposedly elicited similar human reactions. Consider the account of a one-year-old encountering a Copley portrait of his father: "He sprung to it, roared, and schriched, and attempted gripping the hand ... and when any of us askt him for Papa, he always turned, and pointed to the Picture."[2] Accounts of Copley's verism are not limited to the innocent eye of the gullible infant but extend to sophisticated patrons and artists, who repeatedly paid tribute to Copley's ability to capture a forceful likeness. Articulating the engaging quality of a Copley portrait, John Adams wrote in 1817 that "you can scarcely help discoursing with them, asking questions and receiving answers,"

2. Thomas Ainslie, Quebec, to Copley, 12 November 1764, in *Letters of Copley and Pelham* 1914/1972, p. 30.

Fig. 3 John Singleton Copley

Portrait of Sarah Henshaw, ca. 1770 (pastel on paper, 24 × 17¾ in. (61 × 45.1 cm)), hanging in the Queen Anne Sitting Room at Bayou Bend Collection and Gardens

The Museum of Fine Arts, Houston, the Bayou Bend Collection, Gift of Miss Ima Hogg

Fig. 4 John Singleton Copley
Epes Sargent, ca. 1760

Oil on canvas, 49⅞ × 40 in. (126.5 × 101.6 cm)
National Gallery of Art, Washington, D.C., Gift of the Avalon Foundation

3. The Verplanck Room in the American Wing, Metropolitan Museum of Art, New York, also provides a sympathetic period environment for viewing Copley's Verplanck portraits. See Barker 1950b, p. 82.

4. Temple Franklin reported Benjamin West's comments about Stuart's virtuosity to his grandfather Benjamin Franklin in 1784 (McLanathan 1986, pp. 52–5). For Stuart's comment regarding Copley's portrait, see Benjamin 1880, p. 20.

5. A committee comprised of John Neagle, C.G. Childs, and Walter Strickland drafted a memorial essay to Stuart in which they praised him as "gifted with that power of hand which so admirably counterfeited life upon the canvas, one whose pencil was as the wand of a magician, matchless and beautiful." See Whitley 1932/1969, p. 214. Further, Dunlap mentions that while Stuart "lay a bed for weeks ... Copley and West had the industry of ants ... " (Dunlap 1834/1969, p. 167).

a striking observation when one considers the dimly lit space in which a Copley portrait might typically be displayed in the eighteenth century, as the pastel portrait of Sarah Henshaw at Bayou Bend Collection and Gardens suggests (fig. 3).[3] No less a painter than Gilbert Stuart (1755–1828), himself known for his ability to "nail the face to the canvas," once challenged the viewer of Copley's portrait of Epes Sargent (fig. 4): "Prick that hand and blood will spurt out".[4]

These testimonials help to define the province of the Copley portrait as it hovered somewhere between artifice and reality. But if Copley's critics observed a magical quality of illusionism in his images, they did not assume it was achieved by sleight of hand. Unlike Stuart, whose admirers claimed he wielded a "magical wand" instead of a brush, the Copley who emerged in the literature was not a conjurer but a laborer.[5] Observers consistently referred to Copley's determination and vigor, noting the artist's exhaustive efforts to match the sitter's skin tone with pigment, a process that Stuart, now reversing himself, claimed resulted in "labored flesh" resembling "tanned leather."[6] And few accounts of the artist neglected to mention the numerous sittings Copley required of his subjects, particularly the twenty visits Mrs. Mifflin (fig. 73 on p. 108) endured.[7] Accounts of the artist invariably included the terms "work," "labor," "mechanical," and "industry." Regarding Copley's portrait of Josiah Quincy (fig. 5), Stuart exclaimed: "there is as much work in one of those hands as I put in a whole portrait. Why, I could take off that wig ... The industry of Copley was marvelous."[8]

Stuart's comment about Copley's work and industry discloses as much about the observer as it does about the observed, marking Stuart's effort to portray himself as a natural genius. Stuart implies that he captures a likeness swiftly, perhaps effortlessly, while Copley seems methodical and dogged by contrast. Stuart's use of the term

Fig. 6 John Singleton Copley
Portrait of a Lady, 1771
Oil on canvas, 48½ × 29½ in. (123.2 × 100.3 cm)
Los Angeles County Museum of Art, Museum Acquisition Fund

6. Charles Robert Leslie reported West's comments about Copley's "tediousness" to Dunlap (Dunlap 1834/1969, p. 126). John Neagle recounted Stuart's comments about the leathery quality of the flesh in Copley's portraits (*ibid.*, p. 217).

7. Peale 1855.

8. As recounted to Mason by Mrs. Charles Amory (Martha Babcock Amory) in 1825 (Mason 1879, II, p. 164).

John Singleton Copley
Mrs. Clark Gayton, 1779 (cat. 7)

"industry" suggests several meanings of the word understood in the early nineteenth century: a trade, cleverness, and also systematic work, a term that then seemed to identify Copley as a mechanic fashioning highly finished products. Stuart's interpretation of Copley's industry suggests the production of portraits with great deliberation but without thoughtful consideration, that will appeal to the innocent eye but not to the more sophisticated one because they are little more than likenesses. His paean to Copley's industry and work, then, can hardly be viewed as flattering. Copley earnestly participated in the widespread effort during the eighteenth century to elevate the social status of an artist from the ranks of a mechanic to that of a gentleman practising a noble liberal art. But Stuart mocks Copley's diligence and condemns his art to the mechanical sphere.

This characterization of Copley – as an artist whose hard work and diligence ensured his success, according to a story-line that many champion as characteristically American – has, for the most part, endured for almost two hundred years. More than

9. Dunlap emerged among the first of Copley's biographers to articulate Copley's changing style as a condition related to national identity: "But Copley was, when removed to England, no longer an American painter in feeling" (Dunlap 1834/1969, p. 117). During the late 19th and early 20th century, accounts that linked style with colonial culture began to emerge in full force. In Copley's American portraits, Henry Tuckerman found the "hardness of the outlines, and the semi-official aspect of the figures, correspond exactly with the spirit of those times," asserting that Copley "unconsciously embodied the peculiarities of his age" (Tuckerman 1867, p. 76). Not all early 20th-century accounts, of course, found correspondences between style and colonial temperament in their assessments of Copley. Sadakichi Hartmann cast Copley in a role that supported his belief that class struggle provoked the Revolutionary War. He placed Copley among the aristocrats who left the colonies, taking Royalist art aficionados with him and leaving a vacuum to be filled by a more democratic, or characteristically "American" art (Hartmann 1901, I, p. 32). Few would now support this reductive view of the war, its effect on American cultural life and Copley's role within it, but it does suggest the extreme way in which Copley was made over to accommodate one theory of American identity. By the 1930s, perceiving the freer brushwork of Copley's manner in England to be pretentious and insincere, critics found that Copley's American period, by contrast, reflected rugged individuality, a characteristic especially championed in an era celebrating the common man. The artist Marsden Hartley went so far as to say that the dissonant harmonies he found in Copley's paintings reflected the "natural acridity of the Yankee temperament" (Hartley [ca. 1930], p. 177). See Prown 1966, I, pp. 1–2, for an introduction to the historiography of Copley, and Carrie Rebora's comprehensive discussion of the literature on Copley, 'Copley and Art History: The Study of America's First Old Master,' in New York, Boston, Houston, Milwaukee 1995–6.

10. Samuel Isham remarked that Copley's American "surroundings forced upon him a greater sincerity, which seems also to have corresponded with his temperament." The dryness and the hardness he – like Benjamin West and Joshua Reynolds more than one hundred years earlier – perceived in Copley's art merely reflected the temperament of the colonials, as "serious, self-reliant, capable ... men to be depended on." Isham implicitly favors Copley's American work, finding his English paintings had "less personality," being virtually inseparable from those of his English contemporaries (Isham 1905/1942, pp. 33–4, 38). Caffin, however, found the London environment "meretricious" to Copley, who "came under the fascination of that pretentious grandiloquence which was passing for the 'grand style' in Europe; and [one] may judge from the rapidity with which

any other colonial American artist, Copley has come to represent the myth of the American colonial as a singularly determined and honest breed. By the mid- to late nineteenth century, historians such as Henry Tuckerman identified Copley's stylistic traits with the colonial model of hard work, simplicity, and directness by locating those virtues in the hard edges and meticulous details of the artist's realism.[9] When, after his depature abroad, the relative linearity of Copley's early brushwork, as in his portrait of an unknown lady (fig. 6), gave way to freer handling, as in *Mrs. Clark Gayton* (cat. 7, also illus. on p. 17), later historians such as Samuel Isham and Charles Caffin viewed the change as evidence of degeneration.[10] Even many of Copley's twentieth-century critics have found his stylistic change once abroad simply un-American – the criticism has surfaced notably during periods of national crisis such as economic depression or world war, for instance in the accounts of Oskar Hagen and Oliver Larkin.[11]

Copley's so called decline and loss of colonial innocence insinuated itself into the literature on American art during the early decades of the nineteenth century when many members of the American Academy of Fine Arts sought to create and nurture a 'national' art. Accounts of American art of this period often made reference to the heartiness of the colonial artist who risked contamination when exposed to the refinement (or decadence) of foreign schools. Metaphorically pairing the colonies with a sturdy plant, *Analectic* magazine of 1815 feared the graft of foreign artifice on the "wild and vigorous stock of ... [colonial] genius," as if America could only blossom, in the fullness of time, in isolation on native soil.[12] These warnings, constructed to caution American artists about the perils of expatriation, did not prevent American artists from traveling abroad but they were reminded when they did, as William Cullen Bryant phrased it to Thomas Cole, to "keep that earlier, wilder image bright."[13]

The isolationist argument for American progress created an atmosphere for negative interpretations of Copley's English career. Once Copley had left the fertile American landscape, itself increasingly associated with American identity, his roots would be said to have decayed in England's depleted soil, and his English paintings would be condemned by twentieth-century historians for their seeming artifice. Under the influence of these nationalistically charged viewpoints, critics largely fashioned their estimation of Copley to accommodate evolving theories of American identity.

But what about the artist himself? If Copley's later historians in large part located colonial traits of innocence, determination, and simplicity in his colonial portraits, is it possible that Copley, using different strategies, also did? In other words, did he exploit the notion of a colonial 'innocent eye' awaiting foreign cultivation? And, if so, to what end? The perception of Copley as a colonial innocent that has emerged in the twentieth-century literature reveals a paradoxical relationship to the artist's own efforts at presenting himself and, possibly, his art. Copley, like any artist marketing his work, was conscious of the perception of provincial innocence and naiveté and used it, as necessary, to orchestrate an extraordinarily successful career in the colonies and in England.

Copley believed that American colonial culture was severely limited regarding painting. His complaint that the colonists considered it like "any other usefull trade ... like that of a Carpenter or shew maker, not as one of the most noble Arts in the World," has already been quoted. Copley criticized his unsophisticated observers as if he were surrounded by philistines, once writing bitterly to an artist abroad that he imitated this mannerism, that at heart he was disposed toward it" (Caffin 1907, p. 21).

11. Oskar Hagen asserted that Copley improved in technique abroad, but, having foresworn the American tradition of so called independence, fell into the "British trap" of artifice and over-sophistication. His definition of an American tradition was so rigid as to omit any place at all for Gilbert Stuart because "the colonial tradition had no use for virtuosity." Virtuosity, he argued, was a "symptom of art in an aged civilization," and since he constructed America as "primitive," painterliness simply could not exist (Hagen 1940, pp. 123, 146–8). Oliver Larkin characterized Copley as a cowardly draft dodger, accusing the artist of copying a Correggio in Parma while Charlestown burned (Larkin 1949/1960, p. 64).

12. *Analectic* 1815, p. 368.

13. See 'The Perils of Vision: Art, Luxury and Republicanism' in Harris 1966, pp. 28–53. See also Bryant 1829, p. 96.

14. Public Records Office, London, 25 January 1765, cited in Prown 1966, I, p. 45 note 2.

15. See Breen 1988.

16. Copley refers his half-brother Henry Pelham to Smibert's copies of Raphael's paintings of the Holy Family and Titian's *Venus and Cupid*, for example. See Copley to Henry Pelham, Rome, 14 March 1775, in *Letters of Copley and Pelham* 1914/1972, p. 304, and Copley to Henry Pelham, Parma, 25 June 1775, in *Letters of Copley and Pelham* 1914/1972, p. 340. References to William Allen's collection appear in Copley to Henry Pelham, New York, 29 September 1771, in *Letters of Copley and Pelham* 1914/1972, pp. 163–5.

17. Lord Lyndhurst to William Dunlap, London, 27 December 1827 (Dunlap 1834/1969, p. 104).

18. For example, Copley to Benjamin West, Boston, 12 November 1766, in *Letters of Copley and Pelham* 1914/1972, p. 51, in which he mentions his yearning "to acquire that bold free and gracefull stile of Painting that will if ever, come much slower from the mere dictates of Nature, which has hither too been my only instructor."

19. Copley to Francis M. Newton, Boston, 23 November 1767, in *Letters of Copley and Pelham*, 1914/1972, pp. 63–4.

20. See Barrell 1986.

preserving a likeness was the "main part of the excellency of a portrait in the oppinion of our New England Conoseurs."[14] He repeatedly recognized and resented the limitations of painting in America, where portraiture enjoyed popularity, while history painting, the highest genre an artist could practice in the academic hierarchy and the focus of Copley's ambition, languished. But amid these repeated criticisms of colonial culture, Copley worked the perception of provincial naiveté to his own benefit.

It was true that his fellow colonists underappreciated history painting, but for Copley to describe the colonies as visually starved hardly characterizes the rich colonial environment that existed. As the economic historian T.H. Breen reminds us, American colonial society was thoroughly English and reflected English standards of taste, largely transmitted through manufactured goods.[15] As for painting, a profession Copley insistently distinguished from artisan trades, sophisticated aesthetic material was available in John Smibert's well appointed studio in Boston, with its copies of Old Master paintings and portfolios of European and English mezzotints, as well as in chief justice William Allen's home in Philadelphia, where Copley studied copies of paintings by Titian, Correggio, and Van Dyck.[16] America's first art historian, William Dunlap, doubted the claim of Copley's son that his father "never saw a decent picture, with the exception of his own" until he left for England.[17] Since this claim echoed Copley's own writings, his son probably gathered the information from the artist's letters, or reiterated sentiments the artist himself expressed during his lifetime.[18] Again, in his letter accepting admission to the Society of Artists of Great Britain, to which he was elected in 1766 while still in Boston, Copley exaggerated the disadvantages of home: "their is neither precept, example, nor Models, to form the taste direct and confirm the practice" of art.[19] These sorts of complaints allowed Copley to magnify his own talent as it developed in the colonies. By making reference to colonial naiveté and, in particular, colonial primitiveness, Copley could advertise abroad his astonishing talent even before he left colonial soil.

By claiming a state of innocence, Copley drew attention to his desire and potential for "improvement," a term that reverberates throughout Anglo-American eighteenth-century literature, whether in agricultural treatises that encouraged more efficient means of production through the process of fencing lands for greater yield, or in etiquette books that advised the unimproved on matters of manners and morals. These sorts of books proliferated during a century when a Lockean model of nurture over nature informed English culture. Education, not natural proclivity, according to this model, would lead to personal and public improvement and, ultimately, to the prosperity of England. Appeals for "improvement" proved a potent form of nationalism, since they created an environment which encouraged the notion of England as a world power.

The exponential gain in English wealth based on trade during this period introduced new moral and political problems that thinkers argued could be contained by "improvement." As John Barrell has noted, these national concerns emerged in aesthetic treatises as well, particularly Sir Joshua Reynolds's lectures to the Royal Academy.[20] By 1780, Reynolds argued explicitly what he had long hinted: that the artistic profession would be validated through its active promotion as a civilizing agent in a world where familiar structures and institutions were shifting. Reynolds argued that England would never rise above the "rank of a barbarous nation" without the acquisition of excellence in art. He noted that the riches brought by trade provided the means for acquiring this excellence but that too great a concern for the means rather than the end would promote only a primitive state.[21] By claiming that enlightened artists extolling public virtue through their art could prevent a society of merely economic men, Reynolds constructed a role for English artists to play in the expanding circle of trade. Increased trade brought riches, but not necessarily enlightenment. Without art, England would never rise above the status of the primitive.

Copley's incessant complaints about the absence of artistic appreciation in the colonies should thus be understood as more than the sign of discontent. His desire for improvement and claims of innocence worked to his advantage because they signified his participation in the eighteenth-century intellectual notion of progress; they forged a role for him in the larger project of civilizing America and demonstrated to those whose help he sought abroad, such as Sir Joshua Reynolds and Benjamin West, his yearning to be a part of a larger program in which artists would serve as civilizing agents in a society transformed by a market economy.

The letters of Copley consistently reveal his own artistic ambitions and his cultural aspirations for the colonies, which were, he wrote, "intirely destitute of all just Ideas of the Arts."[22] He demonstrated his earnestness in letters soliciting advice from West, Reynolds, and the distinguished Swiss pastellist Jean-Etienne Liotard.[23] To his European and colonial contacts, Copley claimed repeatedly that America would one day be an enviable environment for the arts.

To John Greenwood, his friend and fellow artist who was traveling in Europe, he expressed his particular pleasure that the arts were "travilling Westward," and hoped that they would travel quickly so that the colonies would acquire the refinement of a civilized society.[24] America, otherwise, would always have the innocence associated with the primitive, and would be nothing more than a trading post. Nourished by eighteenth-century aesthetic treatises by Daniel Webb and George Turnbull that promoted a position among the arts – the sure mark of a civilized society – for England, Copley had ambitions that America should be a worthy region in the Anglophone world. He conceived his role as an American to consist in being a patriotic citizen in an English civilization defined by its preoccupation with progress. Jonathan Clarke, Copley's brother-in-law, did not appeal to Copley's filial duty or to any other consideration when he warned him about moving abroad in 1772. Instead, he appealed to Copley's desire for colonial progress, warning him that talented men leaving the colonies would eventually stunt the colonies' "improvement."[25]

Copley, then, echoed Reynolds in his desire to play a part in the eighteenth-century notion of the "progress" of civilization, in which artists would prevent the state from succumbing to conditions of barbarism and so called primitivism. Yet he played on the perception of his provincial origins as primitive, once remarking, "We Americans seem not half-removed from a state of nature," an exaggerated reference to American "primitiveness."[26] Copley's pronouncement of innocence is similar in spirit to West's when he equated the *Apollo* Belvedere with a Mohawk warrior before his learned European audience.[27] Stuart, delighting in the sound of exotic placenames, gave himself a "native" pedigree when he told a group of Londoners that he was "born six miles from Pottawoone, and ten miles from Poppasquash, and about four miles west of Connonicut, and not far from the spot where the famous battle with the warlike

21. Reynolds 1769–90/1959/1975, *Discourse IX* (16 October 1780), lines 15–24, p. 169.

22. Copley to Captain R.G. Bruce(?), 1767(?), in *Letters of Copley and Pelham*, 1914/1972, p. 64.

23. See, for example, Copley to West, 13 October and 12 November 1766, and Captain R.G. Bruce's discussions with Reynolds about Copley in Captain R.G. Bruce to Copley, London, 4 August 1766, and London, 11 June 1767, in *Letters of Copley and Pelham* 1914/1972, pp. 49–52, 41–43, 52–5. To Liotard, Copley wrote, "You may perhaps be surprised that so remote a corner of the Globe as New England should have any d[e]mand for the necessary eutensils for practiceing the fine Arts, but I assure You Sir however feeble our efforts may be, it is not for want of inclination that they are not better, but the want of oppertunity to improve ourselves. however America which has been the seat of war and desolation, I would fain hope will one Day become the School of fine Arts . . ." in Copley to Jean-Etienne Liotard, Boston, 30 September 1762, *ibid.*, p. 26.

24. Copley to John Greenwood, Boston, 25 January 1771, in *Letters of Copley and Pelham* 1914/1972, p. 105.

25. Jonathan Clarke to Copley, London, 20 December 1772, *Letters of Copley and Pelham* 1914/1972, p. 190.

26. Copley implies the civilized behavior of the British as revealed through their landscapes in a letter to his wife, Susanna Clarke Copley, London, 11 July 1774 (Amory 1882, pp. 27–8).

27. John Galt, *The Life and Studies of Benjamin West, Esq.* (1816), in von Erffa and Staley 1986, p. 2.

Fig. 7 J. Bretherton
Christian Frederick Zincke and Jean-Etienne Liotard
(in oval)

Engraving from Horace Walpole, *Anecdotes of Painting in England*, vol. 4, p. 91

28. As recounted by Dr. Waterhouse to Dunlap (Dunlap1834/1969, p. 190).

29. See Wind 1938–9, II, pp. 116–27, for a discussion of American painters' references to *mirabilia* (the exotic).

30. See Breen 1990, pp. 325–50.

31. West's comments to Copley were conveyed in letters, Reynolds's through Copley's agent Captain R.G. Bruce. Bruce wrote to Copley, 4 August 1766, that his *Boy playing with a Squirrel*, submitted to the Society of Artists exhibition of 1766 to overwhelming praise from West and Reynolds, nonetheless elicited criticisms such as "Hardness in the Drawing, Coldness in the Shades, An over minuteness" and "to liney, which was judgd to have arose from there being so much neetness in the lines," in *Letters of Copley and Pelham* 1914/1972, pp. 41–5. Regarding his second submission, *Young Lady with a Bird and Dog*, to the Society of Artists exhibition of 1767, West wrote to Copley, London, 20 June 1767, and quoted Reynolds, who criticized the painting for its lack of general effect: "Each Part of the Picture being Equell in Strenght of Coulering and finishing, Each Making to much a Picture of its silf, without that Due Subordanation to the Principle Parts ...", in *Letters of Copley and Pelham* 1914/1972, pp. 56–8.

Pequots was fought."[28] West, Copley, and Stuart fashioned themselves in a manner common during the eighteenth century in their repeated references to distant lands. For example, Liotard, whom Horace Walpole accused of adopting Middle Eastern attire to attract customers intrigued by foreign countries, also made references to exotic lands that brought identification with the fashionable 'other,' and it proved an attractive marketing device, witness his portrait of Christian Frederick Zincke (fig. 7). Both West and Copley, once abroad, included either Native Americans – as in West's *Death of General Wolfe* (fig. 57 on p. 79) – or blacks – as in Copley's *Watson and the Shark* (cat. 4) – in their history paintings as references to help identify the distant lands considered so appealing and so essential to British prosperity.[29] If it served them, being American could have primitive or exotic associations advantageous to an artist eager to practice his profession in new surroundings. More than that, by making reference to colonial outposts, the source of new English wealth but also of contention, both artists played on England's image of itself as a world power.

Copley's art engaged the subject of trade, however indirectly, in ways that caused consternation among conservatives such as Reynolds, who recognized the promises and perils of increased trade but did not address them in his art. American lands, colonized for the mutually beneficial mercantile system in which raw materials would be exchanged for finished products, soon emerged as the largest market for British manufactured goods. The colonies *were* a kind of trading post, in which portraiture was, as Copley complained, just another trade. But portraiture in the colonies was also a means by which trade assumed a face. Consistent with T.H. Breen's analysis of colonial culture, the extraordinary attention artists such as Copley spent on rendering fabrics, jewels, and other expensive stuffs drew notice to the wealth and prosperity of the colonies brought about by a mercantile society.[30] It may be that Copley's insistent materialism, his precise portrayal of polished mahogany surfaces and the sheen of expensive fabrics, reminded Reynolds and West of the dangers of an unimproved state, one flourishing because of trade but not yet sufficient in cultural refinements. On one hand, Copley satisfied his colonial clients because he glorified their new wealth by emphasizing their material goods. He understood his colonial market. But to those he wanted to emulate, such as Reynolds and West, Copley's insistent materialism connoted vulgarity; the "lineyness" and "overminuteness" West and Reynolds condemned in his art drew attention to the particular rather than the general, the part rather than the whole, the stuffs rather than the idea.[31] Despite his desire for success in London circles, Copley had a compelling financial motive to remain in the colonies and to retain the particularity of his style, which had proved so attractive to the New England clientele responsible for Copley's dramatic rise in social status. While Copley's development from the linear to the painterly represented progress, as it was understood in the eighteenth century, it was the particular art market at a given time and place that guided Copley's stylistic change, as he alternately fashioned himself – with great industry – as an innocent, a primitive, and eventually, a sophisticate.

Once abroad, Copley emphatically asserted his desire to be a part of the eighteenth-century notion of the progress of civilization in his first public presentation of himself in paint, *The Copley Family*, a *tour de force* of artistic self-fashioning which he exhibited to great acclaim at the Royal Academy of 1777 (cat. 1). Here, Copley followed Reynolds's proscriptions and joined his cause. Copley's family might be

John Singleton Copley
The Copley Family, 1776–77 (cat. 1)

fashionably dressed in stylish surroundings, but their material goods do not distract the viewer from understanding the picture's larger message. Copley loosens his brushwork, softens his lines, and draws attention to his status as a gentleman connoisseur not of the New England type he had earlier deplored, but of the London type to which he had long aspired. Gripping a set of drawings, the artist links himself to an antique urn, the celebrated Medici Vase, and to an Italianate background including what appears to be a Renaissance church. Newly returned from the Grand Tour, a prerequisite for status as a gentleman and a serious artist, Copley announces his right to be a part of Reynolds's elect group, the Royal Academy, to which he was elected, in fact, just one year later. Copley proved that promoting innocence had its advantages because, in one grand image, he demonstrated the reward of seeking improvement by displaying this badge of civility, London style. Copley had arrived, and over the next thirty-eight years he not only emulated London style, he helped to invent and market it in new, unprecedented ways.

The Challenge of New Horizons

Copley's "rough and perilous Asent" "of that Mighty Mountain where the Everlasting Lauriels grow"[1]

WILLIAM L. PRESSLY

Born in Boston in 1738, John Singleton Copley spent the second half of his career in London, then the art capital of the English-speaking world. As early as 1766 he had sent portraits from Boston to London for exhibition at the Society of Artists, and on 10 June 1774 he sailed for England, leaving behind in America his wife and four children. Intent on improving himself as a painter by studying the masterpieces of classical sculpture and Renaissance painting, he almost immediately, on 26 August, set off for Rome, reuniting with his family in London in October of the following year.

In 1776, Copley exhibited for the first time at the Royal Academy, which had been founded in 1768: he submitted a conversation piece, probably the painting *Mr. and Mrs. Ralph Izard* (fig. 68 on p. 94), which he had executed in Rome. Later that year he was made an associate member of the Royal Academy, and in 1777 he exhibited four pictures, one of which was a portrait of his family (cat. 1, also illus. on p. 22), his most complex group portrait and his largest painting up to that time. Given its size and complexity, he obviously intended this work as the centerpiece of his announcement, after having settled in the English capital, of his considerable abilities as a portrait painter. In addition, it was a personal celebration of his family's reunion after a separation that had lasted for over a year.

The three adults in *The Copley Family* are the artist himself, who stands in the background, his father-in-law, Richard Clarke, who is seated in front of him, and his wife, Susanna, on the settee at the right. One contemporary reviewer complained in a newspaper critique of 26 April 1777 that the artist's own placement within the composition distanced the artist to such a degree that he no longer seemed part of the family circle: "The figure of the gentleman, leaning behind with some plans in his hand, seems also to be od[d]ly placed, and not properly one of the family."[2] Copley, wearing a dark-blue brocade dressing gown over the shoulder of which appears to be draped a cape with a fur-trimmed collar, leans on a plinth that in a later grisaille sketch can be more clearly read as supporting a column.[3] He is part of a structured, man-made world of right-angled architecture and decorated vases, and the papers in his hand denote his engaged, intellectual pursuits. His father-in-law, even with a frolicking child on his lap, remains properly composed, an *exemplum* of dignified *gravitas*. Copley's wife, on the other hand, while still serious in demeanor, is closely linked with two of her children in a complex interweaving of arms. The colors of her clothes are brighter than those of the men, and she is associated with fertile nature by the floral patterns on her shoe and on the fabric of her footstool and settee and by the blooming vine behind her.

The youngest of the children, grasping the traditional toy of whistle and bells with coral, is seated on Richard Clarke's lap at the left. When Copley began the group portrait he intended this child as his son Clarke, appropriately associating him with the grandfather for whose family he had been named. The child, though, had been left behind in Boston because of frail health, and sometime after learning of his death in January 1776 the artist must have decided to replace him with their fifth child, their daughter Susanna, born in October 1776. The eldest son, John Singleton Copley, Jr., receives his mother's undivided attention, while Mary nestles next to her on the settee at the right. Elizabeth, the eldest child, stands at the composition's center, linking the two pyramidal groups.

Copley takes pains to distinguish the children's world from that of the adults. The adults are somber and reflective, while the three youngest children display a

1. The phrasing in quotation marks is a reordering of a statement Copley made in a letter of 25 January 1771 to the artist John Greenwood. The sentence is quoted in full and in context on page 25 below.

2. *The London Packet or New Lloyd's Evening Post*, 25–28 April 1777, p. 1.

3. This sketch is in the Museum of Fine Arts, Boston. It is identified as preparatory to Robert Thew's unfinished engraving of 1789, rather than as preparatory to the painting itself, in Boston 1980, no. 12, and in Miles 1994.

contrasting, joyous vitality. Again Elizabeth provides a link. Dressed in white with a pink sash, she is associated with the bright gaiety of her siblings, but her demeanor and her self-contained pose, her right hand resting on her left wrist like her father's, more closely reflect the seriousness of the adults. The doll, whose attire most closely resembles hers, has been poignantly cast aside at the far left. Within the context of a family portrait, Copley celebrates childhood with its sense of promising renewal that will soon give way to more sobering cares, and the emphasis on the stream in the background is a conventional reminder of the transience of life. The painting is calculated to demonstrate the artist's ability not only to capture surface appearance but also those profounder realities that underlie it.

Yet, why had Copley made the bold decision to start again in London after having enjoyed such a productive and prosperous career in Boston? In June 1774, when he left America, he was just a few weeks shy of his thirty-sixth birthday. Invariably his career is compared to that of his compatriot Benjamin West, who had also been born in 1738, and the comparison was very much on Copley's own mind as well as that of his contemporaries. West had left Philadelphia to study in Rome as early as 1760, and it was there, during a three-year sojourn, that he reached artistic maturity. He arrived in London in 1763, a stop on his way back to Philadelphia that soon became permanent once he realized his opportunities. He went on to become, in 1768, a founding member of the Royal Academy of Arts and in 1792, after the death of Sir Joshua Reynolds, its second president. Copley, on the other hand, came to maturity in colonial Boston, though he achieved in this provincial center a level of excellence in portraiture that places him in the foremost ranks of the world's painters.

Copley was largely self-taught, and his success was due as much to his intelligence and the driving force of his ambition as it was to his natural abilities. In composing in 1773 a letter of introduction for the artist, the Philadelphia physician Dr. John Morgan came very close to the truth, even when indulging in the hyperbole customary on such occasions: "Perhaps History cannot furnish a single Instance of any Person, who with so little Assistance from others, and so few Oppertunities of seeing any thing worth studying has by the force of his Genius and by close Application to study Nature, arrived to such preheminance in Painting as Mr. Copley."[4] Copley had surpassed the models available to him in Boston in terms of paintings and painters, including the meager materials left by his stepfather Peter Pelham, a mezzotint engraver and portrait painter. He was not content, however, to dominate his surroundings but wanted to compare himself to his European contemporaries as well as to the Old Masters. Until he could see their work for himself, he had to face the nagging insecurities of falling short of an imagined standard. In 1766, he had sent a portrait to the Society of Artists in London, the most important venue for exhibition before the creation of the Royal Academy two years later, and was relieved and pleased when the picture, *Boy playing with a Squirrel*, a portrait of his half-brother Henry Pelham, was well received. While Reynolds and West offered him encouraging words of praise, their advice that his style was overly minute, his color too cold in the shades, and his drawing too sharp-edged and linear proved counter-productive,[5] as Copley's submission the following year was decidedly inferior.[6] The artist had to see rather than merely be told how to proceed.

In the 1760s Copley had written his friend and patron Thomas Ainslie, collector of customs in the Port of Quebec, that he was intent on "improveing in that charming Art

4. Dr. John Morgan to Isaac Jamineau, Philadelphia, 24 November 1773, in *Letters of Copley and Pelham* 1914/1972, p. 210.

5. Reynolds's criticism was given secondhand in a letter to Copley of 4 August 1766 from Captain R.G. Bruce, London, while West's was contained in his letter to Copley of the same date. Both are published in *Letters of Copley and Pelham* 1914/1972, pp. 41–5.

6. See *Young Lady with a Bird and Dog* (Mary Warner?), reproduced in Prown 1966, I, fig. 164.

which is my delight, and gaining a reputation rather than a fortune."[7] He added that, of course, fortune can be acquired while in pursuit of reputation, the one reinforcing the other. The artist had, like his colonial peers, a healthy respect for material prosperity – indeed his English colleagues were to label him as miserly and greedy, characteristics that had been ingrained by a somewhat impoverished childhood – but, as the quotation makes clear, he also burned to excel. In order to succeed, Copley was well aware that he needed to study the works of the Old Masters. On 25 January 1771 he wrote to John Greenwood, a fellow artist who had left Boston in 1752 eventually to settle in London: "Your tour through Europe must have affoarded you great pleasure and the more so as you have had so many Capitol Picture[s] in you[r] possession. I should think myself happy in such an oppertunity of contemplating the works of those Renowned Masters. I sincerely rejoice in Mr West's successfull progress towards the summit of that Mighty Mountain where the Everlasting Lauriels grow to adoarn the brows of those Elustrious Artists that are so favour'd of Heaven as to be able to unravel the intricate mazes of its rough and perilous Asent."[8] While Copley writes of West, the context makes clear he wishes to scale that same mighty mountain, an ascent of Parnassus, at least in his own mind, that can only be fully attempted from an European vantage point.

Although driven to compete in an international arena, it was still difficult for Copley to give up a prosperous practice to relocate in Europe. As he wrote to Captain R.G. Bruce in 1767, practical considerations offered a strong counter inducement: "I would gladly exchange my situation for the serene climate of Italy, or even that of England; but what would be the advantage of seeking improvement at such an outlay of time and money? I am now in as good business as the poverty of this place will admit. I make as much as if I were a Raphael or a Correggio; and three hundred guineas a-year, my present income, is equal to nine hundred a year in London. With regard to reputation, you are sensible that fame cannot be durable where pictures are confined to sitting-rooms, and regarded only for the resemblance they bear to their originals. Were I sure of doing as well in Europe as here, I would not hesitate a moment in my choice; but I might in the experiment waste a thousand pounds and two years of my time, and have to return baffled to America. Then I should have to take my mother with me, who is ailing: she does not, however, seem averse to cross the salt water once more; but my failure would oblige me to recross the sea again. My ambition whispers me to run this risk; and I think the time draws nigh that must determine my future fortune."[9]

Ambition finally won out only after the mounting turmoil in America threatened to disrupt the art market severely, and, as the political situation deteriorated at home, the artist departed for Europe to accept the challenge of learning from and competing with the best the Western tradition had to offer. Just how daunting this challenge was should not be underestimated. Not only had he matured outside the major artistic centers, but he also had to contend with the eighteenth-century belief that art was in decline. Raphael and Michelangelo had achieved a level of excellence that was thought impossible to equal, and there were no contemporaries who could even measure up to such seventeenth-century masters as Rubens and Poussin. For Copley it would be hard enough to take on the challenge of competing with Reynolds and Gainsborough in the sphere of portraiture, not to mention the courage required to confront the Old Masters

7. Copley to Thomas Ainslie, Boston, 25 February 1765, in *Letters of Copley and Pelham* 1914/1972, p. 33.

8. Copley to John Greenwood, 25 January 1771, in *Letters of Copley and Pelham* 1914/1972, pp. 105–6.

9. Cunningham 1831/1837/1868, V, pp. 164–5.

Fig. 8 John Singleton Copley
Galatea, ca. 1754
Oil on canvas, 37 × 52 in. (94 × 132 cm)
Museum of Fine Arts, Boston, purchased from Picture
Fund

Fig. 9 Augustinus after Gregorio Lazzarini
Galatea Triumphs upon the Waves
Engraving

10. Copley to Pelham, Parma, 25 June 1775, in
Letters of Copley and Pelham 1914/1972, p. 340.

as well. His confidence, though, proved equal to the task. Coming of age in Boston ulti-mately provided a psychological distancing that was more of a help than a hindrance. Writing back to Henry Pelham from Italy, he offered the following observations: "You are to remember that the works of the great Masters are but Pictures, and when a man can go but a very little beyond his cotemporarys he becomes a great Man. the differ-ence between Raphael, Titiano, [Michael] Angelo and the common run of moderately good Artists, is not so great as one would Imagin from the Praises bestow'd on those Great men. but they are the first Artists and they merit the Most elaborate Praises from the World."[10] The purpose of this passage is of course to overcome his younger half-brother's insecurities by encouraging him to attempt high art, but one senses the artist's conviction that the laurel crown is indeed within reach.

Fashioning a History Painter

Having made the leap from America to Europe, the true test for Copley, if he were to accept the prevailing academic standard, was not in portraiture but in history painting, which was considered to be art's most exalted genre. History painting's high-minded subject matter was drawn from a repertoire limited to the Bible, classical history and mythology, and epic poetry. These texts were the primary source for those ennobling 'universal' values embodied in the Western tradition. In depicting these subjects, the artist was to avoid ordinary reality, choosing instead an heroic, idealizing standard, though grounded on the study of the human figure. By a process of selection and distil-lation, the artist was to eliminate the particular and the individual to achieve a general idea of nature perfected. Fortunately each painter did not have to begin anew in order to arrive at this ideal standard, because he or she could build on the work of the past. The art of the ancients was cited as the most important source for forms embodying the ideal, and the modern artist was encouraged to study and imitate this rich artistic her-itage. Imitation, however, was not to be confused with copying, for one was to select and build on artistic models without slavishly parroting the original.

Earlier, as a teenager in Boston, Copley had tutored himself by 'copying' historical compositions. One such work that survives is his *Galatea* (fig. 8), which is based on an engraving after Gregorio Lazzarini's *Galatea Triumphs upon the Waves* (fig. 9). The differ-ence between Copley's painting and its model is noteworthy. Even as a youth of sixteen or seventeen, he made numerous adjustments in translating the black-and-white print into a relatively large oil-painting. His prudish draping of the goddess is less surprising than the numerous, more subtle changes he made in order to 'improve' the composi-tion, such as extending the pearl-laden shell held by the nymph at the left beyond the line of the hill in the background or re-angling Neptune's triton at the right. This is not the passive response of an overawed apprentice but rather demonstrates an aggressive confidence in his approach to tradition. Yet Copley is not known to have executed dur-ing his American years any history paintings that are independent conceptions, and once he had established himself in his profession in Boston, he devoted himself exclu-sively to portraiture.

America had offered limited opportunities not only in terms of instruction but also in patronage. As Copley complained, portraiture in its most limited sense was all that was desired: "... was it not for preserving the resembla[n]ce of perticular persons, paint-ing would not be known in the plac[e]. The people generally regard it no more than any other usefull trade, as they sometimes term it, like that of a Carpenter tailor or shew maker, not as one of the most noble Arts in the World."[11]

Upon arriving in Rome, Copley would have joined the large contingent of British artists whose unofficial headquarters was the English Coffee House in the Piazza di Spagna. His time was too limited, however, to indulge in a great deal of socializing, as he was determined to take full advantage of this opportunity to study and sketch classical art and Renaissance and Baroque masterpieces. In the winter he also set himself to work on a major original conception, *The Ascension* (fig. 10), a biblical subject that aspired to emulate such illustrious predecessors as Raphael and Poussin. While the canvas is relatively small, the project was a highly ambitious one, the artist hoping his work would later be commissioned as a large altarpiece. In a letter back to Henry Pelham, he described in detail his painstaking efforts to build up the composition, each of his figures being carefully worked out in relationship to the whole and in the detailing of the parts.[12] The scene shows the Mount of Olives forty days after the Crucifixion when Christ last appeared to the eleven apostles. Christ ascends, while angels, described in the Bible as "two men ... in white apparel" (*Acts* 1:10) approach from the right. The

Fig. 11 Raphael
The Transfiguration, 1518–20

Oil on panel, 159¹/₂ × 109¹/₂ in. (405 × 278 cm)
Pinacoteca Vaticana, Rome

Fig. 10 John Singleton Copley
The Ascension, 1775

Oil on canvas, 32 × 29 in. (81.5 × 73.5 cm)
Museum of Fine Arts, Boston, bequest of Susan Green
Dexter, in memory of Charles and Martha Babcock
Amory

11. Copley to Benjamin West or Captain R.G. Bruce(?), 1767(?), in *Letters of Copley and Pelham* 1914/1972, pp. 65–6. These sentiments are echoed in a letter from Copley to West, Boston, 24 November 1770: "You are sensable in this country the hands of an Artist is tied up, not having it in his power to prosicute any work of fancy for want of meterials" (*Letters of Copley and Pelham* 1914/1972, p. 97).

12. Copley to Pelham, Rome, 14 March 1775, in *Letters of Copley and Pelham* 1914/1972, pp. 295–9.

choice of an almost square format is unusual for an Ascension, but Copley carefully distinguishes between the heavenly sphere and the earthly one.[13] The apostles all wear colored garments, for the most part darker at the center of the composition, and are positioned against a generalized, muted landscape background. As in Raphael's *Transfiguration* (fig. 11), an important source of inspiration for him, gesture and facial expression offer a visual language of emotions, but Copley, a novice at history painting, while tightly grouping the apostles, over-indulges in histrionic gestures. Christ's own dynamic pose is a somewhat awkward mixture of a reference to the Crucifixion and a gesture of blessing with His left hand. Copley represents Heaven in the form of an energizing light, and it is in the dynamic nature of his sky that he is most successful.

One of *The Ascension*'s admirers was Gavin Hamilton, a Scottish artist, fifteen years older than Copley, who had long been a Roman resident.[14] Hamilton proved influential in directing the American's interest toward Homeric subject matter, having himself in the 1760s projected six illustrations to *The Iliad*.[15] In a letter dated 14 March 1775 Copley mentions to Pelham, "I could wish to accompany it [*The Ascension*] with one of another kind, one of a Clasick subject, that of the Reconciliation of Achilles and Agamamnon, a very sublime Subject."[16] If he depicted this episode from Book 19, it has not survived, but a previously unidentified drawing (cat. 20) is an illustration of an earlier Homeric scene from Book 17, the fight between the Achaians and Trojans over Patroclus's body.[17] Menelaus, assisted by Meriones, struggles beneath the burden of "the weighty corse" (Pope's translation, Book 17, line 802). Ajax, supported by his brother, turns to face the Trojan charge led by Hector wearing Patroclus's armor and by Aeneas. Copley employs dramatic contrasts of dark and light, which are in keeping with Homer's imagery through this book, as in the lines, "Such o'er Patroclus' body hung the Night,/ The rest in sunshine fought, and open light" (426–7). In the episode depicted in the drawing, Homer compares the storm of war to an inflamed city where "sheets of smoke mount heavy to the poles" (line 830), and Copley shows a pulsating darkness rising above and behind the noble corpse.

While Copley's illustration for Book 17 may not have advanced beyond this drawing, he did find time to complete the painting *Priam Beseeching Achilles for the Body of Hector*, now known from the engraving after it (fig. 12).[18] This subject is identical to one already attempted by Hamilton (fig. 13), and Copley, again finding his way in history painting, is heavily in the Scotsman's debt. In both, Priam is on his knees, kissing and bathing with tears Achilles's hand, which had recently been stained with Hector's blood. Priam has entered the enemy's camp in order to reclaim his son's body, which can be seen in both works tied to Achilles's chariot beneath a moonlit sky. The lone woman in each composition is Briseis, the source of the earlier quarrel between Agamemnon and Achilles.

Although relying heavily on Hamilton's work, Copley also shows creative independence. He chooses, in the manner of the Caravaggisti, to conceal his light source, and to highlight dramatically the attendant at the left who is seen from behind. The shadow of this figure, who is possibly Automedon, Achilles's charioteer, extends into the viewer's space, and it is through him that one enters the composition and is instructed how to respond. Copley also chooses as a model for Achilles the figure of *Laocoön* (see fig. 63 on p. 86), one of the most celebrated sculptures of antiquity and one appropriate to a scene from the Trojan War.

13. The squarish proportions do not reflect his ultimate intent, as he wrote his half brother that he envisioned the altarpiece he hoped to paint based on this sketch as measuring "24 feet by 18" (Copley to Pelham, Rome, 14 March 1775, in *Letters of Copley and Pelham* 1914/1972, p. 301).

14. Copley reported to his half-brother, "Mr. Hamilton is lavish in its praises, and says he never saw a finer Composition in his life, and that he knows no one who can equil it; that it is a subject the most difficult I could have ingaged in, that there is no subject but I can compose with less Dificulty" (Copley to Pelham, Rome, 14 March 1775, in *Letters of Copley and Pelham* 1914/1972, p. 300).

15. Copley already apparently knew Homer well, presumably in translation, as when he was in Paris on his way to Rome, he wrote to his half-brother in regards to Rubens, " ... with what an easey flowing out line he Draws his figures, smooth and easey as the flow of Homer's Verse" (Copley to Pelham, Paris, 7 September 1774, in *Letters of Copley and Pelham* 1914/1972, p. 250).

16. Copley to Pelham, Rome, 14 March 1775, in *Letters of Copley and Pelham* 1914/1972, p. 300.

17. The drawing listed as "Unknown Subject, studies from the antique [?]" in Prown 1966, II, fig. 335, is also a preparatory study for *The Battle over Patroclus's Body*.

18. See Prown 1966, II, p. 360, for a discussion why the engraving, published in 1799, dates so much later than the painting it reproduces.

Fig. 12 A. Fogg after John Singleton
Copley
Priam Beseeching Achilles for the Body of Hector,
4 June 1799

Engraving, 17⅞ × 22 in. (45.4 × 55.7 cm)
The Fogg Art Museum, Harvard University Art
Museums, Gray Collection of Engravings Fund

Fig. 13 Domenico Cunego after Gavin
Hamilton
Priam Redeems the Dead Body of Hector, 1775

Engraving, 17½ × 24¾ in. (44.3 × 63 cm)
University of Glasgow

Despite Copley's interest while in Italy in depicting scenes from the *Iliad*, classical subjects play a smaller role in his œuvre than in that of many of his contemporaries. A painting such as *Venus and Cupid* of *ca.* 1779,[19] for example, is a modest, though charming, composition that may only be preparatory to an allegorical portrait of a mother and child. Instead, on his return to London, his primary concern in the area of history painting was with biblical subject matter.

While visiting Parma in 1775, Copley had written his half-brother encouraging him to attempt historical subjects: "... I don't think a Man a perfect Artist who on occasion cannot Paint History ...".[20] For himself, he had already begun to master the necessary training, but in this same letter he added that he would now require commissions before undertaking this type of picture: "... but portrait painting I shall pursue, unless tempted to some things in history by any that may wish to imploy me in that way."[21] Yet once he was back in London, despite an absence of patronage, ambition led him to undertake such projects even without support. These pictures, though few, were, like *The Ascension*, all drawn from the Bible and were all uncommissioned.

In 1777, at the same time he exhibited *The Copley Family* and two male portraits, the artist also showed *The Nativity* (cat. 2), a picture intended to announce his prowess as a history painter. The painting was well promoted, a mezzotint after it appearing two years later, and eventually two more prints were to follow, one published in Boston and the other in Paris. Mrs. Copley was the model for Mary, who, along with the Christ Child, is awash in radiant white at the composition's still center. Both the raking light and the group of Saint Joseph and the shepherds set up a strong diagonal that continues through Mary's reclining figure. The ox (in this case oxen) and ass at the right are traditionally included in the Nativity as a reference to Isaiah's verse, "The ox knoweth his owner, and the ass his master's crib; *but* Israel doth not know, my people, doth not consider" (Isaiah 1:3). Here the animals, along with the dog, threaten to upstage the human attendants.

Writing in 1796, John Williams, under the pseudonym Anthony Pasquin, criticized with wicked humor Copley's conception: "The immaculate mother reclines unconscious of her divinity, and is made to regard the *Salvator Mundi* with an air of despondency, rather than ineffable joy; and her white drapery is so inveterately modern, that it furnishes a lively notion of a female haberdasher in the third week of her *accouchement*."[22] Mary's melancholy reverie over her infant is hardly inappropriate, but it is surprising to the degree that Copley employs the same solemn expression for his wife in *The Copley Family*. The references to the lack of divinity and the emphasis on fashionable fabrics are standard charges leveled against portrait painters, who were thought to be particularly inadequate in achieving a generalized and elevated treatment when attempting the grand style. After the somewhat faltering beginnings of *The Ascension* and *Priam Beseeching Achilles for the Body of Hector*, *The Nativity* shows Copley starting to overcome those defects arising from his lack of academic training, wisely pursuing in this work a less complex composition and a cast of characters more closely rooted in portraiture.

Copley's next religious painting, *Samuel Relating to Eli the Judgments of God upon Eli's House* of 1780 (cat. 10), was also apparently uncommissioned. Having been elected a full academician in February of the previous year, he was required to submit a diploma piece, and Jules Prown speculates this canvas may have been intended for this purpose,

19. See Prown 1966, II, fig. 386.

20. Copley to Pelham, Parma, 25 June 1775, in *Letters of Copley and Pelham* 1914/1972, p. 339.

21. *Letters of Copley and Pelham* 1914/1972, p. 340.

22. Pasquin [Williams] 1796, p. 137.

Detail of cat. 10, John Singleton Copley,
Samuel Relating to Eli the Judgments of God

Fig. 14 Benjamin West
St. Peter Denying Christ, ca. 1778–79

Oil on canvas, 48³/₄ × 49 in. (124 × 124.5 cm)
The Royal Collection © Her Majesty Queen Elizabeth II

23. Prown 1966, II, p. 276 note 4. He goes on to
speculate that Copley may have withdrawn the
picture after finding a buyer. To the press cutting
describing Copley's picture mentioned by Prown,
one should also add the following: " ... nor may we
dismiss this article [on paintings in the Royal
Academy annual exhibition], without noticing his
historical picture below stairs, of *Samuel and Eli*, on
which too much commendation cannot well be
bestowed; it is in every respect *a picture*; finished in
every part, with a precision, and roundness, which
makes the whole an outline; and the character of
the child Samuel, is so divine, and has such an air
of truth and simplicity about it, that this picture
alone, is a considerable acquisition to the Arts in
this country" (*The Morning Chronicle*, 22 May 1780,
p. 2).

24. See von Erffa and Staley 1986, no. 350.

25. For a summary of the evidence pointing to
Copley as the author of the head of St. Peter in the
British Royal Collection version of *St. Peter Denying
Christ*, with Gilbert Stuart supplying the other two
figures of Christ and the woman, see von Erffa and
Staley 1986, no. 351. As these authors state, "The
circumstances under which Copley and Stuart
would have painted a joint copy after West (if this
painting is indeed that) can only be guessed at."
While over his career West instructed numerous
American artists such as Stuart, Copley of course
does not fall into this category.

26. See von Erffa and Staley 1986, no. 271.

27. *Ibid.*, p. 31.

particularly as it is described in 1780 as hanging in the Royal Academy's new
quarters.[23] If *The Ascension* looks back to Raphael and *Priam Beseeching Achilles for the Body
of Hector* to Hamilton, *Samuel Relating to Eli the Judgments of God* pays homage to, while
also competing with, West, as the head of Eli is based on West's composition *St. Peter
Denying Christ*, the first version of which he had exhibited at the Royal Academy in
1779.[24] The version of *St. Peter Denying Christ* reproduced here (fig. 14) was a gift to
George III, and there is speculation that the figure of St. Peter in this canvas is actually
by Copley.[25] West had also been at work at this time on painting *Hannah Presenting
Samuel to Eli*,[26] a project that may have suggested to his countryman the subject matter
for his own picture. Certainly, during the 1770s, the two artists would appear to have
been on good terms and in close contact, with Copley even painting West's portrait.
Throughout his career, Copley continued to measure himself against his colleague's
work, and, as Alan Staley points out, the influence was not all one way, for in the 1770s
in his use of brushwork West responded to Copley's example.[27]

   In *Samuel Relating to Eli the Judgments of God upon Eli's House*, Copley abandons the
multi-figured compositions of his earlier history paintings to focus only on two well
integrated figures. His son served as the model for the young Samuel, who is shown
revealing to Eli, the high priest of Israel, the Lord's unsettling judgment. It is the first
evidence of Samuel's having been chosen as the Lord's Prophet, and his hand pointing
heavenward is a traditional prophetic gesture. The detailed treatment of fabrics, the

Rembrandtesque gleam of golden threads and medals, and the expressive *pas de deux* played out by the hands and faces are marshalled into a monumental design which flows from the lower left through the rising columns at upper right. By choosing a low point of view and introducing the oversized ewer at upper left, the artist adds to the scene's sense of awesome grandeur. One of his contemporaries who mentioned seeing this work in the rooms of the Royal Academy referred to it as "masterly",[28] and it is indeed a bravura performance.

Whether or not *Samuel Relating to Eli the Judgments of God* was begun with the Academy in mind, this picture did not become Copley's diploma piece, and surely as a consequence of his tardiness, the Academy passed a regulation on 10 December 1781 stating that an academician's election was considered as having been declined if a diploma work had not been submitted within a year. Copley prudently submitted *The Tribute Money* (cat. 14) as his diploma piece a year later, and, as has been pointed out, the subject itself – "Render ... unto Caesar the things which are Caesar's; and unto God the things that are God's" (St. Matthew 22:21) – is a wry reference to the painting as the artist's 'tribute.'[29]

While the borrowing of West's head of St. Peter for Eli can be seen, at least in part, as an act of homage, *The Tribute Money* is clearly a challenge to West, intentionally competing with his *Christ Blessing Little Children* (fig. 15). West had given this last painting to the Royal Academy around 1780 to help decorate its quarters in New Somerset House, and from the beginning the architect, Sir William Chambers, envisioned giving it a prominent position over the fireplace in the Assembly Room,[30] the position it enjoys in Henry Singleton's *The Royal Academicians Gathered in their Council Room, 1793, to Judge the Work of the Students* (fig. 53 on p. 73) dated 1795. In Singleton's painting, *The Tribute Money* can also be seen (cropped) at the upper right, hanging on an adjacent wall.[31]

Despite West's having executed *Christ Blessing Little Children* for the Royal Academy, it is not one of his finest efforts. Sentimental in approach, soft in focus, and with the figures stretched over a wide format (presumably from the beginning he intended it as an overmantel), it lacks the concentrated energy of Copley's tight focus. The mustached, turbaned figure at the left of West's canvas reappears in Copley's, as does the pensive disciple with hand to mouth at the right, who becomes the Pharisee looking out of the composition to challenge the viewer's response. West's Christ, a bland interpretation of the works of Murillo, gives way to the heroic, semitic features of Copley's commanding figure, who is far more than a match for his five challengers. Each of Copley's characters is individualized to a higher degree than is usual for history painting, but by tightly compressing his group, a result of his study of Rubens,[32] he maintains a compositional unity. In this comparison with West's picture, one which, as we have seen, Copley wanted his audience to make, his work is clearly superior. Soon his rivalry with West was to become public. Even Singleton in his painting of the academicians of 1795 shows Copley, who is standing with his cane beneath the cast of *The Laocoön*, competing for attention with West, who is shown seated in the president's chair and wearing a hat as befits his office. But by 1782 in his diploma piece Copley was already challenging his countryman within and on the Academy's walls.

While in the genre of history painting Copley was not the equal of some of those who had inspired him such as Raphael and Rubens, his history pictures deserve more attention than they have received. It was second nature to his contemporaries to collect

28. See Prown 1966, II, p. 276 note 4.

29. *Ibid.*, p.293.

30. Von Erffa and Staley 1986, no. 330, date West's picture to 1781 on the basis of the caption in Valentine Green's 1782 mezzotint reproducing it which describes it as having been painted in 1781. However, Chambers included West's painting in his elevation of the Assembly Room wall, now in the Soane Museum, London. If this drawing was executed in preparation for the room's layout then West's picture may have been executed as early as 1779. In any case, it already formed a prominent part of the Academy's holdings when Copley undertook his diploma piece.

31. This is not to say that Copley knew when he painted his picture that it would necessarily hang in the same room with West's, only that it would join the same collection. Also, the arrangement in Singleton's painting cannot be taken as gospel. The casts presumably were not in the Council Room, and he could have taken liberties with the paintings as well, although there is no evidence that this was the case.

32. Prown points out Copley's indebtedness to the engraving after Rubens's *Christ Giving the Keys to St. Peter* (Prown 1966, II, p. 294).

Fig. 15 Benjamin West
Christ Blessing Little Children, 1781
Oil on canvas, 44½ × 83¼ in. (113 × 211.5 cm)
Royal Academy of Art, London

the work of the Old Masters, but when patronizing living artists they tended only to commission portraits, be it of themselves, of their horses (sporting art), or of their estates (landscape). The imaginative sphere of history painting was to be honored, but the artist living next door should be discouraged from making the attempt to aspire to this level. In 1766, after West had completed a painting of the classical subject of Pylades and Orestes,[33] the picture, as his colleague James Northcote relates, received high praise, with numerous people visiting his home to see it: "But the most wonderful part of the story is, that, notwithstanding all this vast bustle and commendation, bestowed upon this justly admired picture, by which Mr. West's servant gained upwards of thirty pounds for showing it, yet no one mortal ever asked the price of the work, or so much as offered to give him a commission to paint any other subject. Indeed there was one gentleman so highly delighted with the picture, and who spoke of it with such great praise to his father, that he immediately asked him the reason he did not purchase, as he so much admired it, when he answered – 'What could I do, if I had it? – you would not surely have me hang up a modern English picture in my house, unless it was a portrait?'"[34]

Fortunately for West he did not long have to endure this state of affairs, soon obtaining important supporters and within a few years even becoming historical painter to King George III, a situation that was to offer unparalleled opportunities. West went on to create an impressively large number of history paintings, including works from the classical past, mythological and religious subjects, and scenes illustrating Renaissance and Baroque epics, but in receiving support he remained the exception rather than the rule.

Despite the fact that one of the principal reasons for the founding of the Royal Academy in 1768 was to establish in England a school of history painters, this genre met with little encouragement. In the 1770s, artists such as Angelica Kauffmann, John Hamilton Mortimer, and James Barry valiantly produced historical paintings for an often indifferent public. Sir Joshua Reynolds himself was to attempt the occasional work of this type, but few persisted in pursuing this exalted genre in the face of inadequate patronage. Copley, however, even without support, never backed down from the challenge of confronting the Old Masters. From 1780 onwards he proved himself to be

33. See von Erffa and Staley 1986, no. 186.

34. Northcote 1818, I, pp. 142–3.

an accomplished history painter. Yet these religious pictures, while a more important part of his œuvre than is usually acknowledged, are not the major achievement of his English period. It was his pioneering exploration of contemporary history painting that proved his greatest legacy.

Contemporary History Painting: Brave New World

The phrase 'contemporary history painting' was, from the conventional point of view, an oxymoron. History painting and painting of contemporary life were necessarily mutually exclusive concepts. Only an idealized and imagined past could provide subject matter suitable for portrayal in a heroic mode. Events drawn from the modern world were obviously too familiar and ordinary to allow for the distancing required by the grand style. It was a prime example of familiarity breeding contempt, and an artist who wished to treat a contemporary hero in the manner reserved for such figures as Christ or Achilles invited ridicule.

Benjamin West, however, defied academic dogma by depicting a modern subject in the grand style with his picture *The Death of General Wolfe* (fig. 57 on p. 79), which he executed in 1770 and exhibited at the Royal Academy in the following year.[35] Because of misinformation supplied fifty years after the fact by John Galt, West's biographer, commentators often focus on the erroneous issue of dress. According to Galt, King George III remarked to the painter that he had been informed that the dignity of the subject had been impaired by his having represented the characters in modern military costume, "observing that it was thought very ridiculous to exhibit heroes in coats, breeches, and cock'd hats."[36] This complaint is of course just what one would expect from upholders of the academic standard, but Galt goes on to quote West as saying that in an earlier conversation Sir Joshua Reynolds, the disapproving president of the Royal Academy, had "concluded with urging me earnestly to adopt the classic costume of antiquity, as much more becoming the inherent greatness of my subject than the modern garb of war."[37] While Reynolds painted portraits of his contemporaries in classical guise, such a masquerade for the soldiers on the Plains of Abraham would have been patently absurd, and one doubts he ever espoused any such view. The question was never whether or not to depict the protagonists in classical or contemporary dress but whether or not a contemporary subject should be treated in the exalted rhetoric that had formerly been exclusively reserved for history painting. West was not even the first to depict Wolfe's death, George Romney and Edward Penny having done so before him, but their more modest efforts should be termed narrative paintings.[38] West deliberately set out to elevate and monumentalize this contemporary subject in terms of scale and composition to the level of high art, and in this he was successful. He took many of the elements already present in Penny's painting but translated them to a more exalted plane, adding a host of respectful mourners, a more graceful Lamentation pose for Wolfe, and the dramatic grandeur of an open vista punctuated with the majestic sweep of storm-laden clouds. As Edgar Wind has pointed out, by choosing an event that took place in remote Canada and including such exotic details as the Indian and colorful frontiersman, West achieved the requisite distance in terms of place rather than time.[39] As Galt insisted, even if for the wrong reasons, West did occasion a revolution in the arts.

Copley, another American painter who had been born outside the class structure

35. In Copley's first letter from London, 11 July 1774, he wrote his half-brother Henry Pelham, "I have seen Mr. West's Death of General Wolf, which is sufficient of itself to Immortalize the Author of it" (*Letters of Copley and Pelham* 1914/ 1972, p. 226).

36. Galt 1820, II, p. 46.

37. *Ibid.*, p. 47.

38. Romney exhibited his painting in London at the Free Society in 1763, and Penny exhibited his the following year at the Society of Artists. While Romney's picture has not survived, Penny's is now in the Ashmolean Museum, Oxford, with a version also at Petworth House.

39. Wind 1938–9.

on which the academic hierarchy of genres was so strongly dependent, was the first artist to follow up on West's innovation, and contributed even further to its development when in 1778 he exhibited at the Royal Academy *Watson and the Shark* (cat. 4). West had taken for his subject the death of a national hero at the moment he had secured North America for the British Empire, a moment that was already one of utmost consequence. Copley's story, on the other hand, while an exciting one, was hardly momentous for anyone other than Watson himself. West painted his subject on speculation, hoping his nationalistic theme would appeal to a wide audience, and in this he was far from disappointed, producing several versions, one of which was for the king. While there is no documentation as to how Copley came to select his subject, the presumption, surely correct, is that Brook Watson, a prominent London merchant, commissioned the painting.

In 1749, when just fourteen years old, Brook Watson had gone for a swim in Havana Harbor, where he had recently arrived as a crewman aboard a merchant ship. On seeing a shark approaching, the crew of a boat waiting to take the captain ashore raced to rescue Watson and were finally able to drive off the shark on its third assault, but not before it had mutilated his right leg below the knee. Copley depicts this climactic moment, while Watson's fate is still in doubt.

Copley deliberately elevates his subject, just as West had elevated his, by drawing on the repertoire of the Old Masters, and despite the dynamic nature of the moment being depicted, with the shark furiously charging in to seize its prey, the artist's borrowings from the grand style lend a frozen monumentality to the whole. Copley's critics were more concerned with factual 'errors' such as why the harpooner's hair blows in the wind when the sea and sails in the background are calm or why the boat does not tilt more to starboard, but these writers miss their mark just as have those military historians who never tire of pointing out West's inaccuracies in his *Death of General Wolfe*. Both paintings depend on the heroic, idealizing world of history painting to transcend the merely factual, and in the case of *Watson and the Shark* so grand a conception demands a significance beyond the retelling of the event itself.

Modern critics have contrived a number of explanations for the painting's deeper purpose, relating it to the aesthetic experience of the Burkean sublime, particularly in terms of America's mythic perceptions of the sea, the turmoil of the American Revolution with its threat of political dismemberment, and the social issues raised by the prominent role of the black seaman.[40] None of these arguments is mutually exclusive; all in greater or lesser degree could have formed part of the conscious or unconscious intention, but the primary context for explaining the painting's use of ennobling, grand-manner rhetoric is religious.[41]

The man in the prow armed with a boat hook consciously evokes images of St. Michael casting out Satan or the related subject of St. George slaying the dragon; the two seamen straining to reach Watson are borrowed from figures in Raphael's *The Miraculous Draught of Fishes* and Rubens's similar conception of the same subject; and the pose of Watson himself harks back to the possessed boy in Raphael's *Transfiguration* (fig. 11), a work that in Copley's own estimation "has always been allowed to be the greatest picture in the world."[42] According to the Bible, this youth, before being delivered from his affliction by Christ, "oft-times ... falleth into the fire, and oft into the water" (St. Matthew 17:15). Both he and Watson anguish for a merciful deliverance.

40. See respectively Stein 1976; Abrams 1979; and Boime 1989. The last two articles, while well researched, at times force their material into insupportable conclusions.

41. The religious reading was first pointed out in Jaffe 1977. The religious perspective has also been ably expanded upon in Miles 1993.

42. Copley to his wife, 5 November 1774, quoted in Prown 1966, II, p. 250. The relationship of Watson to Raphael's youth was first pointed out by Stein 1976, pp. 102–3.

Watson himself felt the image to be didactic in content, for when in 1803 he bequeathed the painting to Christ's Hospital, London, a school for poor boys, he wrote it should hang in the hall of the hospital "as holding out a most useful Lesson to Youth."[43] That lesson is one of salvation. Copley elevates Watson to the level of Everyman, flailing in a sinful world where the Jaws of Hell threaten to consume him body and soul. Watson's rescuers represent that Christian community who return him to the safe harbor in the background, a scene dominated at the horizon by a radiant sky, against which are silhouetted the cross of the cathedral at the far left, the crosses on the tops of the rounded convent towers, and those formed by the masts and crossbars of the ships at anchor. An exciting tale of a brush with death is transformed into a larger religious allegory in keeping with its monumentalizing presentation. Both West's *The Death of General Wolfe* and Copley's *Watson and the Shark* employ a transcendent spirituality for nationalistic purposes, West describing the Christ-like sacrifice of the military hero, Copley the individual who is saved to become a contributing member of that same community.

On 7 April 1778, a few weeks before *Watson and the Shark* was on exhibit, William Pitt, 1st Earl of Chatham, collapsed in the House of Lords, dying five weeks later. Chatham, the architect of Britain's imperial expansion during the Seven Years War, had suffered a stroke when attempting to reply to the Duke of Richmond's speech in favor of American Independence. While sympathetic to American aspirations for greater freedoms, Chatham could not tolerate the break-up of the empire he had helped to create. Both West and Copley fastened on this subject as suitable for history painting, but West eventually left the field to his rival, producing only a small painting which was never exhibited (fig. 16). If the two drawings that are based on West's composition are by Copley, as is thought (see fig. 17),[44] then he had knowledge of West's design before beginning his own, a large canvas that arrives at a different solution (fig. 18). Horace Walpole, the noted writer, compared the two conceptions to Copley's detriment: "Mr. West made a small Sketch of the death of Lord Chatham, much better expressed & disposed than Copley's. It has none but the principal person's present [42 figures in all]; Copley's almost the whole peerage [56 figures], of whom seldom so many are there at once, & in Copleys most are meer spectators, but the great merit of West is the principal Figure which has his crutch & gouty stockings, which express his feebleness & account for his death. West wd not finish it not to interfere with his friend Copley."[45]

In West's conception, Richmond shares center stage with Chatham, and Copley may have wished to avoid a pairing that could be interpreted as showing the pro-American speaker on one side with the literal collapse of his opposition on the other. While still giving Richmond a place of prominence, he moves him to the right and reorients him to face inward. By shifting Chatham to the right as well, he places him beneath one of the Armada Tapestries that provided the room's decor. Chatham's view of Britain's imperial mission lay in promoting the control of the seas as a means to commercial dominance, rather than in a land-based empire, and his expiring beneath this image of England's greatest maritime victory is appropriately symbolic. Yet Walpole's comment gets to the heart of the difference between Copley's conception and West's, though one may disagree with his preference for the latter. West's version, while by no means unedited and unidealized, is closer to ordinary reality, emphasizing

43. Watson's will is in the Public Record Office, London, and this portion is quoted in Boston, Detroit, Washington 1993, p. [5].

44. The other drawing is in Prown 1966, II, fig. 400. Prown tentatively accepted these drawings as by Copley in his publication of 1966 (II, p. 281), but in 1977, after West's oil sketch resurfaced, he wrote the respective owners that he felt they were by West (copies of these letters are in the National Gallery of Art file on its drawing). Neither von Erffa nor Staley, however, accepted them as being by West, and their book characterizes the drawings as appearing to be free copies after West's painting presumably by Copley (von Erffa and Staley 1986, no. 104). The drawings are indeed far more closely related to Copley's style than to West's. A curious detail in the drawings is the hat placed at Chatham's feet. In both West's and Copley's paintings, the Earl Bathurst, the Lord Chancellor, is shown wearing a black hat as befits his office. Chatham, on the other hand, like the other peers, would have been hatless, and the inappropriate detail of the fallen hat is in neither artist's final composition.

45. Quoted in Prown 1966, II, pp. 280–1, from "Walpole's Book of Materials, 1771," Lewis-Walpole Library, Farmington, Conn. (1785), p. 113.

Fig. 16 Benjamin West
The Death of the Earl of Chatham, ca. 1778–86

Oil on canvas, 28 × 35¾ in. (71 × 90.8 cm)
Kimbell Art Museum, Fort Worth, Texas

Fig. 17 Attributed to John Singleton Copley
Study for *The Death of the Earl of Chatham*, 1779

Pencil and white chalk on gray-green paper, 12⅛ × 19½ in. (31 × 49.5 cm)
National Gallery of Art, Washington, D.C.

the frail human being beneath the imposing robes. Copley, in contrast, strives for epic grandeur. The benches seen in his early sketch (fig. 17), which are like encroaching coffins, are swept away as the space is enlarged and Chatham himself is pushed further into the middle ground and to one side. Distanced from the spectator and with his head facing the light, he is like a Baroque saint about to join his Redeemer.

In the hierarchy of genres, history painting, as we have seen, is intended to show man not as he is but as he should be. Portraiture, on the other hand, even when idealizing the sitter, is more closely rooted in reality. Even West's *Death of General Wolfe* was vulnerable to the charge of being a glorified group portrait as numerous officers, almost none of whom was present, crowd around their expiring leader. Copley's *Death of the Earl of Chatham* is indeed 'mired' in portraiture, but with American pragmatism the artist attempted to turn the tables by arguing that "uniting the value of living characters to the dignity of an Historical Fact" is "an advantage that will be rising in estimation in every succeeding age, and which no other Picture extant has to boast of in any degree equal to this."[46] According to Copley, then, portraiture, properly introduced, enhances the value of history painting for posterity. Yet, despite his success in aggrandizing his scene, literal truth continues to make inroads in diluting the grand style.

The Death of the Earl of Chatham is a landmark work for yet another reason. Nationalistic subjects such as *The Death of General Wolfe* and *The Death of the Earl of Chatham* appealed to a larger audience than did the canonical subject matter of history painting, and Copley was boldly innovative in marketing these works. West had exhibited his contemporary history paintings at the Royal Academy as had Copley his *Watson and the Shark*, but after completing *The Death of the Earl of Chatham*, a work that required a considerable investment in time given its numerous portraits, Copley displayed his picture in 1781 in a private venue that opened just days after the Royal Academy's own annual exhibition. He not only hoped to profit from the admission charge but also from the sale of the picture after it had been exhibited and from the sale of the print reproducing it, for which he had contracted. While he encountered difficulties because he asked too high a price for the painting and had to wait far longer than desirable for a print of quality, he did point the way to reaching an expanding audience for high art.

The Death of the Earl of Chatham also began Copley's business relationship with John Boydell, the innovative printseller and art promoter who was soon to become Lord Mayor of London. In 1779 Boydell had urged the Guildhall to commission a painting instead of a sculpture as a memorial for the Earl of Chatham, and when his efforts proved unsuccessful, he arranged to accept subscriptions on Copley's behalf for the projected print after his painting.

Boydell was closely involved in Copley's next contemporary history painting, *The Death of Major Peirson* (cat. 18). He had first engaged the artist to execute a picture of the seventeenth-century subject of Charles I demanding in the House of Commons the five impeached Members, but this work was delayed when *The Death of Major Peirson*, for which Boydell paid the artist £800, was substituted in its place. On its completion in 1784, the artist again mounted a private exhibition, displaying this work along with *The Death of the Earl of Chatham* in a room in the Haymarket. After this showing, Boydell kept *Peirson* on view in his second-floor gallery at his shop at 90 Cheapside in the City and oversaw the production of the print after it.

46. *Proposals for Publishing, by Subscription, an Engraved Print, from the Original Picture, now painting by John Singleton Copley, R. A. Elect, representing the Death of the Late Earl of Chatham, to be engraved by Mr. John Keyse Sherwin*, London, 29 March 1780, p. 2.

Fig. 18 John Singleton Copley
The Death of the Earl of Chatham, 1779–81

Oil on canvas, 90 × 121 in. (228.5 × 307.5 cm)
On loan to the National Portrait Gallery, London, by
courtesy of the Tate Gallery, London

The Death of Major Peirson far surpasses *The Death of the Earl of Chatham* in its brilliant theatricality and stirring appeal to patriotic sentiments. It depicts the death of a gallant young officer, killed while leading a counter-attack against French troops invading the island of Jersey. The scene is the central market square of St Helier on the morning of 6 January 1781, with the smoking chimney in the background and the crisp light the only indication that this is a winter's day. In the center, officers, all of whom are identifiable portraits, support their fallen leader, while his black servant exacts instant retribution by shooting the French soldier who had killed Peirson. The engagement was a side-show to what was taking place in America, but everyone could enjoy an image in which the French were cast as the enemy, their traditional role in Francophobic England.

Copley took pains to authenticate such details as the appearance of the square and the correctness of the uniforms, but again he took those liberties allowed by poetic license to elevate his subject, transcending mere reportage in order to achieve the exalted level of history painting. Richard Saunders has also pointed out that Copley's editing of the literal truth was not always just for pictorial effect. The artist deliberately

Fig. 19 John Singleton Copley
The Siege of Gibraltar, 1783–91

Oil on canvas, 214 × 297 in. (543 × 754 cm)
Guildhall Art Gallery, London

played down the role of the Scottish Highlanders of the 78th Regiment to highlight that of the English Grenadiers of the 95th Regiment, thereby making his subject more appealing for the English audience to whom it was addressed.[47]

Although handled with greater grace, the pose of Major Peirson with his torso arched back, his hair flowing freely, and one arm dangling down recalls that of Patroclus in Copley's earlier Roman drawing (cat. 20). Again, like West, Copley uses the rhetoric of traditional history painting to ennoble modern life. Around the spring of 1783, when contemplating embarking on a painting commemorating the installation of the new Order of St. Patrick, he wrote an unidentified Irish nobleman whose support he was seeking, "Being fully persuaded that modern subjects are the properest for the exercize of the pencil and far more Interesting to the present Age than those taken from Ancient History I have as much as possible employed myself in Events that have happened in my own time."[48] Greater interest on the part of the public means greater profits on the part of the artist, but, if the subject of Peirson is preferred to that of Patroclus, all of the heroic possibilities formerly reserved for the Greek hero are here transferred to the youthful English officer.[49]

Copley's other point "that modern subjects are the properest for the exercize of the pencil" presumably alludes to the artist being better able to recreate, albeit in an idealized manner, the 'facts' of contemporary life. Although the image is carefully planned and manipulated, there is the sense of a heightened 'photographic' truth which might be felt to be inappropriate in portraying a distant classical past. The single drop of Peirson's blood suspended in mid-air to the left of his dangling hand reinforces this sense of an instantaneous moment captured for eternity.

Homer devotes a full book of *The Iliad* to the fight over Patroclus's body, which instigates the most sustained and fierce battle of the entire epic. In the painting of Peirson, the ferocity is again due to the body, Copley skillfully having personalized the conflict. The British forces, galvanized by the magnitude of their loss, prove irresistible as they sweep from left to right to certain victory. With only a few exceptions, even the

47. Saunders 1990.

48. Quoted in Prown 1966, II, p. 297.

49. Saunders also associates the figure of Peirson with the classical warrior that I am identifying as Patroclus (see Saunders 1990, pp. 34–5). With his usual prescience, Robert Rosenblum has been even more specific in connecting *The Death of Major Peirson* with the antique past: "The almost balletic fall of the young Peirson into the arms of his fellow officers is as elegant and noble as the scene of Achilles mourning the dead Patroclus in the new wave of Homeric illustrations that began in the 1760s ... The horrors of war, the unavoidably ugly facts known to all, are here translated into a high-minded drama that might almost bring the Trojan Wars up-to-date" (Rosenblum and Janson 1984, p. 18).

Fig. 20 Augustus Pugin and Thomas Rowlandson
John Singleton Copley's The Siege of Gibraltar *as seen in the Interior of the Court of Common Council at the Guildhall*, 1808–10

Colored etching and aquatint from Rudolph Ackermann, *Microcosm of London*, vol. 2

50. Quoted in Howgego 1958, p. 38.

51. Copley to Pelham, Rome, 14 March 1775, in *Letters of Copley and Pelham* 1914/1972, p. 301.

52. If *The Battle of La Hogue* was begun as early as 1774 or 1775, as has been suggested (see von Erffa and Staley 1986, no. 90), then it may have also influenced the underlying structure of Copley's *Watson and the Shark*: the compact group of attacking English sailors in the foreground of West's picture slopes upwards to the right from a base composed of rescued seamen to climax in a dramatic assault.

French rifles lean rightward as the engagement threatens to become a rout. The pressure of the onslaught within this compact, urban square splits the fleeing factions into two vectors. One is composed of the women and children, terrified non-combatants who rush into the viewer's space, and the other is composed of the French troops who retreat not out of the painting's right-hand side but through the court house doorway surmounted by the royal coat of arms in the background. This building, the symbol of British justice and rule, stands ready to swallow and expel these disturbers of civil order.

Copley's next contemporary history painting, *The Siege of Gibraltar* (fig. 19), commemorates another British military triumph. In an attempt to retake the Rock of Gibraltar, which it had lost to England in 1704, Spain, aided by France, had begun an extended siege on 11 July 1779, and in 1782 intensified its pressure by mounting a formidable assault from the sea with the launching of floating batteries. The garrison forces, under the command of General George Augustus Eliott (raised to the peerage as Lord Heathfield in 1787), successfully parried this threat, destroying ten of the ships sent against them, and the later arrival of Admiral Howe's fleet dispersed the remaining opposition.

In this instance the subject had not been of Copley's choosing. The commission was from the Corporation of London, which, as stated in a committee resolution, determined that "an Historical Painting will be the most suitable mode for the Court of Common Council to express its respect to the Gallant Conduct of General Eliott, Governor of Gibraltar, Lord Viscount Howe, Commander of the Fleet, and the rest of his Majesty's Officers, Soldiers and Sailors employed in its [Gibraltar's] defence and relief."[50] This committee approached both Copley and West, and, although on this occasion West competed with his colleague, Copley secured the prize, thanks in part to the favorable reception given to *The Death of the Earl of Chatham* and to *The Death of Major Peirson*, on which he was still working. He eventually was to concentrate only on the destruction of the floating batteries, relegating Admiral Howe's relief to a predella painted by Dominic Serres, but his work, as completed, is still by far his largest painting, measuring almost eighteen by twenty-five feet. It dominated the Common Council room – as can be seen in Pugin and Rowlandson's print of this chamber (fig. 20) – where it not only lauded Britain's imperial might but also testified to the impressive possibilities opened up by municipal patronage on a grand scale. When he had been in Rome working on *The Ascension* (fig. 10), Copley had written his half-brother of his hope that he might receive a commission to render his sketch as an altarpiece measuring "24 feet by 18."[51] Thanks to the Corporation of London, he finally had a commission on this grand scale, creating a secular altarpiece celebrating Britain's benevolent empire.

When Copley initially conceived his subject, he decided to depict the action as seen from the water with Gibraltar in the background, and surely in choosing such a point of view he was thinking of challenging West's *The Battle of La Hogue* (fig. 21), a picture of an engagement of 1692 that his rival had exhibited at the Royal Academy as recently as 1780.[52] West focuses on the rescue of French seamen in the composition's center, but the fighting rages around them, even to the point that one sailor ungallantly uses his fist to dispatch a drowning opponent at lower right. Copley embraces instead an image of British magnanimity with several naval officers and crews risking their own lives in the aftermath of victory to rescue the enemy amidst their exploding ships, "a display of humanity," as stated in his proposal for the subscription to his print, "that highly exalts the British character."[53]

Under pressure to include portraits of the defenders in the garrison, Copley radically reconfigured his design, introducing at the right a cluster of prominent officers. The demands of portraiture again pull against those of history painting as the Rubensian inferno is confined to the left and pushed farther into the background, while the officers pose in the size of life for posterity. The viewer, too, is no longer a part of the epic maritime struggle, having now been placed on land with the parapet extending across the bottom edge almost to the left-hand corner. General Eliott, seated on a white horse, points toward the carnage, his pose having been described as "in the attitude of giving directions, and applauding the succour afforded the vanquished foe, after the destruction of the floating batteries."[54] Whether or not the gesture is quite so nuanced is debatable. It is, of course, the commanding gesture later used to such telling effect in the artist's *Saul Reproved by Samuel* (fig. 22), but in this instance Copley, to underscore Eliott's benign intentions, removes from his final composition the blazing cannon seen in the earlier oil sketch between the legs of the officer directly beneath Eliott's outstretched hand.[55]

In his original agreement for the commission of *The Siege of Gibraltar* from the City of London, Copley had stipulated that he "will undertake the work for one thousand guineas, hoping the advantages of an Exhibition of the Picture and the publication of a Print from it will compensate him for the time and study requisite for completing so large a work."[56] It took him eight years to finish this ambitious project, and in the spring of 1791 he had to have a tent erected in Green Park in order to show it because of its large size. Complaints from the aristocratic residents north of the park required him to move the tent several times, until George III, referring to Buckingham House, advised the artist to "Push it up nearer to my Wife's house – she won't complain."[57]

Copley is recorded as having said that 60,000 people attended the exhibition,[58] and, with a one-shilling admission charge, he would have received approximately £3,000, some of which was needed to cover expenses. Given that he had spent the better part of eight years on this project and had to alter the conception from the original proposal, he felt justified in requesting an additional 500 guineas from the Corporation beyond the thousand already agreed upon.[59] After lengthy and humiliating negotiations, he eventually received only 100 guineas more. He was also to be disappointed in the sale of the print, which, when it finally appeared in 1810, was met with indifference by a public saturated with images of more recent and significant campaigns.

Although this venture was not the commercial success Copley had hoped to achieve, it did help to forge new ways of marketing contemporary history paintings. On 5 May 1795 he exhibited at Spring Gardens *Charles I Demanding in the House of Commons the Five Impeached Members*, the subject he had been engaged to paint as early as 1781 for Boydell but had put aside when *The Death of Major Peirson* was substituted in its place. From its inception, this work was probably conceived as a pendant to *The Death of the Earl of Chatham*, its scene from the House of Commons complementing the one from the House of Lords. Once the grand style, formerly limited to scenes from the Bible, classical antiquity, and epic poetry, was employed in the service of contemporary subjects, it could then be applied to any era, medieval or Renaissance as well as modern. A subject such as *Charles I in the House of Commons* required antiquarian research on Copley's part

53. *Proposals for Publishing by Subscription, An Engraving, from the Historical Picture, of the Siege and Relief of Gibraltar, painted by John Singleton Copley, R. A. Now Exhibiting in a Pavilion, erected by the gracious Permission of the King, for that Purpose, in the Green Park,* London [1791], p. 2.

54. These lines, which are from the committee minutes made after a visit to the artist's studio, presumably reflect what the artist told the committee. (G.R.O. MSS 4.16, Cttee, 3 July 1787, quoted in Howgego 1958, p. 40).

55. This officer is Lieutenant General Sir Robert Boyd, who also forms part of the study for Major General August de la Motte (cat. 35) as the figure in outline on the left.

56. Quoted in Prown 1966, II, p. 312.

57. Quoted *ibid.*, II, p. 331.

58. See *ibidem.*

59. There are twenty shillings in a pound and twenty-one in a guinea. The difference between the two is more than monetary, guineas being the preferred payment for gentlemen.

Fig. 21 Benjamin West
The Battle of La Hogue, ca. 1775–80
Oil on canvas, 60 × 84¹/₂ in. (152.5 × 214.5 cm)
National Gallery of Art, Washington D.C.

to recapture likenesses of the participants. Yet the ensuing focus on portraiture made this seventeenth-century scene more akin to his contemporary ones than to his biblical paintings. Perhaps because of the less than topical nature of this seventeenth-century subject, its exhibition failed to generate much enthusiasm.

On 22 May 1799, Copley attempted his last private showing of this type. In another tent erected for the occasion, while re-exhibiting *The Death of the Earl of Chatham* and *Charles I in the House of Commons,* he displayed *The Victory of Lord Duncan* (fig. 40 on p. 63), depicting the surrender of the Dutch Admiral DeWinter to Admiral Duncan on the deck of the *Venerable* on 11 October 1797. Although at the very end of his life Copley was still attempting history paintings of modern subjects, *The Victory of Lord Duncan* was the last that he privately exhibited and contracted for engraving. In the nineteenth century these one-man exhibitions of one or a few paintings were to become more common, and, in France, Jacques-Louis David was to follow Copley's lead in exhibiting privately in Paris his *Intervention of the Sabine Women* as early as 1800.

History Painting: The Late Years

Despite an absence of patronage, Copley until the end of his career persevered in executing biblical subjects, an integral part of the traditional standard by which ambitious artists were to be judged. At the Royal Academy in 1796, he exhibited *Abraham Offering Up Isaac,* a work inspired by Rembrandt's conception of this same subject, and two years later *Hagar and Ishmael in the Wilderness,* its pendant, both works now known only from the mezzotints after them. In 1798 he also exhibited *Saul Reproved by Samuel for Not Obeying the Commandments of the Lord* (fig. 22). Although this is the largest of his surviving religious paintings, unlike its predecessors it was not engraved, Copley presumably finding even this market to be unrewarding. For his subject he returns to the story of Samuel, who, now as an old and revered Prophet, condemns Saul, King of Israel. Despite having been instructed to lay waste to the Amalekites and their possessions,

Fig. 22 John Singleton Copley
Saul Reproved by Samuel for Not Obeying the
Commandments of the Lord, 1798
Oil on canvas, 67 × 85¹⁄₂ in. (170 × 217 cm)
Museum of Fine Arts, Boston, bequest of Susan Dexter
Greene in memory of Charles and Martha Babcock
Amory

Saul had spared their king and the best of their livestock, causing Samuel to reject him
for his disobedience.

"And Samuel said unto Saul, I will not return with thee: for thou hast rejected the
word of the Lord, and the Lord hath rejected thee from being king over Israel.

And as Samuel turned about to go away, he [Saul] laid hold upon the skirt of his
mantle, and it rent.

And Samuel said unto him, The Lord hath rent the kingdom of Israel from thee
this day ..." (1 Samuel 15:26-28)

Samuel, positioned against the black smoke rising from the ravished lands of the
Amalekites, imperiously turns to pass judgment on the recoiling king. For Samuel's
pose, Copley looks back to Caravaggio's *The Calling of St. Matthew* (fig. 23), which he
would have seen in Rome. Caravaggio shows Christ as twisting his body around in
order to point after having walked beyond a group of figures. Christ's limp, outstretched hand evokes the hand of Adam in Michelangelo's celebrated *Creation of Adam*

Fig. 23 Caravaggio
The Calling of St. Matthew, 1599–1600
Oil on canvas, 126³/₄ × 134 in. (322 × 340 cm)
Contarelli Chapel, San Luigi dei Francesi, Rome

on the ceiling of the Sistine Chapel, while for Samuel's hand Copley chooses as his model the more forceful one of God in this same fresco. Like Caravaggio, Copley uses light and shade for dramatic intensity, although opting for more graduated contrasts.

The subject is an interesting choice for its uncompromising harshness. Samuel rebukes Saul with devastating finality for not having waged total war, and the force of this gesture sends shock waves through the entire group. The imposing horse and attendant anchoring the composition's right-hand edge are related to the colossal sculptures of the *Horse-tamers* on the Quirinal Hill in Rome, but they go on to surpass their well known prototypes. The characterization of the agitated horse is as electrifying as any of George Stubbs's animals attacked by lions or West's foaming steeds in his 1796 version of *Death on the Pale Horse*,[60] and, while the attendant wears a blue, skin-tight garment worthy of one of Henry Fuseli's mannerist figures, his idealized proportions have nothing in common with Fuseli's exaggerated effects. The last painting Copley exhibited at the Royal Academy was *The Resurrection*, a now missing picture of 1812. Thus, to the very end of his career, he was attempting the type of religious picture that had been the mainstay of artists working in the grand manner.

Copley's religious pictures, firmly anchored in the traditional category of history painting, differ from his scenes of more recent events, and it is instructive to compare his *Saul Reproved by Samuel* to his depiction, never completed, of a moment that occurred in 1685, *Monmouth before James II Refusing to Give the Names of his Accomplices* (fig. 24). In the biblical subject the figures fill the space, whereas in the painting of English history they are smaller players on a larger stage. Yet the organization is similar, a figure striding away from his king, while, at the same time, turning back. But in *Monmouth before James II* the power relationships are reversed. Monmouth, the illegitimate son of Charles II, had plotted to overthrow his uncle James II, counting on Protestant support against this Catholic king. Captured and condemned to death for treason, he was granted a last interview. In the late nineteenth century, John Pettie, following Lord Macaulay's interpretation in *The History of England*, shows the young duke, hands bound behind him, groveling at his uncle's feet (fig. 25). Copley, on the other hand, highlights those accounts of the duke's defiance, as in David Hume's *History of Great Britain*: "James, finding such symptoms of depression and despondency in the unhappy prisoner, admitted him to his presence, in hopes of extorting a discovery of his accomplices: But Monmouth would not purchase life, however loved, at the price of so much infamy. Finding all efforts vain, he assumed courage from despair, and prepared himself for death, with a spirit, better suited to his rank and character."[61] In Copley's presentation, James II is literally diminished, and of course the viewer knows that, whatever Monmouth's personal fate, the Protestant faction will soon supplant its king. *Monmouth before James II*, no less than *Saul Reproved by Samuel*, is about the rejection of a monarch. Despite the differences in their approach to history painting and although in the more remote biblical subject the artist is less circumspect in his chastisement of a king, similar sentiments inform both: the difference between the modern subject and the biblical one is not so great as might at first be imagined.

Portraiture

Copley, of course, did not abandon portrait painting upon settling in London: it remained for him, as it did for the majority of his English colleagues, a major source of

60. See von Erffa and Staley 1986, no. 403.
61. Hume 1770, VIII, p. 242.

Fig. 24 John Singleton Copley
Monmouth before James II Refusing to Give the Names of his Accomplices, ca. 1795
Oil on canvas, 66¹/₂ × 88 in. (169 × 223.5 cm)
Fogg Art Museum, Harvard University Art Museums, gift of Edward D. Bettens to the Louise E. Bettens Fund

Fig. 25 John Pettie
The Duke of Monmouth's Interview with James II, 1882
Oil on canvas, 36³/₄ × 51³/₈ in. (93.5 × 130 cm)
© Manchester City Art Galleries

62. For discussions of this work, see von Erffa and Staley 1986, no. 546, and Prown 1986.

63. Cited in von Erffa and Staley 1986, p. 462.

patronage. In 1777, when he exhibited *The Copley Family* (cat. 1), Sir Joshua Reynolds and Thomas Gainsborough were the most prominent of the English portrait painters, and once again Copley could not have helped but measure himself also against the work of his countryman Benjamin West. When composing his own family piece, he surely knew West's family picture of 1772 (fig. 26), which commemorates the birth of Benjamin, their second son, in August of that year.[62] Coincidentally, West exhibited his family picture in the Royal Academy exhibition of 1777, probably in remembrance of his father who had died in the previous year, and Copley must have welcomed a comparison with his own canvas. The two works are on a different scale and in different keys. West depicts with subdued restraint a simple interior inviting contemplation, Copley a sumptuous elegance opening onto an Italianate setting, signaling his mastery of the fashionable grand manner. A reviewer in *The General Advertiser* criticized West for exhibiting a painting of such a personal subject,[63] but it is the quality of the presentation itself, not the subject, that is so intensely personal, and Copley's image, while as carefully constructed, is more in the nature of self-promotion. While West stresses his more austere Quaker roots, Copley presents himself as having left behind his provincial origins as he ably assumes the trappings of an aristocratic, cultural elite.

The Copley Family had the desired result, the artist receiving a commission from Sir William Pepperrell, another American expatriate, whose family portrait (cat. 3) was exhibited at the Royal Academy in the following year. The Pepperrells were among those prominent Loyalists who fled Boston because of the Revolution, and the painting celebrates the birth of a male heir, the longed-for son arriving after the births of three daughters. The composition again bears comparison to a work by West, a family portrait (fig. 27) traditionally identified as of Richard Brinsley Sheridan and his wife Elizabeth Linley with their son Thomas, who had been born on 17 March 1775. At

Fig. 26 Benjamin West
The Artist's Family, 1772
Oil on canvas, 20$\frac{1}{2}$ × 26$\frac{1}{4}$ in. (52 × 66.5 cm)
Yale Center for British Art, Paul Mellon Collection

Fig. 27 Benjamin West
The Sheridan Family(?), ca. 1775
Oil on canvas, 89$\frac{3}{4}$ × 63$\frac{1}{4}$ in. (228 × 160.5 cm)
Walker Art Gallery, Liverpool

64. For a detailed discussion of the picture in these terms, see Lovell 1991.

65. *The Morning Post*, 25 April 1778, p. 2.

their core, both West's and Copley's works allude to the theme of the Holy Family, the heroic nudity of the two male heirs discreetly borrowed from the Christ Child. Such allusions are a part of the ongoing secularization of religious imagery also to be seen in the work of their colleagues and already encountered in West's *The Artist's Family* (as well as later in *The Copley Family*). These borrowings were not intended as sacrilegious pillaging of the Old Masters but rather as the sanctification of modern family life. The type of fictive, irrational juxtapositions found in West's *Sheridan* and Copley's *Sir William Pepperrell and his Family*, where luxurious trappings and unexplained, grandiose architectural elements are combined with a sense of boundless, park-like scenery, is a commonplace in portraiture of this period, and of course had already been adopted by Copley in his own family portrait. Yet the narrative offered in *Sir William Pepperrell and his Family* is even more of an invented fiction than one usually encounters, in that Elizabeth Pepperrell had died in Boston three weeks after her son had been born in July 1775. To a large extent, then, the portrait is about the denial of loss, the loss of this wife and mother as well as the wealth represented by the family's sizable American holdings.[64]

The picture was Copley's largest work up to this time, exceeding the measurements of *The Copley Family* and *Watson and the Shark*, the artist thereby insuring that his painting would not be overlooked. Yet while *Watson and the Shark*, which was exhibited at this same time, received a favorable response, *Sir William Pepperrell and his Family* did not, one critic praising the former as "among the first performances of this exhibition" while contemptuously dismissing the latter as "a mere daubing."[65] Perhaps the reviewer found it excessive in its colorful and luxuriant profusion. In any event, the work was to spawn no immediate progeny, Copley returning to portraits of single figures.

Perhaps the painting Copley exhibited in 1778, "Portrait of a lady; three-quarters," is the work now tentatively identified as *Mrs. Seymour Fort* (cat. 6). This portrait, while

Fig. 28 Joshua Reynolds
Anne, Countess of Albemarle, 1759(?)

Oil on canvas, 49³/₄ × 39³/₄ in. (126.5 × 101 cm)
Reproduced by courtesy of the Trustees, The National
Gallery, London

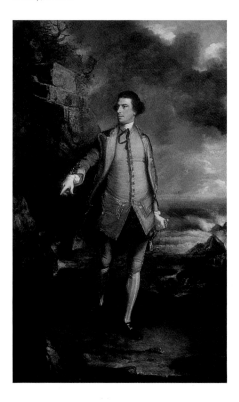

Fig. 29 Joshua Reynolds
Commodore Augustus Keppel, 1753–54

Oil on canvas, 94 × 58 in. (238.8 × 147 cm)
National Maritime Museum, Greenwich

related in style to his American œuvre, does demonstrate a more assured freedom in its handling of brushwork. The sitter is shown 'knotting,' holding a golden shuttle in her right hand while knotting the thread with her left. The other end of the thread disappears into the elegant work-bag hanging from her arm. In England and France, knotting was a favored pastime for ladies, acceptable even at court, as it avoided the appearance of idleness while allowing the practitioner to display feminine grace and dexterity. With younger sitters it is the coquettish aspects that are emphasized, while with older women it is industriousness that is celebrated.[66] In England, knotting becomes almost an act of piety, the Protestant equivalent of the Catholic telling of the rosary.[67] Reynolds could appropriately show Anne, Countess of Albemarle engaged in knotting (fig. 28), and Copley's middle-class sitter is even more regally presented than the countess in terms of her red velvet chair with its carved gilded frame and the bold patterning of the animated red drapery behind her, but at the same time his sitter is a great deal more accessible, inviting an intimacy that the countess denies.

In 1780, Copley exhibited at the Royal Academy his impressive full-length portrait of Major Hugh Montgomerie (cat. 9), a work in the grand manner that coincides with the beginnings of Montgomerie's political career, as he was first elected to Parliament in this year as Member for Ayrshire. The painting, though, celebrates Montgomerie's service as a captain in the French and Indian War of twenty years earlier. His pose is an adaptation of Reynolds's admired portrait of Commodore Augustus Keppel (fig. 29), which in its turn is based on the graceful authority of the celebrated *Apollo Belvedere*. In placing Montgomerie on a high, shallow foreground with sparse vegetation where he is silhouetted against a turbulent, battle-torn sky, Copley also relies on Reynolds's more recent portrait of Colonel John Hayes St Leger (fig. 30), exhibited just two years before. Copley, however, provides a narrow middleground, where Montgomerie's troops almost effortlessly sweep over the Cherokees they have been sent to subdue. The artist portrays the Indians as savages worthy of extinction, an American version of the biblical Amalekites who were so deserving of divine retribution. Not only do the Cherokees give way, but even the clouds respond to the pressure of Montgomerie's authoritative gesture, parting under the force of his pointing finger.

In 1782, Copley painted two portraits of Americans. One was of Henry Laurens (fig. 31),[68] a former president of the Continental Congress and, after his release from the Tower of London, a peace commissioner for the United States. The green drapery above Laurens's head forms a regal canopy, but there is a decided tension between the grandeur of the setting and the short, restless figure occupying it. Copley's image is a perceptive variation on the creative interplay between Baroque formulae intended for aristocracy and the assertive independence of the self-made man, explored by Hogarth in his 1740 portrait of Captain Coram, which then, as now, was on public view in London's Foundling Hospital.

Copley's portrait of Elkanah Watson (cat. 11) also comments on America's place in the new world order. In his memoirs, Watson, a native of Plymouth, Massachusetts, relates the story of the painting's dramatic completion: "The painting was finished in most admirable style, except the back-ground, which Copley and I designed to represent a ship, bearing to America the intelligence of the acknowledgment of independence, with a sun just rising upon the stripes of the union, streaming from her gaff. All was complete save the flag, which Copley did not deem prudent to hoist under present

Fig. 30 Joshua Reynolds
Colonel John Hayes St Leger, 1778
Oil on canvas, 94^1/$_2$ × 58 in. (240 × 147 cm)
Waddesdon Manor (The National Trust)

Fig. 31 John Singleton Copley
Henry Laurens, 1782
Oil on canvas, 54^1/$_8$ × 40^5/$_8$ in. (137.5 × 103 cm)
National Portrait Gallery, Smithsonian Institution,
Washington, D.C.

66. For an article on Copley's *Mrs. Seymour Fort (?)* in
the context of knotting, see Townsend 1966.
Townsend points out that knotting does not appear
to have been practiced at this time in America.
When Copley showed Mrs. Thomas Mifflin indus-
triously employed in a double portrait of 1773, she
is depicted working a fringe loom (fig. 73 on p. 108).

67. The second stanza of the poem *The Royal
Knotter*, first published in 1704, makes this point
when praising Queen Mary:

Bless'd we! who from such Queens are freed,
Who by vain Superstition led,

circumstances, as his gallery is a constant resort of the royal family and the nobility. I
dined with the artist, on the glorious 5th of December, 1782, after listening with him to
the speech of the King, formally recognizing the United States of America as in the
rank of nations. Previous to dining, and immediately after our return from the House
of Lords, he invited me into his studio, and there with a bold hand, a master's touch,
and I believe an American heart, attached to the ship the *stars and stripes*. This was, I
imagine, *the first American flag hoisted in old England*."[69]

Watson, thirty-four years Laurens's junior, represents a younger generation that
will be involved in building the fledgling republic. A merchant, he had ardently supported the Revolution and had earlier journeyed to France with dispatches and money
for Benjamin Franklin. In 1782 he carried other dispatches to London, and the two

legible papers on the desk allude to his extensive commercial connections which spanned the Atlantic Ocean, the one, "Mess. Watson & Cossoul/ Nants," referring to his partnership with a Monsieur Cossoul in Nantes and the other, "John Brown Esqr/ Providence," to his continuing relationship with the Rhode Island merchant to whom he had been apprenticed.

Copley portrays Watson elegantly attired with a hat in his right hand and a letter and cane in his left, leaning against a substantial plinth while musing on a bright future. As Watson's memoir makes clear, the radiating sun plays a symbolic role, but one that is more complex than the simple reference to the birth of the republic would suggest. In his *First Discourse*, delivered on 2 January 1769, Sir Joshua Reynolds had recapitulated the common trope of the arts' westward migration: "IT has been observed, that the ARTS have ever been disposed to travel westward. *Greece* is thought to have received them from her more eastern neighbours. From the *Greeks* they migrated into *Italy*; from thence they visited *France*, *Flanders*, and *Holland*, enlightening, for a time, those countries, though with diminished lustre; but, as if the ocean had stopped their progress, they have for near an age stood still, and grown weak and torpid for want of motion. Let us for a moment flatter ourselves that they are still in being, and have at last arrived at this island."[70]

Copley, whose correspondence amply demonstrates his admiration for Reynolds's *Discourses*, had echoed these same sentiments in his letter of 25 January 1771 to John Greenwood: "It gives me great pleasure to find the Arts travill[i]ng Westward so fast it gives me hopes they will one Day reach this Country however destitute at present it appears of every affection for them."[71] The sun's westward passage, so prominently displayed in *Elkanah Watson*, is the seal on this longed-for migration: what from the vantage point of England is a sunset is a sunrise in America. The two columns in the painting also speak of duality. The one in back is lower and plain, while the one above Watson is elevated and fluted, another promise of the resplendent future that he is portrayed as envisioning.

In 1782 Copley also executed two portraits of boys, *Midshipman Augustus Brine* (cat. 12) and *Richard Heber* (cat. 13), that demonstrate in their free-flowing backgrounds his stylistic break with the tightly executed works of his American period. The two sitters exhibit a calm self-assurance, their hand-on-hip pose a favorite one for males that ultimately derives from a martial type. *Charles Callis Western and his Brother Shirley Western* (cat. 15), exhibited at the Royal Academy in the following year, is another example of Copley's depiction of the special bonds between children and animals, though here the boy commands whereas in the case of the earlier portrait of Mary Elizabeth Martin[72] and the later one of the three daughters of George III (cat. 33), the girls only react with, rather than control, their bounding spaniels.

Along with *Charles Callis Western and his Brother Shirley Western*, Copley exhibited at the Royal Academy in 1783 his portrait of William Murray, 1st Earl of Mansfield (fig. 32). Born in 1705, Lord Mansfield was nearing the end of a distinguished judicial career as well as an important political one, during which one of his chief opponents had been Lord Chatham. Copley had already portrayed Mansfield in *The Death of the Earl of Chatham* (fig. 18), where he is seated at the table at the left, and a newspaper report found this portrayal implicitly critical of Mansfield's conduct on this occasion: "Lord Mansfield is distinguished from the Rest by being drawn sitting, while the sympathetick

Are always telling Beads;
But here's a Queen, now, thanks to God,
Who, when she rides in Coach abroad,
Is always knotting Threads.

This three-stanza work is included under poems ascribed on doubtful authority to Sir Charles Sedley in Pinto 1928, II, p. 148.

68. The painting reproduced here may be a replica of the original, which by one account was destroyed in a fire in 1861. See Prown 1966, II, p. 425.

69. Watson 1968, pp. 202–3.

70. Reynolds 1769, p. 3.

71. Copley to John Greenwood, Boston, 25 January 1771, in *Letters of Copley and Pelham* 1914/ 1972, p. 105.

72. Reproduced in Prown 1966, II, fig. 291.

Fig. 33 James Gillray
Judge Thumb, 27 November 1782
Etching, 13⁹/₁₆ × 9³/₄ in. (35.2 × 24.8 cm)
Prints and Photographs Division, Library of Congress

Fig. 32 John Singleton Copley
William Murray, 1st Earl of Mansfield, 1783
Oil on canvas, 88 × 57¹/₂ in. (223.5 × 146 cm)
By courtesy of the National Portrait Gallery, London

73. *The St. James's Chronicle*, 9–12 June 1781, p. 4.

74. See Prown 1966, II, p. 285.

Alarm had brought up all the Members of the House. This has a fine Effect on those who know that Lord Mansfield must have felt some secret Satisfaction at the probable Exit of a Man who had ever been his Scourge and his Terrour. ... Lord Mansfield, it is said, was distinguished, because he was the only Nobleman applied to who would not sit for his Picture. His Refusal was attended with Appearances of Unconcern for the Memory of Lord Chatham; and the Painter has very properly expressed that Unconcern by fixing him in his Chair, while the whole House is on Tip-Toe to observe an interesting Event."[73] Mansfield apparently did sit for the painter,[74] but he

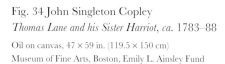

Fig. 34 John Singleton Copley
Thomas Lane and his Sister Harriot, ca. 1783–88
Oil on canvas, 47 × 59 in. (119.5 × 150 cm)
Museum of Fine Arts, Boston, Emily L. Ainsley Fund

presumably would not have been pleased with Copley's characterization of him as coolly indifferent to his long-time rival's fate.

There has been speculation as to why in 1783 Copley would again be painting Mansfield's portrait, given the presumption of the chief justice's displeasure with his earlier portrayal.[75] If a newspaper report is to be believed, it was a commissioned piece but not from Mansfield himself: "Mr. Copley's picture of Lord Mansfield was painted for Mr. Justice Buller. Various other Portraits of his Lordship are, we understand, at this time bespoke by different gentlemen of the law, either on the Bench, or high at the bar."[76] Francis Buller had good reason to flatter Lord Mansfield. It was because of his recommendation that Buller had been appointed in 1778 to the chief justice's court at the extremely young age of thirty-two. Buller also desperately needed favorable press at this time, as he had recently been skewered by James Gillray in the satire *Judge Thumb* (fig. 33), published on 27 November 1782, where Gillray attacks him for his ruling that a husband might lawfully beat his wife with a stick provided it were no thicker than his thumb. Gillray transforms Judge Buller into a street vendor of thumb-like canes who gives new meaning to the 'cries' of London.

Like Buller, Copley had much to gain by flattering Lord Mansfield. Although the artist's final conception is still rooted in his earlier portrayal, the tone has changed utterly. The passive figure in *The Death of the Earl of Chatham* now forcefully eyes the viewer, while firmly gripping a rolled legal document as a commander would his staff or truncheon.

Thomas Lane and his Sister Harriot (fig. 34) is another example of the fresh inventive-ness of Copley at this period. The fashionably attired figure reclining in a landscape with book in hand is borrowed from Joseph Wright of Derby's portrait of Sir Brook

75. Jules Prown succinctly states the problem: "What is puzzling is that less than two years later Copley painted a full-length seated portrait of Lord Mansfield, in which the expression and the head position are substantially different from the figure in the history painting. Mansfield could hardly have been pleased by Copley's dramatization of his indifference, and it is almost inconceivable that he would subsequently commission a portrait by Copley. Perhaps Copley, realizing the extent of his tactlessness and the professional danger of offend-ing great and powerful lords, painted the portrait *gratis* as an act of contrition" (Prown 1966, II, p. 285). A few pages later he also speculates that "he may have simply received a regular commission for it" (II, p. 298).

76. *The Morning Chronicle*, 30 April 1783, p. 3.

Fig. 35 Benjamin West
Queen Charlotte, 1779
Oil on canvas, 101 × 71$^{1}/_{2}$ in. (256.5 × 181.6 cm)
The Royal Collection ©Her Majesty Queen Elizabeth II

77. Reproduced in Nicolson 1968, II, pl. 219a.

78. One such example is Hogarth's portrait of *David Garrick with his Wife* in the Collection of Her Majesty the Queen.

Boothby, exhibited at the Royal Academy in 1781,[77] while the idea of Harriot interrupting her contemplative brother is adapted from the popular subject of a wife as a surrogate Muse disturbing her husband.[78] Copley makes all the more daring the reconfiguring of these elements by his dramatic cropping of Harriot's figure at the right.

Copley's image (cat. 16) of his step-niece, Mrs. Daniel Denison Rogers, of *ca.* 1784 marks another break with the past. The canvas, rapidly executed, conveys a dynamic spontaneity, and in its broad style and conception it shows a stronger debt to George Romney than to Reynolds or Gainsborough. The windblown sitter, silhouetted against a light sky, turns her back to make eye contact with the viewer. The figure's rightward lean is echoed and supported by the inclining tree at the right, while the delicate protruding foliage reinforces the leftward motion of fluttering ribbons, hair, and garments. The billowing scarf dominates the distant vista at the left, as Mrs. Rogers is in sprightly command of her animated environment.

From 1783 until 1796, when he recommended showing portraits on a regular basis, Copley exhibited only three times at the Royal Academy, one portrait in 1785, two in 1786, and one in 1793. Three of these paintings, *The Three Youngest Daughters of George III* (cat. 33), exhibited in 1785, *The Sitwell Family* (fig. 37) of the following year, and *The Red Cross Knight* (cat. 38) of 1793, show him at his most original, each piece representing a new point of departure. This is not to say that after this time Copley ceased to create portraits of high quality, only that he retreated from these bold experiments with new formulae when they failed to generate commissions.

The Three Youngest Daughters of George III was Copley's first opportunity to paint members of the royal family, offering him a chance to break into a select inner circle.[79] The painting is second in size only to *Sir William Pepperrell and his Family* in terms of his portraits up to this time, and in his zealousness to succeed he required such lengthy sittings that the complaints reached the king.[80] The final conception shows Princess Amelia riding in her monogrammed carriage with Princess Sophia sitting behind and Princess Mary pulling in front while holding aloft a tambour. The fictional terrace is ablaze with exotic flora and fauna, vegetation also spilling over the walled gardens rising up on the left-hand side. Windsor Castle is seen in the distance, where the banner streaming over the Round Tower declares that the king is in residence.

The concept of an older child, usually a boy, pulling a younger sibling in a carriage is not an unusual one in eighteenth-century portraiture, and it had already been used in the context of a royal, English portrait. At the Royal Academy in 1780, West had exhibited *Queen Charlotte* (fig. 35), where all her children born up to that time appear before Windsor Castle in the background at the left. In this group, Prince Octavius is shown in a carriage being pulled by Prince Ernest and pushed by Prince Adolphus while their sisters and elder brothers look on. Copley excerpts this minor, subdued passage to bring it front and center.[81] Just the year before, in 1784, Gainsborough had executed his painting *The Three Eldest Princesses: Charlotte, Princess Royal, Augusta, and Elizabeth*, where the sitters are shown with a graceful decorum suitable to their status.[82] In the case of the three youngest princesses, Copley had greater license to introduce exuberant gaiety, though still maintaining in their expressions a dignified reserve befitting royalty.[83] His buoyant conception hints at such classical prototypes as the Triumph of Flora or even, given the grapes above and the upraised tambour, the Triumph of Bacchus, processions that often were portrayed as performed by children.

Upon its exhibition, the painting received a devastating critique from John Hoppner, who, writing anonymously, failed to mention that he had three individual portraits of the same sitters in the same exhibition: "What delightful disorder! Why, you have plucked up harmony by the roots, and planted confusion in its stead! Princesses, parrots, dogs, grapes, flowers, leaves, are each striving for pre-eminence, and opposing, with hostile force, all attempts of our wearied eyes to find repose!"[84] While Hoppner was clearly prejudiced, his reservations had already been sounded in earlier, essentially favorable reviews, as in the following excerpts: "the whole is disfigured with a glare of vines and flowers very hurtful to the eye";[85] "If there be any fault it is, that the artist, in

79. For the evidence suggesting the work was uncommissioned, see Prown 1966, II, p. 312 note 2.

80. William Dunlap publishes an amusing letter from the artist Charles Robert Leslie concerning the sitters' impatience: "... during the operation, the children, the dogs, and the parrots became equally wearied. The persons who were obliged to attend them while sitting complained to the queen; the queen complained to the king and the king complained to Mr. West, who had obtained the commission for Copley. Mr. West satisfied his majesty that Copley must be allowed to proceed in his own way, and that any attempt to hurry him might be injurious to the picture, which would be a very fine one when done" (Dunlap 1834/1969, I, p. 126). See the previous note for the evidence that the work was uncommissioned. West, a favorite of the king, presumably only helped to secure the sittings for Copley rather than a royal commission.

81. West also executed a reversed version of this portrait with the addition of a child that shows the carriage moving from right to left as in Copley's composition (Von Erffa and Staley 1986, no. 558).

82. This painting, which in the 19th century was severely cut down, is reproduced in London 1994, no. 9. The mezzotint after it, showing the original composition in its entirety, is also reproduced in this catalogue (no. 45).

83. In this regard, Copley's Rococo exuberance is closer to Gainsborough's *Giovanna Baccelli* in the Tate Gallery, where the sitter is shown executing a twirling dance with a tambourine resting in the flowers in the corner. Gainsborough's sitter was a celebrated dancer, whose portrait had been commissioned by her lover, the Duke of Dorset, and one doubts such a charmingly lighthearted approach would have been appropriate to an adult, titled sitter.

84. *The Morning Post*, 5 May 1785, p. 2.

85. *The London Chronicle*, 26–8 April 1785, p. 406.

Fig. 36 Philipp Otto Runge
The Hülsenbeck Children, 1805–06

Oil on canvas, 52^{1}/$_{2}$ × 57^{1}/$_{2}$ in. (133.5 × 146 cm),
Kunsthalle, Hamburg

86. *The General Advertiser*, 28 April 1785, p. 3.

87. *The Universal Daily Register*, 28 April 1785, p. 2.

88. *The Public Advertiser*, 29 April 1785, p. 2.

89. See Prown's description: "In the distance a blue sky above Windsor Castle is touched with light reds, yellows, and pinks of the sunset" (Prown 1966, II, p. 314). While the foreground is fictitious, the view of Windsor in the background is from the southwest looking toward the northeast. I would like to thank the Hon. Mrs. Jane Roberts, curator of the Print Room at Windsor, for pinning down the point of view. She also points out in her letter of 26 August 1994 that the Queen's Lodge does not appear in Copley's painting as suggested by Sir Oliver Millar (Millar 1969, text vol., no. 712). Rather, the buildings in addition to the Round Tower appear to include the Tennis Court and Burford House/Lower Lodge.

90. As noted earlier, Copley had already exhibited a work at the Royal Academy in 1776 that had been listed in the exhibition catalogue as "a conversation piece." If, however, this painting is *Mr. and Mrs. Ralph Izard*, it is a more formal presentation than that of *The Sitwell Family*.

91. *The Daily Universal Register*, 2 May 1786, p. 3.

92. The worst review appeared in *The Morning Post*, where the critic challenged Copley's right to call himself an academician based on this performance: "The picture before us is, in every part, such a stranger to the inspirations of genius, that in spite of the meretricious glare which flashes on us, and seems intended for delusion, that did we not know others of the distinguished order of Academicians capable of exhibiting things of EQUAL mediocrity, we should pronounce it the performance of a mere TYRO in the art. To enter minutely on this

his drapery, has introduced too much *coxcomb* [*i.e.*, foppishness] among the children";[86] "we could wish that the back ground had been more subordinate, and that his eye had been attentive to that greatness of distribution which alone constitutes fine Art";[87] "Copley's children want only to be pruned of the leaves and flowers to be very pretty."[88]

These viewers were taken aback by the painting's bright exuberance, by its equation of childhood with bursting vitality, with the opulent profusion of nature's burgeoning growth. The picture is about beginnings, and it is a sunrise rather than, as has been said, a sunset that gladdens the sky in the background.[89] One wonders if the German artist Philipp Otto Runge knew Bartolozzi's 1792 engraving after Copley's painting when conceiving his own inventive picture *The Hülsenbeck Children* (fig. 36). Like Copley, Runge associates childhood with towering plants, with an arm raised in energetic activity, and with the baby's bare feet peeking out from under its dress, but he, of course, offers a middle-class image rather than an aristocratic one, turning the royal carriage back into a pumpkin.

The Three Youngest Daughters of George III, like *The Copley Family* and *Sir William Pepperrell and his Family*, is a group portrait, but in 1786 Copley exhibited *The Sitwell Family* (fig. 37), a type of group portrait more specifically classified as a conversation piece. Such works, which were extremely popular in the eighteenth century, are on a more intimate scale, placing their sitters within a setting reflecting their actual environment.[90] This descriptive genre was closer to middle-class taste than to an aristocratic one that emphasized grandeur, as in the invented settings of the earlier group portraits. The German-born artist Johan Zoffany, who had first arrived in England around 1760, had made a specialty of this type, raising it to new levels. However, in 1783, Zoffany had left London for India, and *The Sitwell Family* may be Copley's attempt to stake his claim to this popular segment of the English market.

Copley's conversation piece is built around the narrative incident of the eldest brother, Sir Sitwell Sitwell, playfully collapsing the house of cards so meticulously constructed by Francis and Hurt, his two brothers. Mary, their sister, establishes the stabilizing center around which this domestic drama is played out. The artist daringly places the large window on the back wall in the composition's center, drawing the eye to an enchanting vista while framing Mary in its ambient light. The motif of the house of cards, which alludes to the fragile nature of all human endeavors, is a common *vanitas* theme in both French and English portraits of children. Copley, however, is careful to introduce this theme of instability – in the collapsed card-house and the overturned toy wheelbarrow – within the well appointed setting of a room in the Sitwell home, so that the ultimate message is a comforting one of domestic tranquility and security. Even when life's card-houses should collapse, one can always count on the fact that the sanctuary of the Sitwell house will remain. Like *The Three Youngest Daughters of George III*, the painting is a virtuoso performance of its kind, but although one critic praised it as "a beautiful high finished piece"[91] (and the work is indeed meticulous in its execution), the other commentators were at times brutally scathing.[92] Again, the departure proved a dead end for the artist.

Occupied with *The Siege of Gibraltar* and perhaps discouraged by his lack of critical success, Copley did not exhibit again at the Royal Academy until 1793, when he displayed *Portraits of John, Elizabeth, and Mary Copley as the Red Cross Knight, Fidelia and Speranza* (cat. 38), a painting that casts his children as characters from Edmund

Spenser's *The Faerie Queene*. John, as the Red Cross Knight, approaches Elizabeth as Fidelia (Faith) and Mary as Speranza (Hope), who, in the context of the poem (Book 1, canto 10), dwell in the House of Holinesse. The painting again demands attention by its large scale, and it was the artist's first and most ambitious attempt at allegorical portraiture, a genre in which the sitters are identified with gods, heroes, or virtues, thereby associating them with ennobling characteristics. While this genre is an old one, Reynolds had given it new life within an English context, turning duchesses, for example, into such flattering guises as Venus and Hebe. As we have seen, to a certain extent contemporary history painting involves the introduction of portraiture into history painting. Allegorical portraiture, on the other hand, arrives at a similar mixture but from the opposite direction, introducing historical or epic subjects into portrait painting. Since the sitters portray someone other than themselves, the artist runs an even greater risk of slipping from the sublime into the ridiculous, and Copley's aggrandized casting of his progeny as Spenserian characters comes perilously close to such a danger.

Copley was not the first to use *The Faerie Queene* for the purposes of allegorical portraiture, as West, Reynolds, George Stubbs, and Maria Cosway had done so before him.[93] West had even employed the same subject, exhibiting *Fidelia and Speranza* (fig. 38) at the Royal Academy in 1777. This last painting almost certainly depicts sisters,[94] de-emphasizing the figures of the Red Cross Knight and Una, who can be seen approaching in the distance at the left. West's somewhat static portrayal is more typical of allegorical portraiture, helping to underscore the boldness of Copley's design in its insistence on so strong a narrative element. Because of its ambitious complexity, one contemporary reviewer with tongue in cheek described Copley's canvas as "an allegorical, historical, poetical, and portraitical picture from *Spenser's Fairy Queen*."[95] Another unsympathetic critic went out of his way to underscore the tension between appearance (*i.e.*, the Spenserian allegory) and reality (*i.e.*, the Copley children) in his snide aside, "We should certainly have mentioned it as a great impropriety in the *Red-Cross Knight*, that he does not look at the Ladies – if we did not recollect that they are his Sisters."[96]

The painting was also criticized for technical deficiencies in terms of its poor draftsmanship and raw coloring.[97] Conservation on the picture in preparation for this exhibition has made it possible finally to see it much as it must have originally appeared. Examination reveals that it was indeed hastily executed, Copley obviously hurrying to meet the exhibition deadline. Yet, to modern eyes, the lack of high finish seems a less than damning flaw. What has emerged is a truly dynamic composition. The Red Cross Knight, boldly out of scale, strides in from the left with an impact worthy of the armored ghost of Hamlet's father, a favorite moment in the eighteenth-century London theater. The two women are ethereal visions, conjuring up a world of angelic purity in contrast to the Christian knight's active, masculine presence. It is an imaginative conception which again failed to ignite his contemporaries, and Copley's only other allegorical portrait is the more conventional *Mrs. Richard Crowninshield Derby as St. Cecilia*, exhibited at the Royal Academy in 1804.[98] In terms of his English portraits, Copley did not fail his public, rather it failed him.

Conclusion

Although after exhibiting *The Red Cross Knight* Copley had another twenty-two years to

picture, would be giving a history of defects; we shall therefore dismiss it with a wish, that when this artist again exhibits pictures so little redounding to the fame of an Academician, that the respectable capitals of R. A. may not succeed the name of the Exhibitor" (16 May 1786, p. 3).

93. All of these artists had exhibited allegorical portraits drawn from *The Faerie Queene* at the Royal Academy. West was the first, exhibiting *Mary Hall as Una* in 1772 and *Fidelia and Speranza* in 1777. Reynolds exhibited *Miss Mary Beauclerk as Una* in 1780 and Stubbs *Isabella Saltensell as Una* in 1782. In this last year Maria Cosway showed *The Duchess of Devonshire as Cynthia* and two years later *Mrs. Braddyll and her Son as Astrea instructing Arthegal*. Several of these works are reproduced in Bradley 1979–80.

94. For a discussion of this work as a portrait, see von Erffa and Staley 1986, no. 222.

95. *The London Chronicle*, 27–30 April 1793, p. 412.

96. *The True Briton*, 1 May 1793, p. 3.

97. The critic in *The St. James's Chronicle* complained, "The figure of the Knight is not well drawn" (27–30 April 1793, p. 4), while the one in *The London Packet* commented, "the colouring is raw, and even the drawing in many places bad" (29 April–1 May 1793, p. 4). Numerous other contemporary descriptions are given by Ellen G. Miles in her helpful catalogue entry (Miles 1994).

98. Reproduced in Prown 1966, II, fig. 651.

live, his most imaginative work was behind him, and after 1800 the quality of his work also suffers a decline. His failure late in his life runs counter to the cherished notion that great artists only get better with time, developing an incomparable old-age style that outstrips their public's comprehension, as did, for example, Titian, Rembrandt, and Turner. In Copley's case, the seeds of his decline were already present from the beginning. In England, while he became freer in his brushwork and employed a higher key in his range of colors, the essentials of his working method remained the same. Throughout his career, Copley carefully and slowly built up his compositions, conceiving the whole in terms of the sum of the parts. In Europe, he boldly experimented with multi-figured compositions, for which he relied heavily on preparatory drawings that he 'squared up' for transfer. Such a procedure again involved painstaking processes,

Fig. 37 John Singleton Copley
The Sitwell Family, 1786
Oil on canvas, 61½ × 71 in. (156.2 × 180.5 × cm)
Reproduced by kind permission of Sir Reresby Sitwell

Fig. 38 Benjamin West
Fidelia and Speranza, 1776
Oil on canvas, 54³/₄ × 42¹/₂ in. (139 × 108 cm)
Putnam Foundation, Timken Art Gallery, San Diego

requiring physical as well as mental stamina. As he got older, Copley simply could no longer sustain the effort required to produce works of superior quality.

It is unproductive to argue which is better, Copley's American or his European work. He had already achieved greatness in his colonial portraits, but the European experience considerably opened up his range of possibilities, and he showed in middle age a remarkable ability to continue to learn and experiment. As an American artist wedded to the particular and the real, he was always highly sympathetic to portrait painting, and in England in this genre he pursued his mastery of group compositions and the grand manner and added to his repertoire the conversation piece and allegorical portraiture. From his Roman sojourn to the last years of his life, he attempted history painting, the *sine qua non* of high art, but in this category, as was the case with so many of his contemporaries, he was less successful. It is no accident that his finest religious painting, *Samuel Relating to Eli the Judgments of God upon Eli's House*, is the one most closely related to portraiture in that it consists of only two figures, both of which are firmly grounded in specific models.

Copley's greatest achievement in England was his development of contemporary history painting, a category that requires the merger of portraiture with the grand style. Freer than the majority of his London colleagues from the oppressive weight of academic tradition, he was able to pursue independently the course first charted by his countryman Benjamin West, imaginatively exploiting this genre's potential. As we have seen, with such paintings he achieved an almost immediate success, *Watson and the Shark* appearing as early as 1778. In the nineteenth century, pictures of important contemporary events often degenerate into prosaic reportage, but Copley's depictions, while indebted to portraiture, never lose sight of the idealizing heroism of the grand style. Even he was never to surpass the brilliant combination of epic drama and intense realism to be found in his *Death of Major Peirson*, a painting which was completed within a decade of his arrival in Europe. Copley also demonstrated a practical brilliance in his innovative marketing of such paintings, exhibiting these works privately outside the walls of the Royal Academy while orchestrating the creation and sale of reproductive prints.

Benjamin West proved a strong influence on Copley during the whole of the English phase of his career, first as a model worthy of emulation and then as a rival to be excelled. While Copley's personal competition with West produced negative results in terms of the political advancement of his career, particularly within the Royal Academy, it did help to energize his art, stimulating him to surpass his rival on his own terms. Copley believed himself the better artist, and he was right. Yet he never received West's acclaim. Differences in their reception had to do with their personalities and with their timing, West arriving as a young man in London, where he was perceived as a *Wunderkind* from the American wilderness, while Copley, arriving more than a decade later, was perceived as one more American fleeing the colonial war. The mighty mountain that Copley climbed turned out to be higher than the one West ascended, but, despite the originality of his achievement, he could never entirely escape his compatriot's long shadow.

The History
Theater

Production

and Spectatorship in Copley's

The Death of Major
Peirson

EMILY BALLEW NEFF

(Opposite page) Detail of cat. 18

1. *The Morning Herald, and Daily Advertiser*, 22 May 1784. According to this account, the royal family "appeared equally well pleased with a performance that does so much honor to the Officer whose fate is thereby celebrated, and the Artist by whose pencil it is produced. The King on being told it was painted for Mr. Boydell's gallery of curious drawings, pictures, and c., spoke in high terms of his public spirit, and encouragement of the Arts!"

2. Altick 1978, p. 105.

3. According to *The Morning Herald, and Daily Advertiser*, 21 May 1784, the exhibition on

On 21 May 1784, King George III cut short his morning ride, returning to Buckingham Palace with unusual haste to see John Singleton Copley's recently completed *The Death of Major Peirson* (cat. 18).[1] A painting that celebrated English superiority in warfare with dash and glamour – for military martyrdom did have a glamorous veneer in the eighteenth century – *The Death of Major Peirson* did not fail to earn the approval of the King. According to *The Morning Herald*, he devoted nearly three hours of study to its "various excellencies, in point of design, character, composition, and colouring." Whether fact or fancy, the King's reported enthusiasm and due diligence to the arts of England conferred a royal stamp of approval on the painting the very day Copley moved it to rented rooms at 28 Haymarket for a two-month exhibition. Three years before, in his first one-picture exhibition – a genre he essentially invented as well as popularized – Copley had shown to great acclaim *The Death of the Earl of Chatham* (fig. 18 on p. 39).[2] As for *The Earl of Chatham*, Copley charged a one-shilling entrance fee for *The Death of Major Peirson*. At the same time he provided a brochure describing the historical event and soliciting a subscription for an engraving after the painting.[3]

Representing the death of a valiant hero as his troops counter-attacked and defeated French invaders, *The Death of Major Peirson* helped shape the popularity of the painted and printed 'death tableaux' that emerged during the mid- to late eighteenth century in England.[4] In 1771, Benjamin West had introduced to Royal Academy circles, with great fanfare, *The Death of General Wolfe* (fig. 57 on p. 79), a painting that capitalized and expanded on the cult of military heroes. Subsequent to *The Death of Major Peirson* the cult continued to gain momentum with popular images of such contemporary wartime events as Admiral Nelson's victory at Trafalgar in 1805 (fig. 39) and the Duke of Wellington's defeat of Napoleon at Waterloo in 1815.

Copley's monumental painting was displayed before a British public riding a wave of patriotic fervor. In the context of the looming loss of the American colonies, the event of 1781 depicted in *The Death of Major Peirson* had been a much needed

Haymarket was open daily except Sundays from morning until evening. The exhibition ran for two months before moving to Boydell's gallery, see below, pp. 67f.

4. The rise of 18th-century contemporary history painting, usually attributed to Benjamin West and his seminal *The Death of General Wolfe*, actually began flourishing following England's victory in the French and Indian War in the 1760s. At fashionable Vauxhall Gardens, visitors could see Francis Hayman's patriotic renditions of English military success in *The Surrender of Montreal to General Amherst* (1760) and *Lord Clive meeting Mir Jafar, Nawab of Murshidabad, after the Battle of Plassey* (1762). In 1762, Richard Wright exhibited paintings of recent British naval engagements at the Society of Artists, and again at the Society of Artists in 1763 George Romney exhibited *The Death of Wolfe*, followed by Edward Penny's version of the event shown one year later. See Allen 1987, pp. 62–70; also Carter E. Foster, 'History and Heroes: The Military Narrative in the Wake of Benjamin West,' and Amanda M. Eggers, 'Popularity and Power: Images of the Duke of Wellington,' in Providence 1991, pp. 47–52 and 53–60; and Peter Cannon-Brookes, 'From the *Death of General Wolfe* to the *Death of Lord Nelson*: Benjamin West and the Epic Composition,' and David Alexander, 'Patriotism and Contemporary History, 1770–1830,' in *Painted Word* 1991, pp. 15–22, 31–43.

5. Prown 1966, II, pp. 311–12. The Corporation solicited advice and proposals from Benjamin West and Copley. The latter convinced the committee that he could consolidate the military and naval event into one painting, whereas West proposed two separate paintings. Copley may have also won over the committee by taking the commission for a low figure, assured that its exhibition and print subscription would repay him for his efforts. See also Howgego 1958, pp. 38–9.

6. Prown 1966, II, p. 312. See cat. 33 for further discussion.

7. Copley's subsequent military compositions include *The Siege of Gibraltar* (*The Defeat of the Floating Batteries on 13 September 1782*), 1783–91; *The Victory of Lord Duncan* (*Surrender of the Dutch Admiral DeWinter to Admiral Duncan, 11 October 1797*), 1798–9; *The Battle of the Pyrenees*, 1812–5 (Museum of Fine Arts, Boston); and *The Siege of Dunkirk*, 1814–5 (College of William and Mary, Williamsburg, Virginia).

8. The representation of the military has not been of particular interest or fashionable for the 20th-century art historian. Notable exceptions include articles devoted to West's *The Death of General Wolfe* (see Fryd 1995 for the most recent treatment of the subject to date, and for full bibliographic citations), Ayres 1993, and, for 19th-century French military painting, Maarinan 1988.

morale-booster, much as England's stunning success in defending Gibraltar in 1782 was to be one year later. Filled with complex narrative twists, *The Death of Major Peirson* represents a highly mythologized version of a skirmish between the British and the French on 5 January 1781, when French troops invaded the British-held Isle of Jersey, prized for its strategic location in the English Channel. Captured by the French, the British Lieutenant-Governor Moses Corbet signed a capitulation relinquishing English control of the island. Major Francis Peirson, a twenty-four-year-old captain of the 95th Regiment, ignored his superior and mounted a successful counter-attack in St Helier, the principal town of Jersey. At the moment of British victory, however, Peirson lost his life; according to popular lore, his black servant avenged his untimely death.

Copley's spine-tingling account of these events takes place in the market square of St Helier, the center of which is marked by a bronze statue of George II and which includes a cupola-topped court house, identified by the royal arms above its door. While British reinforcements march over Town Hill at upper left, clearing their path with a barrage of fire, British and French soldiers engage in battle in the foreground. At lower left, a sergeant covers his overflowing wound as he heroically gestures toward his dying superior in a pose that anchors the base of the pyramidal composition and leads the viewer's attention to the central group. The sergeant's gesture is answered by the frightened women and children fleeing the scene and running for safety at right. The central group of officers of the 95th and an officer of the Jersey militia (Captain Clement Hemery, in black), amid British flags and standards and the smoke of musket fire, carry the heroic Peirson away from a battlefield strewn with fallen weapons and toppled hats among the dead and dying. Despite the chaos of battle and tone of pathos, an officer (Captain Malcolm McNeil) points out the French enemy to the black servant who with model steadiness avenges the untimely death of the young hero. The persistent diagonals formed by the marching soldiers and their bayonets, the flagmasts and swirling smoke, the steep hill, and the exaggerated orthogonal lines created by the building at right, combined with the contrasting passages of brilliant light and deep shadow, intensify the drama and convey the terror and confusion of battle. The building at right presses inward, and Town Hill hovering over the scene blocks the distance so that the picture appears ready to implode at any moment. As in Copley's subsequent paintings of contemporary English military successes – such as *The Siege of Gibraltar* (fig. 19 on p. 40) and *The Victory of Lord Duncan* (fig. 40) – *The Death of Major Peirson* is an epic nationalist picture that conveys the heat of battle, a surprise victory, and model heroes through dazzling displays of paint. Not even Benjamin West could make war appear both so noble and inhuman, glamorous and visceral, triumphal and tragic.

Within five years of the extraordinary debut of *Watson and the Shark* (cat. 4) at the Royal Academy in 1778, Copley had entered the top rank of history painters in England, becoming one of the few artists to achieve success in both critical and popular terms, and winning the patronage of the City as well as the King. On the basis of his success with *The Death of the Earl of Chatham*, and of his progress of *The Death of Major Peirson*, both of which were viewed by the Court of Common Council of the Corporation of the City of London at the artist's Leicester Square studio in 1783, the City of London awarded Copley the largest commission of his career. For the Court of Common Council Room, Copley would commemorate the 1782 British success in the defense of Gibraltar and the defeat of the Spanish floating batteries by painting a

Fig. 40 John Singleton Copley
*The Victory of Lord Duncan (Surrender of the Dutch
Admiral DeWinter to Admiral Duncan, 11 October
1797)*, 1798–99

Oil on canvas, 111 × 147 in. (281.9 × 373.3 cm)
Dundee Art Galleries and Museums, by permission of the
Trustees of Camperdown House, Dundee, Scotland

twenty-five-foot monument to the military prowess of Sir George Augustus Eliott (later
Lord Heathfield; fig. 41) and Admiral Richard Earl Howe (cat. 36).[5] And, impressed by
the *tour de force* of swashbuckling British heroism in *The Death of Major Peirson*, King
George III soon granted Copley permission to paint *The Three Youngest Daughters of
George III* – as near as Copley ever would come to receiving a royal commission (cat.
33).[6] *The Death of Major Peirson*, the first of his many military pictures, contributed in no
small part to Copley's rising status in the esteemed field of history painting.[7] And yet,
despite its favorable reception in Copley's own day, the painting itself has lapsed into
relative obscurity in modern times.[8] Bold, visually sophisticated, and complex in narrative, the painting eludes easy understanding, offering messages as much about
eighteenth-century artistic and social conventions as about a specific military event.
The painting is, in fact, the climactic work of Copley's English career, his greatest success both artistically and commercially, and the key to understanding the motivating
factors of his evolved painting style, his mature aesthetic theory, and his final mastery
of the English artistic system.

Fig. 41 John Singleton Copley
The Siege of Gibraltar (detail of fig. 19 during conservation): Lord Heathfield, 1783–91
Oil on canvas, 214 × 297 in. (543.6 × 754.4 cm)
Guildhall Art Gallery, Corporation of London

The Problem of Money

The manner in which Copley presented *The Death of Major Peirson* to his London audience illustrates one of the most profound dilemmas of the English artistic system. Although it was the most esteemed category in the academic hierarchy, history painting was not financially remunerative. Furthermore, the question of money for artists was fraught with socio-political problems in the eighteenth century. Copley had a keen perception of those problems, and his masterful manipulation of them to his advantage amounts to a significant achievement.

The English philosopher Anthony Ashley Cooper, 3rd Earl of Shaftesbury, whose theoretical reflections on art profoundly influenced eighteenth-century aesthetics, had made the situation difficult for the artist by decreeing that gentlemen could and should study art, but that painters, because they used their hands, could not be gentlemen and so could never rise above the social status of the "mechanick."[9] Jonathan Richardson, England's first art theorist and a painter by profession, naturally thought otherwise, asserting that the painter was capable of intellectual discourse. The practice of painting did not automatically consign an artist to the lower order of the social structure, he argued, and earning money for one's efforts, moreover, was not dishonorable, because other professions such as the judicature and clergy also received money for the "Exercise of their ... Mind."[10]

9. Shaftesbury's discussion regarding the 'correct' method of portraying *Hercules Choosing between Virtue and Vice* assumed that the painter was not intellectually equipped to compose the image properly. In a manner unusual for the 18th-century patron, he subsequently commissioned the Neapolitan Paolo de Matteis to paint the subject according to his detailed instructions (fig. 59). In other words, he played out the 'proper' relationship between thinker and mechanic; he composed a painting without getting his hands dirty, and left its execution to the craftsman. See Shaftesbury 1714/1727, pp. 347–93.

10. Richardson 1715/1725/1971, p. 29.

Shaftesbury and Richardson's opposing opinions reflect this contested area of artistic practice. If the artistic profession were to be associated with the liberal arts rather than with artisan trades, its practitioners needed to look and act like gentlemen, a mandate that helps explain the prescriptions for social behavior that recur in aesthetic treatises. Richardson argued that as long as artists took money not for the sole sake of acquisition but for the noble fulfillment of the profession, then earning an income was acceptable. The English artist Arthur Pond, for example, supplemented his income from producing mediocre portraits by acting as an advisor to art collectors.[11] He traveled the path of the intellectual and sophisticated artist, and so did not risk being labeled a 'mechanic,' as American colonial artists did when advertising their availability to paint not only portraits but also signs and carriages.

Importantly, Shaftesbury and Richardson engaged the problem of money, social status, and respectability at a time when Britain was emerging as a modern commercialized nation. It should be noted, in this context, that Shaftesbury excluded from status as a gentleman not only the artist, but nearly anyone whose income did not derive from landed estates. In his civic humanist world view, propertied men had the leisure and disinterest to act as patriotic citizens promoting the public good, as opposed to men of commerce whose self-interest, he argued, made them incapable of assuming civic duty.[12] Shaftesbury expressed concerns common to many contemporary political thinkers who recognized that Britain's transformation into a market economy ushered in new moral problems – above all, how a virtuous republic was to be maintained in a market economy motivated primarily by self-interest. Political and economic theorists, satirists, novelists, and aestheticians grappled with this issue, some focusing on the moral degeneracy that was expected to attend the pursuit of trade, others rehabilitating self-interest, reasoning that wealth could only help to refine the nation at large.

Copley's letters indicate he was not isolated from this debate. Early in his career, he reconciled his concern over a growing reputation with a parallel rise in fortune by stating that each would mutually assist the improvement of his art. In 1765, he wrote to his friend and patron Thomas Ainslie: "I assure You I have been as fully imployd these several Years past as I could expect or wish to be, as more would be a means to retard the design I have always had in vew, that of improveing in that charming Art which is my delight, and gaining a reputation rather than a fortune without that: Tho if I could obtain the one while in persuit of the other, I confess I should be so far from being indiferent about either that I would willingly use great diligence for the acquireing of both, and indeed the mutual assistance they would render each other in their progress must naturally excite in me a desire for both, tho in diferent degrees."[13]

Copley wants to convince Ainslie of his anxiety over the issue, and even after indicating a felicitous solution, he softens the materialistic edge by stating that his enthusiasm erupts "in diferent degrees," reputation, of course, superseding financial rewards. In fact, his financial rewards as well as his reputation were great. He married the wealthy Loyalist Susanna Farnham Clarke within five years of his correspondence with Ainslie, and began acquiring property on Beacon Hill, Boston's most prestigious neighborhood. Copley had the trappings of gentility; he married and dressed well, lived in the right neighborhood, and built a grand and exquisitely detailed house.[14] He made his fortune as a portraitist quietly and discreetly. Except for the mezzotints he produced early in his career, he does not appear to have advertised, preferring the system of

11. See Lippincott 1983 for a detailed analysis of the 18th-century art market in London, and Pond's role in defining social distinctions between artisans and artists.

12. Propertied men were expected to take leadership roles in national policy because they were perceived to be without interest. It was argued that because of their wealth and education in moral virtue, they had the leisure and disinterest to become engaged in public life. See Wood 1969, Pocock 1975, and Wood 1992 for the historical analysis of republicanism, and Barrell 1986 and Solkin 1992 for its implications on art.

13. Copley to Thomas Ainslie, Boston, 25 February 1765, *Letters of Copley and Pelham* 1914/1972, p. 33.

14. See cat. 17 for descriptions of Copley's appearance and comportment. See letters written by Copley and Pelham from June through December 1771 for detailed descriptions of Copley's elaborate refurbishing plans for his Beacon Hill house in *Letters of Copley and Pelham* 1914/1972.

15. The one time he did travel afar to paint portraits, New York City, Copley had to be asked twice, and it appears that he may have accepted, in part, to leave the inconvenient atmosphere the remodelling of his Beacon Hill home represented. See Myles Cooper to Copley, New York, 9 January 1769, and Captain Stephen Kemble to Copley, New York, before 17 April 1771, in *Letters of Copley and Pelham* 1914/1972, pp. 75–6, 112. Copley's patron Thomas Ainslie, as early as 1757 and again in 1764, tried unsuccessfully to lure him to Halifax, Nova Scotia, where there were clients who "would be glad to employ you." See Thomas Ainslie to Copley, Halifax, 8 October 1757, and Thomas Ainslie to Copley, Quebec, 12 November 1764, in *Letters of Copley and Pelham* 1914/1972, pp. 23, 30–1.

16. Cunningham 1831/1837/1868, IV, p. 140, and Copley to Captain R.G. Bruce(?), 1767(?), in *Letters of Copley and Pelham* 1914/1972, p. 64.

17. Of the twenty-one historical subjects Copley is known to have painted, only five were commissioned: *The Holy Family with Saint Jerome* (lost), *Watson and the Shark*, *The Death of Major Peirson*, *The Offer of the Crown to Lady Jane Gray*, and *The Siege of Gibraltar*. *The Victory of Lord Duncan* sold during Copley's lifetime, bought by Duncan's aunt for £1000, and *Samuel Relating to Eli the Judgments of God Upon Eli's House* probably attracted a buyer (see Prown 1966, II, p. 276).

18. Prown 1966, II, pp. 278–9.

19. Bacon was also selected to sculpt a memorial honoring George Rodney's 1782 naval success in Jamaica. See Council Minutes 1784.

20. See especially the chapter 'Illustrious Heads' in Pointon 1993, pp. 53–78, describing the tradition and political significance of collecting portrait prints.

21. Boydell founded the Shakespeare Gallery in Pall Mall, exhibiting history paintings of scenes from Shakespeare commissioned from well known British artists. The gallery, although short-lived, did much to promote British artists and to encourage a taste for visiting galleries of art. The most comprehensive treatment of Boydell to date remains Bruntjen 1974/1985, which provides much of the information on Boydell here.

22. Altick 1978, pp. 107–8. Another critic celebrated Boydell, mentioning that "the arts and artists are more indebted [to him] for patronage and encouragement than to all the nobility of England put together" (*V & A Press Cuttings*, vol. 1, p. 291).

23. Altick 1978, p. 106. If Altick is correct in stating that Boydell received a third share of print proceeds, then West would have made the extraordinary sum of approximately £23,000.

24. *V & A Press Cuttings*, vol. 2, p. 512, dated in hand 13 April 1789.

25. *Ibid.*, p. 517.

26. See Prown 1966, II, pp. 290–1 for a full account of the event.

referral business. Patrons in other colonial cities invited him to visit their homes to paint their portraits, but he avoided assuming the role of the lowly itinerant artist, and instead let his clients come to him.[15] Copley may have boasted that he "made as much as if he were a Raphael or Correggio," but he feared that if he left his steady fortune for study abroad, he might have to return to the colonies and "Bury all my improvements among people intirely destitute of all just Ideas of the Arts, and without any addition of Reputation to what I have already gaind."[16] When the political situation of Boston became not only strained but physically threatening, however, Copley embarked on the Grand Tour in 1774, rejoining his family in England in October 1775. His financial future in London, a city filled with talented artists, was not as certain as it had been in the colonies, especially as he at last began to fulfill his lifelong desire to paint histories.

Patrons of history subjects were not plentiful in eighteenth-century England, and collectors traditionally focused on Old Masters rather than contemporary British artists, at least until mid-century. Many collectors hesitated to acquire history paintings, which were physically large, pictorially complex, and consequently high-priced. Copley's successful and influential *The Death of the Earl of Chatham* found only one tentative buyer, the Marquis of Buckingham, who found the price of 2,500 guineas (£2,625) simply too high, and declined. In fact Copley apparently sold only two history paintings throughout his career in England; the others were commissioned, sold by lottery when Copley needed the money, or remained in his studio unsold.[17] The high demand for portraits in Britain provided artists such as Copley with a steady supply of customers, but elaborate commissioned projects like *The Siege of Gibraltar* did not leave much time for the profitable portrait trade. And so the serious artist, like Copley, who aspired to paint in the most noble genre of the academic hierarchy had few opportunities as well as intense competition from his peers.

The Death of the Earl of Chatham, in its conception and its fate, demonstrates the risk and reward the history painter encountered, and the means by which Copley, as well as his contemporaries, could find compensation for their endeavors. With the encouragement of West, Copley began painting *The Death of the Earl of Chatham* on speculation in 1779. He submitted it to the Corporation of London for consideration as a memorial to Chatham after learning of the intention to commission one,[18] but his painting was rejected in favor of a monument to be sculpted by John Bacon, who later won the commission to memorialize Major Francis Peirson as well.[19] *The Death of the Earl of Chatham* had taken the better part of two years for Copley to complete, containing, as it did, life portraits of more than fifty members of the House of Lords. Despite the phenomenal public reception of the picture, Copley did not find a buyer after its exhibition, nor was he able to dispose of it at Christie's auction house in 1788. He succeeded in selling the painting only in 1806, by lottery, for £2,100. However, to profit even more by his endeavors, Copley also realized funds (not to mention publicity and contacts) from exhibition admission fees and from the sale of reproductive prints based on the painting.

The production and consumption of portrait and subject prints burgeoned in the eighteenth century. A taste for prints had long existed, particularly for portrait mezzotints,[20] but in the mid- to late century boomed, to the benefit in particular of the astute entrepreneur John Boydell, Britain's most successful print publisher and promoter of

Fig. 42 Valentine Green after Josiah Boydell
John Boydell

Mezzotint, from *A Collection of Prints, engraved after the most capital paintings in England*
Photograph courtesy of the National Gallery of Art Library, Joseph E. Widener Collection

27. Boydell originally commissioned Copley to paint *Charles I Demanding the Five Impeached Members*, which Copley suspended in favor of painting the event of St Helier. See Prown 1966, II, p. 306 note 5.

28. *The Morning Herald*, 6 August 1784; *V & A Press Cuttings*, vol. 1, p. 269, dated in hand 24 May 1785, but possibly sometime in August 1784: "Mr. Boydell respectfully informs the Nobility, Gentry, and particularly his Subscribers to the Print of the Death of Major Peirson, that the Picture is now to be seen in his Gallery, with the small one, the size of the intended Print, as a companion to the Death of Lord Chatham ... ."

29. *The Morning Herald*, 6 August 1784, as quoted in Prown 1966, II, p. 307 note 8: "Three ovals are placed on the top of the frame, in the centre of which is Mr. Copley's portrait, painted by that able artist, Mr. Stuart. The portrait of Mr. Heath, who is to engrave the subject, is on one side of the frame, and that of Mr. Josiah Boydell, who is to make the drawing, on the other." For more information on the Adam frame, see Harris 1990, pp. 92–7. *Per* Sotheby's, London, 29 July 1953, no. 56, the subject of fig. 43 is listed, without documentation, as *Portrait of Fontaine North*. Charles Merrill Mount identified the subject as Josiah Boydell on the basis of information in the Witt Library, Courtauld Institute files (see Rhode Island School of Design file notes). On the grounds of stylistic similarity to the Wadsworth picture, the

British artists, and, eventually, alderman of the City of London (fig. 42).[21] Boydell began his career as a land surveyor, then turned printseller, importing prints in the 1760s, and by the 1770s becoming the leading exporter of reproductive prints after works by English artists, amassing solely through the print trade a £350,000 fortune. The Prince of Wales called him "an English tradesman who patronizes art better than the Grand Monarque ... the Commercial Maecenas."[22] Boydell recognized the commercial advantages of prints particularly after patriotic subjects, such as *The Death of Major Peirson*, which he commissioned from Copley. The phenomenal success of William Woollett's 1776 reproduction after Benjamin West's *The Death of General Wolfe*, the most popular engraving of the eighteenth century, made £15,000 for John Boydell, £7,000 for Woollett, and an unknown sum for West.[23] In the absence of a commission or patron, and even with one, the print trade offered the aspiring history painter significant compensation for his efforts as well as a form of self-promotion.

The income from prints was not worry-free, however, especially for Copley. Due to the expense of producing prints, publishers sold subscriptions in advance, receiving final payment when the engraver produced the print. Copley published *The Death of the Earl of Chatham* himself, paying Francesco Bartolozzi, one of the best engravers in England, £2,000 to make the print. Instead of the four years he promised, however, Bartolozzi took ten years to engrave his plate, blaming unexpected delays and the need to finish other uncompleted commissions – common problems in the trade. When Copley came to advertise a print subscription for *The Siege of Gibraltar*, one critic lashed at him: "This proposal would come from any other man with a better grace than from Mr. COPLEY, who EIGHT years since received his subscription for the DEATH of LORD CHATHAM; and two years after for Major PEIRSON'S death; and to this hour neither print has been delivered!"[24] Either Copley or another supporter responded that other artists and engravers encountered similar delays,[25] but in spite of this defense such charges seriously damaged the artist's credibility. The situation worsened when Bartolozzi's plate yielded only 2,500 impressions of *The Death of the Earl of Chatham*, enough to fulfill the subscription list, but no more. To recoup the loss, Copley commissioned Bartolozzi's assistant Jean-Marie Delattre to produce a smaller, less expensive print. Copley recognized that poor reproductions also damaged reputations, and so, when the completed plate did not pass his inspection, he went to court to defend himself (but lost despite testimony in his favor from Boydell and West).[26]

The Death of Major Peirson, commissioned for £800 by Boydell, offered a different case, because the buyer changed the rules of the game.[27] Immediately after the exhibition at the Haymarket closed, *The Morning Herald* announced that "The celebrated picture of the death of Major Pierson [*sic*] is fixed up in Mr. Boydell's gallery."[28] The article went on to describe the elaborately carved frame designed by the renowned Neoclassical architect Robert Adam (fig. 46). Ornamented with carved cannons, weapons, British flags, bows, and swags, the magnificent gilded frame was surmounted by one oval and two roundel moldings that contained portraits by the American artist Gilbert Stuart of Copley (at center in the oval; fig. 44), Josiah Boydell, the draftsman for the proposed engraving (fig. 43), and James Heath, the engraver of the picture (fig. 45).[29] Thus, in one grand gesture, Boydell made the very painting into an advertisement for the print (fig. 47),[30] a means to the end of broad dissemination.[31]

At Boydell's shop at 90 Cheapside, the painting's status as an advertisement was

Fig. 43 (top left) Gilbert Stuart
Josiah Boydell(?) or *Fontaine North(?), ca.*
1781–83(?)

Oil on canvas, 23³/4 in. diam. (60.3 cm)
Museum of Art, Rhode Island School of Design

Fig. 44 (top center) Gilbert Stuart
John Singleton Copley, ca. 1784

Oil on canvas, 26¹/2 × 22¹/4 in. (67.3 × 56.5 cm)
By courtesy of the National Portrait Gallery, London

Fig. 45 (top right) Gilbert Stuart
James Heath (1757–1843), 1783–84

Oil on canvas, 22¹/2 in. diam. (57.1 cm)
Wadsworth Atheneum, Hartford, gift of Samuel P. Avery

Fig. 46 Robert Adam
Frame Design for *The Death of Major Peirson*

Watercolor
By courtesy of the Trustees of Sir John Soane's Museum

roughly correct roundel dimensions, and the complementary angles of the sitters' faces, the Rhode Island painting may indeed represent Josiah Boydell.

30. Another print of *The Death of Major Peirson,* engraved by Aloys Kessler, is at the Graphische Sammlung Albertina, Vienna. See also Mayne 1981, pp. 89–90.

31. For example, despite their popularity, neither *The Death of the Earl of Chatham* nor *The Death of Major Peirson* sold easily. Copley placed the former at a Christie's auction in 1788, but it was bought in, and remained with the artist until Alexander Davison won it in a lottery in 1806. The latter,

even more emphasized than in the public rooms in the Haymarket. In the eighteenth century, the corner of Ironmonger Lane and Cheapside included a number of print-sellers' establishments. Cheapside's spectacular appearance elicited comments from enthusiastic visitors from the Continent, including the German tourist Sophie de la Roche, who remarked: "I was struck by the excellent arrangement and system which the love of gain and the national good taste have combined in producing, particularly in the elegant dressing of large shop-windows, not merely in order to ornament the streets and lure purchasers, but to make known the thousands of inventions and ideas, and spread good taste about, for the excellent pavements made for pedestrians enable crowds of people to stop and inspect the new exhibits."[32] Others would comment on the large crowds and the plentiful displays of luxury goods, the "opulence and

Fig. 47 James Heath
The Death of Major Peirson, 1796
Engraving, 22⅜ × 30½ in. (56.8 × 77.5 cm), published by
J. and J. Boydell, 1796

owned by Boydell, appeared in his Shakespeare
Lottery of 1804, remained unsold at his estate sale
at Christie's in 1805, and was acquired by the
artist thereafter.

32. Sophie de la Roche (1786), in *Sophie in London*,
London 1933, as quoted in Bruntjen 1974/1985,
pp. 28–9.

33. Robert Southey, *Letters from England*, London
1807/1951, pp. 49–50, as quoted in Bruntjen
1974/1985, p. 55 note 33.

34. Charles P. Moritz, *Travels, Chiefly on Foot, through
several parts of England in 1782* ..., London 1795/
1924, as quoted in Bruntjen 1974/1985, pp. 55–6
note 33.

splendour of the shops, drapers, stationers ... silversmiths, booksellers, printsellers ... street after street ... the articles themselves so beautiful, and so beautifully arranged."[33] The windows, projecting into the street so that wares could be seen from three sides, were built to enhance the display of goods: one observer commented that the total effect "seemed to me a well-regulated cabinet of curiosities."[34] In sympathy to the rest of Cheapside, Boydell presented *The Death of Major Peirson* as an entertainment in a street of spectacles designed to lure consumers. His shoproom on the second floor consisted of a space eighty by seventeen foot divided into two galleries, sufficiently impressive for one observer to remark that the "rooms appropriated by this truly patriotic Alderman for the reception of his numerous and well chosen collection of drawings, paintings ... form a spectacle, which at once shew the spirit of the compiler, and the improved state of the arts ...."[35] An inner room displayed paintings by modern British artists, topped by a row of portraits of British artists and engravers commissioned from Gilbert Stuart.[36] It was this skylit room, as described by Sophie de la Roche (who received a guided tour from the proprietor himself) that contained, as well as James Northcote's history paintings of Edward IV's sons in the Tower, "the large canvas by Mr. Cosway [*sic*], of General Pierson's [*sic*] death in Guernsey [*sic*]

Fig. 48 John Singleton Copley
William Ponsonby, 2nd Earl of Bessborough, 1790
Oil on canvas, 23 × 18³/₄ in. (58.4 × 47.6 cm)
Courtesy of The Fogg Art Museum, Harvard University
Art Museums, bequest of Grenville L. Winthrop

35. *The Morning Post*, 14 November 1786, p. 2, as quoted in Bruntjen 1974/1985, p. 58 note 41.

36. Bruntjen 1974/1985, p. 63 note 54, enumerates the following portraits of painters and engravers commissioned from Stuart by Boydell from 1783 through 1786: William Woollett, Joshua Reynolds, Benjamin West, William Miller, Richard Paton, Ozias Humphrey, Josiah Boydell, Georg Sigmund and Johann Gottlieb Facius, James Heath, William Sharp, John Browne, John Hall, Richard Earlom. Not mentioned by Bruntjen is the portrait of Copley, which, along with portraits of Heath and Boydell, was incorporated in the Adam frame. For a discussion of Stuart's portrait of Reynolds, see Rather 1993. Copley's portrait of Gibbs 'Fisshe' Craufurd (private collection), dated *ca.* 1780, is similar to Stuart's portrait of Reynolds with its gesture and props. Further research into the connection between the two portraits might be fruitful.

37. Sophie de la Roche (1786), in *Sophie in London*, London 1933, pp. 237–9, as quoted in Bruntjen 1974/1985, p. 29. *The Morning Post*, 14 November 1786, also mentions Copley and Northcote's paintings, the murder of the Scottish King by Opie, a portrait to be hung over the chimney of the Lord Mayor by Miller, Paton's "seapieces", small elegant pictures by Hamilton, and Rev. Mr. Peters's *Apocrypha*, in Bruntjen 1974/1985, pp. 58–9 note 41.

38. *V & A Press Cuttings*, vol. 2, p. 485, unsourced and undated.

during the unexpected landing of the French in the American war. The painting is significant and expressive. It also contains portraits of the officers fighting beside the general, and of the Moor who shot the man dead at the very moment he had taken his master's life."[37]

Such commentary by impressed visitors suggests that, in an age before the first public art museums, Boydell's gallery operated like the modern-day museum in which retail shops occupy spaces next to the entrances and exits. At Boydell's, the consumer could similarly subscribe to or purchase a print as a memento of the visit. As one print advertiser asserted: "The prints of Wolfe and Chatham will probably outlive, by many ages, the marbles of the Abbey, and remain to future antiquarians invaluable proofs of history, when the building itself shall long have been crumpled into dust:– and the names of Lord Heathfield and his gallant companions at Gibraltar, will live to the remotest futurity in the works of Copley and Trumbull, multiplied by the gravers of Bartolozzi and Sharp; and the rock itself scarce prove a more durable monument."[38] At this time mechanical reproduction did not lessen, but rather enhanced, the value of the image. In fact these paintings can be seen as the residue of the larger project of disseminating prints.

With *The Death of the Earl of Chatham*, Copley did not rely merely on the sale of the painting and the subscription of prints: he also capitalized on the portrait aspect of the project. His novel presentation of over fifty lords in a dramatic tableau involved making portraits from life, in sittings that established important contacts for the artist and led to further individual portrait commissions. In the individual portraits of three sitters Copley undertook after *The Death of the Earl of Chatham* – William Murray, 1st Earl of Mansfield (fig. 32 on p. 51); William Ponsonby, 2nd Earl of Bessborough (fig. 48); and John, 2nd Viscount Dudley and Ward (cat. 37) – Copley posed all three, to some degree, enacting the role they played in the larger painting. By this means Copley in the first place saved time, allowing the initial sittings to do double duty and obviating the need to repeat them.[39] Secondly, the finished individual portrait referred both to the individual and to his role in the event narrated in the history painting.

Still more profitable, however, and more controversial, was Copley's invention of the one-picture exhibition. He was to repeat this innovation four times in his career, and was imitated by competitors.[40] He rented his own gallery space to hang *The Death of the Earl of Chatham*, advertised the exhibition like any other spectacle or theatrical event in newspapers, charged an entrance fee, and provided a brochure explaining the subject and soliciting a subscription for an engraving of the picture. This last element is imaginatively depicted in Bartolozzi's engraved ticket for a visit to see *The Siege of Gibraltar* at Green Park, in which a figure at the left processes subscriptions (fig. 49). The novelty of Copley's scheme was not that he exhibited his work independently of official exhibitions: William Hogarth, Nathaniel Hone, Thomas Gainsborough, and others had already recognized the advantages of solo shows, often displaying their work in their own studios, sometimes even charging a fee.[41] The crucial difference lies in Copley's combination of overtly commercial elements, allowing him to gain profit from tickets as well as from advance partial payments for print subscriptions.

However, by inventing the public one-picture exhibition with its attendant fees and subscriptions, Copley challenged the Academy's disdain for self-promotion; his modern strategies foiled the high-minded fiction embraced by Royal Academicians that

Fig. 49 Mr. Copley's Picture of the Siege of Gibraltar as Exhibited in the Green Park near St. James's Palace
Facsimile of ticket of admission to the 1791 exhibition of *The Siege of Gibraltar*, engraved by F. Bartolozzi
British Museum, London

39. *The Siege of Gibraltar* offered a similar opportunity; for example, Copley painted, posthumously, *Colonel George Lewis* (Detroit Institute of Art) in the pose he occupied in the front row of Copley's larger history painting. Copley also painted an individual portrait of Richard Brocklesby, who appears in *The Death of the Earl of Chatham*. See Prown 1966, II, p. 413.

40. Altick 1978, pp. 104–5. Copley's advertisements, however, suggest that he may have included one or two of his earlier history paintings in these exhibitions, such as *The Death of the Earl of Chatham*, perhaps to attract a buyer, or at least to offer spectators another chance to see an already famous painting.

41. In *Voyage du jeune Anacharsis en Grèce* (1788), Abbé Barthélemy mentions that West charged an entry fee to see *The Death of General Wolfe* before he sent it to the Royal Academy, as quoted by Peter Cannon-Brookes in *Painted Word* 1991, p. 58. As early as 1777, the president of the Royal Academy himself was encouraged to hold an independent exhibition: "Then be youself! nor blend your fame/ With Artists of inferior name,/ Do not your moral Works expose/ At *Royal-Academic shows*;/ But those hold forthe, to mend the Town,/ *An Exhibition all your own!*" (Combe 1777, p. 12). I thank Susan Rather for bringing this poem to my attention.

42. For a full account of the episode, see Whitley 1928/1968, I, pp. 356–8. Some critics blamed the Royal Academy itself; *The Ear-Wig* wondered in 1781, "Hey-day! How comes it that we see here no pictures of Loutherbourg, Copley, or Humphreys? – Oh, that's true! Loutherbourg has an exhibition

gentlemen artists painted to bring pleasure and to enlighten, not to entertain and to accumulate wealth. He thus aroused rancor and frustration among Academy conservatives, especially treasurer William Chambers, and exposed the essential problem the gentleman artist faced when he openly engaged in commercial activities.[42]

Copley had initially intended to rent galleries in Pall Mall that had formerly housed the Royal Academy exhibitions, knowing they would lend cachet to his own exhibition. But Chambers, on learning of this, convinced its proprietor, the auctioneer James Christie, to reject Copley's offer to lease the space. In a spirited exchange of letters, Chambers accused Copley of attempting to mount a "raree show," and requested that he move the exhibition from the gallery space to his own home, where "his own presence will not fail to be of service to his views," the last a probable reference to Copley's glorification of the Earl of Chatham's political position.[43] Chambers, in his disdain for self-promotion, was much like the ancient authority on art, Pliny, who disapprovingly recounted an anecdote about Lucius Hostilius Mancinus's exhibiting a battle painting in the Forum and explaining before the gathered audience its intricacies, a manœuvre that secured his election to the consulship.[44] Chambers and the Academy conservatives he represented held self-promotion as beneath them but not beneath their concern. By calling Copley's exhibition a "raree show," connoting the vulgar and freakish, Chambers deemed Copley's exhibition antithetical to the conventionalizing aims of the Royal Academy. Though a Royal Academician, Copley was dismissing its aims for organic unity; he was a part at odds with the whole, conspicuously insubordinate to the group. While Chambers apparently objected to any public display by an academician outside the Academy, a private viewing in an artist's own studio constituted a lesser evil than conspicuous display in public rooms.[45]

Copley allayed Chambers's fears that losing his grand picture would hurt the Royal Academy exhibition; he assured him that he would never presume to think that his one picture could ever have such an detrimental effect. Denied the Pall Mall galleries, Copley rented another prominent public space nearby, the Great Room at Spring Gardens, which had hosted a wide variety of public events, including the former Society of Artists exhibitions, concerts performed by Johann Sebastian Bach and Wolfgang Amadeus Mozart, and even novelty jewelry displays.[46] Featuring crimson curtains and a domed ceiling with paintings representing the Liberal Arts, the Spring Gardens gallery provided a suitably august room to present Copley's extraordinary effort, but its public and commercial nature could only have exacerbated Chambers's concerns.

Chambers feared Copley's exhibition would compete with the simultaneous Royal Academy show, and the assumption has persisted in the literature that Copley's separate exhibition outside the Royal Academy cost the Academy £928 in lost admission fees that year.[47] The Academy in fact earned £2,141 in 1781, an average figure that appears low only in comparison with an unusually high figure, £3,069. 1s., from the preceding year.[48] The high figure from 1780 may be due to the public's desire to see the new Academy headquarters at Somerset House – designed by William Chambers himself. To some degree, Chambers may have felt threatened personally by the one-picture exhibition, not wanting anything to detract from the architectural renovations he had laid out to great symbolic effect just one year before and which, in terms of attendance, appeared so promising. But the question whether Copley's one-picture

Fig. 50 Joshua Reynolds
Sir William Chambers, 1780
Oil on canvas, 50 × 39³/₄ in. (127 × 101.5 cm)
Royal Academy of Art, London

Fig. 51 Joshua Reynolds
Theory, 1779
Oil on canvas, 68¹/₁₆ × 68¹/₁₆ in. (172.7 × 172.7 cm)
Royal Academy of Art, London

of his own, at five shillings [*The Eidophusikon*, or moving picture] – Copley was made an Academician; and, as soon as he reaped such advantageous honors, he no longer ceased to contribute to their show; but he deserted his standard, and levies contributions on the public, for the first work he produced of any consequence – and the

exhibition caused attendance to decrease at the Royal Academy exhibition was more far-reaching than Chambers's seemingly petty complaints, for it embraced critical debates about the status of art as a disinterested profession, and questioned who had access to art and who profited by it.

The Academy had outgrown its initial headquarters in Pall Mall by 1771. While these rooms remained for the time being the location for exhibitions, the administration and school moved to apartments at Somerset House in the Strand.[49] Chambers had begun the task of converting this large complex into a palace of government offices, also housing the Royal Academy, the Royal Society, and the Society of Antiquaries, in 1775. The rebuilding of Somerset House, of which the Royal Academy parts (now occupied by the Courtauld Institute) were unveiled in 1780, represented one of the most important architectural commissions of Chambers's career, so much so that Joshua Reynolds included its Strand façade in the background of his portrait of the architect (fig. 50). Chambers laid out the impressive new spaces to give visual expression to the Academy's aims. The visitor passed through an entrance hall furnished with antique casts and contemporary busts, and walked up a grand staircase to the first floor, which featured the Academy of Antiques (a room for drawing casts after ancient sculptures), the Assembly or Council Room (fig. 53), and a library, of which the ceiling boasted an allegorical painting of *Theory* by Reynolds (fig. 51). Reynolds's full-length portraits of King George and Queen Charlotte hung in the Council Room, visual proof of monarchical support and encouragement (figs. 52, 54). From the first floor, the visitor ascended the stairs again, passed through an anteroom decorated with antique busts in niches as well as painted architectural details to simulate a grand space, and reached the Great Room. Measuring approximately fifty-three by forty-three feet with a thirty-two-foot high ceiling, the Great Room was the largest gallery for exhibiting paintings in England (fig. 55). An inscription in Greek, reading "Let no Stranger to the Muses enter," appeared over the entrance to the Great Room, legible only to the learned or informed. To the Royal Academy enthusiast, the new spaces elegantly set forth the claim of artists to occupy a privileged place in society. An English school of art could now be said to exist, although the new Royal Academy would have its detractors. One critic, for example, called the room of antique casts a "temple of Priapus" and a "naked phalanx of broad-backed ancients" whose nudity repelled female visitors.[50] Charging the Academy with indecency, his underlying concern seems to be directed as much toward the atmosphere of pretension he perceived as to the indelicate situation the galleries provoked for women visitors. The way in which this critic reacted to the elevated claims of the Royal Academy suggests that some doubted the academicians' pose as disinterested civic servants. Just one year after the grand debut of the new, improved Royal Academy, Copley's one-picture exhibition must have appeared a threat against the principles that had been long committed to paper but were now newly enshrined in stone for all to see.

Chambers's charge against Copley, interestingly, does not directly involve the subject of Copley charging an admission fee. The Royal Academy itself charged a shilling fee for the publicly stated reason that it would assure an elegant crowd – "no Stranger to the Muses" would pass through its doors. According to the accompanying catalogue, probably composed by Reynolds and his friend Samuel Johnson, the academicians had not been able "to suggest any other Means than that of receiving Money for

Fig. 52 Joshua Reynolds
King George III, ca. 1780
Oil on canvas, 107^{15}/$_{16}$ × 72^{1}/$_{8}$ in. (274 × 183 cm)
Royal Academy of Art, London

Fig. 53 Henry Singleton
The Royal Academicians Gathered in their Council Room, 1793, to Judge the Work of the Students, 1795
Oil on canvas, 78^{1}/$_{8}$ × 102^{1}/$_{16}$ in. (198 × 259 cm)
Royal Academy of Art, London

Fig. 54 Joshua Reynolds
Queen Charlotte, ca. 1780
Oil on canvas, 107^{15}/$_{16}$ × 72^{1}/$_{8}$ in. (274 × 183 cm)
Royal Academy of Art, London

Fig. 55 Pietro Martini after J.H. Ramberg
The Royal Academy Exhibition at Somerset House, 1787
Engraving
British Museum, London

partial, illiberal conduct of the Academicians, by exciting parties and factions, has disgusted and driven from them Humphreys, with some artists of established, and others of promising genius."

43. *Ibid.* In addition to Chambers slighting Copley for self-promoting tactics, he may also have been referring to Copley's political views, which were, obviously, in sympathy with the Earl of Chatham and for commerce.

44. Pliny, XXXV, 7, lines 22-3, p. 277.

45. Exhibitions in the artist's studio were not unusual. Canaletto, William Hogarth, Benjamin West, and Thomas Gainsborough held exhibitions in their studios. See Altick 1978, p. 101.

46. Altick 1978, pp. 69–72. The Society of Artists of Great Britain received a royal charter in 1765. In 1768, dissatisfied members broke off to form the Royal Academy; see Hutchison 1968, pp. 26–50.

47. For example, Whitley 1928/1968, p. 357, and Prown 1966, II, p. 284. Statistics for Royal Academy exhibition revenues appear in Council Minutes 1768–1950.

48. Admission fees went into a fund used to award monies to needy families of deceased artists, and to offset building expenses. Any deficits in the Royal Academy budget were made up by the royal purse. Fluctuations in the yearly admission fees could vary widely. The £3069. 10s. figure for 1780 represents an unusually high return, one that would not be reached again for sixteen years.

49. Hutchison 1968, p. 51.

50. *V & A Press Cuttings*, vol. 1, p. 191.

51. Hutchison 1968, p. 55.

52. Pears 1988, pp. 127–8.

53. *V & A Press Cuttings*, vol. 3, unsourced, dated in hand 1815.

54. *V & A Press Cuttings*, vol. 2, p. 416, unsourced, undated, but with 1788 clippings. Even customers willing to pay a shilling were not always guaranteed entrance, for, the critic continued, "people not decently dressed, who have offered their money as others, to enter the Rooms, have been constantly refused admittance; – indeed, that strictness is become necessary, where people of fashion and rank are resorting." The exclusivity of these exhibitions was parodied in the press. The Greek inscription at the Royal Academy, for example, "Let no Stranger to the Muses enter," was parodied as "None must venture to enter but people of taste" in a satirical poem, *A dialogue at the Door of the Exhibition Room*: "Stop, stop my dear girl, you need make no such haste/ These three crooked words [greek] spoil our fun;/ None must venture to enter but people of taste,/ And alas! you and I boast of none./ Friend poet, she cry'd, your reason's but poor,/ Since to boast of ourselves is no sin,/ With the artists we'll say – while we lounge at the door,/ No *judges* of taste are within!" (*V&A Press Cuttings*, vol. 1, 193, dated in hand 1780).

Admittance to prevent the Room from being fill'd by improper Persons, to the entire exclusion of those for whom the Exhibition is intended."[51] After all, if the status of the artist were to evolve from the 'mechanic' to the gentleman, then the public exhibitions needed to be filled with the elegant sort, including and especially, the monarch himself, as Ramberg's image asserts (fig. 55).[52] Nonetheless, even the charge for admission could not prevent a situation in which, as one critic wrote, "all our Pictorial Exhibitions, are now thronged with the lower orders of the people, who think a shilling not ill-disposed in chasing them amongst the people of taste, even sailors in their jackets with their doxies on their arms, now elbow the first people of rank at these spectacles with the utmost of familiarity."[53] The deliberate exclusion of a large section of society simply confirmed the hierarchical social structure of the period, a patronage system of obligations and dependencies in which the assumption existed (although increasingly challenged) that only the affluent and educated were equipped to glean the pictures' larger meanings. Because refining their taste and humanizing their minds constituted one of the responsibilities of aristocratic citizens, the argument followed that they should not be distracted by "so many servants crouding at the door, a nuisance they [the directors] cannot remedy ...".[54]

Critics of the Royal Academy entrance fee rarely targeted it for exclusionary tactics based on social class. Instead, they might question the value of royal patronage of the arts during wartime, or suggest that because the Royal Academy enjoyed royal sponsorship, the people's pockets had already been picked.[55] Still others mocked the euphemistic language that denied the commercial aspect of the arts. Lampooning Noel Desenfans, a collector and promoter of a national gallery, one critic claimed: "When he buys pictures, it is out of love for the art; when he sells them, he only parts with them to oblige his friends; and when he exhibits them in Pall Mall, he puts them upon view at one shilling entrance to be sure, but that is to keep out the mob."[56] Such lively and essentially modern debates suggest that confidence in the disinterested nature of the artistic enterprise was questioned if not shattered during this active era of promoting English art. Aware of the debates and recognizing the loophole the one-picture exhibition presented to him, Copley could take advantage of the Royal Academy tradition of charging fees and could personally profit by such a venture without being charged with excessive self-interest. He risked only the taint of self-promotion. If he had not charged, he would have laid himself open to accusations of pandering to the broader public.

Chambers, it should be noted, fought a losing battle. Two years after Copley's exhibition of *The Death of the Earl of Chatham*, Royal Academy member Thomas Stothard exhibited and charged an admission fee for *The Death of Lord Robert Manners* (see fig. 58) at Thomas Macklin's publisher's shop in Cockspur Street, and was soon to be followed by other artists in various public spaces.[57] Copley would exhibit five times outside the Academy, skirting academicians' disdain by continuing to exhibit at the Royal Academy, but saving his history machines for commercial consumption – he gained from £1,650 to £5,000 for *The Death of the Earl of Chatham* and £3,000 for *The Siege of Gibraltar* from entrance fees alone.[58] Copley's one-picture exhibition itself, then, signalled a challenge to the Academy's aims. This message of challenge was indeed reinforced and duplicated by the inner workings of *The Death of Major Peirson* and by its relationship to the theories and facts that lay behind it.

Rules, Forms and the Aims of Expression

Widely read among eighteenth-century British military officers, Humphrey Bland's *A Treatise of Military Discipline* (1727) provides the perfect analogy of hierarchy, deference, and the challenge of authority that Copley implies in *The Death of Major Peirson*. Asserting the importance of deference to military superiors, Bland wrote: "I have, throughout my Book, taken every Occasion to inculcate the Necessity of legal Military Subordination. It has been the practise of all Nations, ancient and modern, even where the People have been blessed with the highest Liberty, never to admit of a military independauce [*sic*] upon their military Superiors; I look upon it as the Band which ties the Whole together, and without it, all our Rules and Forms to be of no Use."[59]

Deference to a military superior provided the key element that made the military system function. Such assertions of the importance of discipline paralleled the art academy's, which required similar rigor. Just as in the military a young soldier's "natural" excessiveness needed to be "checked by the cool reason of men of experience," so Academy students were instructed never to exceed their orders nor to break rules.[60] Further, the structural model of the military, in which deference provided the "Band which ties the Whole together," also parallels contemporary aesthetic treatises for painting. The due subordination of the parts to the whole, in which all elements of a painting would be integrated, assured the general effect of unity demanded in academic treatises. The fact that the Royal Academy even considered instituting uniforms for its Academicians suggests the degree to which it perceived the artistic profession as one achieved through the same kinds of rigorous training as those experienced by the soldier.[61] In *The Death of Major Peirson*, a painting ostensibly about military decorum, Copley also engages the subject of artistic discipline, creating tension by opposing, in both spheres, individual autonomy against authority, chaos against discipline, the natural against the learned.

Copley spent his career before painting *The Death of Major Peirson* mastering the rules by which history painting was bound. Early copies he made in the colonies after European paintings and prints suggest the young artist's ambition to paint historical subjects, a goal that was thwarted for more than twenty years until he sought the more sympathetic artistic environment of England and the Continent.[62] Copley's formal entrance into the world of history painting took place during his 1775 Grand Tour in Italy, where he experienced "an amaising fund of Pleasure and improvement ...".[63] There he completed his first original history painting, *The Ascension* (fig. 10 on p. 27), a scene taken from the New Testament account of *Acts* 1:9–11. *The Ascension* is an awkward although auspicious beginning, demonstrating, when understood in the context of Copley's long letter to his half-brother Henry Pelham describing "in what manner an Historical composition is made", the artist's thorough knowledge of the sequence of tasks required in executing a history painting.[64] This sequence, combining invention and rule according to academic orthodoxy, would produce a painting that compelled the viewer to respond to its message and act accordingly; in this instance, to understand and appreciate the significance of Christ's divinity.[65] To be a history painter, Copley knew he must master the intellectual and technical stages through which the composition would evolve from idea to object: learning history paintings' academic and visual evolution, identifying a suitably lofty subject to paint, and entering into the passions of the subjects. Finally, the artist must maintain a temperament commensurate to the

55. *V & A Press Cuttings*, vol. 1, pp. 183–4, *London Courant*, dated in hand May 1780.

56. *V & A Press Cuttings*, vol. 1, p. 292, unsourced, undated, near 1786 cuttings.

57. The exhibition of *The Death of Lord Robert Manners* appears to be the first commissioned one-picture exhibition. See Altick 1978, p.106. Macklin offered a variation on the payment plan scheme: he charged a shilling entrance-fee to non-subscribers to the print. See Providence 1991, p. 97.

58. This figure is based on Copley's claim that 60,000 visitors attended *The Siege of Gibraltar*. Reportedly, Copley earned £5,000 from entrance fees to *The Death of the Earl of Chatham*. The show ran ten weeks, and at the end of six weeks, 20,000 visitors were said to have attended. If 33,000 visitors attended at the end of ten weeks, at one shilling apiece, entrance fees would have amounted to £1,650. Copley moved the exhibition to the Gresham Lecture Room over the Royal Exchange from 10 July to 1 September 1781, but research has not revealed whether or not he charged an entrance fee there.

59. Bland 1729/1757, p. 4.

60. *Ibid.*, p. 145.

61. Farington 1978–, vol. 1, p. 120, entry for 10 December 1793, alludes to the fact that Reynolds always wanted uniforms or "gowns" for the Royal Academy. Farington himself believed uniforms would "distinguish them as a body" and would express an "impressive respectability."

62. For example, Copley's youthful copies of European paintings, which he knew from mezzotints, include *The Forge of Vulcan*, 1754 (private collection); *Galatea, ca.* 1754 (Museum of Fine Arts, Boston, here fig. 8); and *The Return of Neptune, ca.* 1754 (The Metropolitan Museum of Art, New York).

63. Copley to Pelham, Rome, 14 March 1775, in *Letters of Copley and Pelham* 1914/1972, pp. 294–308.

64. *Ibid.* Unless otherwise cited, all references to Copley's process or his comments about *The Ascension* refer to this letter.

65. Barrell 1986 makes a distinction between paintings that inspire one to act and those designed to exercise the social bonds of society.

subject at hand until the numerous preparatory studies have been sketched and then squared for transfer to a large-scale canvas, and the painting completed.

Copley's letter to his half-brother, in which he wrote that he hoped Pelham would "procure Sir Josh: Renolds's Lectures; They are the best things that have yet appeared of the kind," indicates his devotion to Reynolds's instruction to seek out lofty models for inspiration. Regarding *The Ascension*, Copley wrote that, after imagining the passions and disposition of the subjects (whose "Appostolick Carracter" forbids their being too exaggerated), he chose certain figural groupings and expressions suitable to the subject inspired by the vast stock of pictorial devices and poses from the works of the ancients and the moderns. He turned to Raphael, the 'modern' painter most esteemed among academic circles, and his *Transfiguration*, depicting the New Testament account of Matthew 17:1–20, served as Copley's main source of inspiration (fig. 11 on p. 27).[66] Further, the manner of his appropriation of the composition, and specifically his variation on Raphael's subject, confirm his knowledge of academic dicta on imitation and invention. On the authority of antiquity, literary and artistic theorists understood that copying from approved masters aided the artist's invention. Forwarding the idea that genius is not native but acquired through principle, Reynolds argued that "by being conversant with the inventions of others ... we learn to invent."[67] Borrowing poses and gestures did not indicate plagiarism of any kind, as Reynolds asserted, because copying helped the artist enter into the spirit of the scene, engaging that "play of mind" that distinguished an artist from a 'mechanic.'[68] Appropriation from venerated models, what Horace Walpole called "wit," and Nathaniel Hone "conjuring," conferred an artistic pedigree on the painting and, by extension, the artist.[69] By using venerated art of the past to inspire his own invention, the artist provided a distinguished lineage for his own painting. The erudite viewers who recognized *The Ascension*'s connection with Raphael's *Transfiguration* indicated their own and, of course, the artist's fluency with the Old Masters, proving an additional element in the communicative spirit of historical painting. Copley repeated such patterns of appropriation in *The Death of Major Peirson* as well.[70]

Imitation also formed part of the "generalization" Reynolds believed was integral to high art. According to Reynolds, artists would correct nature by adapting and adjusting examples of great art from the past through models in nature. According to this principle, Copley looked to Raphael as well as to nature (represented by, quite literally, himself, a model, and a wooden lay-figure) as he improved his composition for *The Ascension*. Still working out his ideas through sketches, Copley improved the details of the figures' drapery, enlisting the aid of a lay-figure wrapped with wet cloth in order to capture the folds and creases, a method he had practiced in New England.[71] Once he had set the general outlines, Copley indicated the areas of shadow and light, and refined the subjects' gesture and expression, which, he wrote, "should always be determined by feeling it yourself" with the aid of a looking-glass. Next, he transferred the drawings to the canvas and used a live model to refine the positions of the figures further.[72] Throughout the process, Copley noted that frequent reference to the work of Raphael "kept the fire of the Imagination alive ... sometimes a fortnigh[t] would pass before I could invent a single figure." Copley emphasizes to his half-brother this fitful and fiery mental spirit, a theatricality that formed a critical part of making serious art.

The central question of narrative and visual unity, an issue that had long been

66. In the letter of 14 March 1775, Copley also mentions the importance of Raphael's *'School of Athens'* and his cartoon of *The Death of Ananias* as artistic models.

67. Reynolds 1959/1975, *Discourse VI*, 1774, lines 169–70.

68. Lawrence Lipking uses this felicitous phrase to describe Reynolds's definition of "imitation," in Lipking 1970, p. 176.

69. *Ibid.*, pp. 176–7.

70. See Prown 1966, II, pp. 305–6, for possible sources for *The Death of Major Peirson*, such as Pieter Soutman's engraving after Rubens's drawing of Caravaggio's *The Entombment of Christ* and Paulus Pontius's engraving after Rubens's *The Massacre of the Innocents*. Other interesting comparisons (I thank A. Thereza Crowe and Laura K. Griffis) include Michelangelo's *Crucifixion* of *St. Peter* and Rubens's *The Consequences of War*, for the dying Peirson and the woman fleeing with arms upraised.

71. In his letter, Copley reminds Pelham of his use of the lay figure in the colonies: "when I was uncertain of the effect of any figure Or groop of figure[s] I drew them of the sise on a peace of Paper ... just in the way you have seen me proceed with Draperys, etc., in my portraits." Presumably Copley did use sketches in working out the compositions of his colonial portraits, although only one, possibly, survives (see Dublin, London, Paris, Liverpool, Cambridge 1976–7, cat. 1 and pl. 1, for a purported study by Copley for his colonial portrait of *Elizabeth and Mary Royall*, ca. 1758, Museum of Fine Arts, Boston).

72. Copley's drawings reveal a grid used in the process of squaring for transfer to a canvas, although no grid appears through X-radiography or infrared reflectography on Copley's English canvases. See introduction to cats. 19–32.

 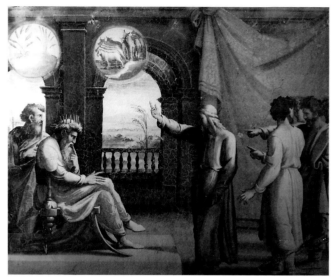

Fig. 56 School of Raphael
The Interpretation of the Dreams to the Brothers and
The Interpretations of Pharoah's Dreams, 1519
Fresco
Vatican Loggie, photograph courtesy Vatican Museums

discussed in aesthetic theory, involved Copley at an early stage, though his narrative skills remained untapped during his career as a portrait painter in colonial America and it was only after study abroad that he at last fully understood it. To his half-brother Copley described Raphael's *The Interpretation of the Dreams to the Brothers* and *The Interpretation of Pharoah's Dreams* which he had seen in the Loggie at the Vatican (fig. 56): "As there was nothing that could lead to the explination of the story, as he could only Paint a young lad talking to several Persons who stood round him, he has represented in the Sky the Dreams ... The same where Joseph interprets the Dream of Pharoh, he has put against the Wall ... two round tablets on which he has painted the Dreams, so that one must instantly know the Story (if he is not quite stupid) as soon as he casts his eye upon it." Copley's fascination with Raphael's solution to the problem of continuous narrative reveals the enthusiasm of a neophyte to painting histories, eager to share his discovery with his half-brother of even more limited exposure. But his commentary, more importantly, reveals that he understood the academic significance of 'instantaneity,' an element of unity which he had learned from lengthy discussion of the subject in treatises on painting.

In choosing Raphael's *Transfiguration* as the model for his *Ascension*, Copley must have known that lack of unity was at issue in Raphael's composition. A conspicuous figure in Raphael's painting is the possessed boy, brought to Mount Tabor by his mother, who appears at lower right. Richardson specifically criticized *The Transfiguration* on the grounds that the fitful boy distracted the viewer and compromised the pictorial and narrative aspect of the general effect that defined good painting – an infraction upon narrative sequence that Copley would not make in *The Ascension*.[73] The account in *Acts* notes that after Christ ascended, two angels appeared to instruct the Apostles to prepare for Christ's second coming, which, Copley writes, "would naturally ingage those that were next to them." Raphael's figures gaze and gesture to both Christ and the possessed child – scattered movements that Copley avoids in his composition by keeping all figures focused on Christ. One angel gestures toward Christ, and both figures affected by the angels keep their bodies aligned toward Him, the figure at left directing the viewer's gaze upon the central form with his worshipful hands. Such sub-

73. Richardson 1715/1725/1971, p. 57.

tleties of composition reveal Copley's acute understanding of academic theory and his concern with the standards of unity to which he would adhere until undertaking *The Death of Major Peirson.*

Unity occupied a lofty realm in academic theory. From the Renaissance to the eighteenth century, theorists gleaned prescriptions for artistic unity from such antique sources as Aristotle's *Politics* and *Poetics* and Longinus's treatise on dramatic writing, *On the Sublime.*[74] Longinus used the human form as an analogy for unity, arguing that its constituent parts made no sense except as they connected to a larger body. Shaftesbury, too, emphasized the importance of unity, warning artists that depicting multiple actions would result in a "confused Heap, or Knot of Pieces, and not a single intire Piece, or Tablature, of the historical kind."[75] For English aestheticians, this unity was equivalent to the "general effect," in which all parts of a painting would be duly subordinated to the general effect of the whole. The lack of this unifying effect was a problem that West and Reynolds recognized in Copley's intricately detailed American portraits, and that Copley grappled with throughout his career.[76] The absence of the general effect would cause viewers to be distracted by parts and conspicuous details, unintegrated elements that would supposedly prevent the viewer from grasping the painting's message, its very *raison d'être.* Although the general effect usually referred to mechanical matters of reconciling line with form, it also, in a broader sense, paralleled the Aristotelian unity so esteemed by the academy as a sign of visual and moral harmony and balance. Count Francesco Algarotti, an eighteenth-century Italian art theorist influential in English circles and familiar to Copley, underscored this position: "the action must be one, the place one, the time one. I need not, I believe, say anything of those painters, who, like the writers of Chinese and Spanish theatre, cram a variety of actions together ... The politeness and learning of the age seem to demand considerations of a more refined nature."[77] Copley carefully observed unity in *The Ascension,* but he challenged it in *The Death of Major Peirson* by manipulating the narrative sequence in a manner that reflects his sensitivity to an alternative idea of the spectators' process of seeing. To some degree, Copley does "cram a variety of actions together," but he does so to maximize the spectators' involvement in the painting.

In the center of the battlefield – the market square of St Helier – a cluster of officers carry away the dying Peirson. His chest dripping with blood, his face a ghostly pallor, his right arm falling lifeless beside him, Peirson's corpse provokes sympathetic gestures and pensive expressions from the surrounding officers. Leaning against a drum, a sergeant at far left nurses his own wound, seemingly oblivious to his pain, and reaches toward Peirson in a gesture of sympathy. While some officers attend to Peirson, others resume battle, leading lines of gun-ready soldiers toward the French enemy at the right. Barely visible at upper left, marching soldiers descend Town Hill, one wounded and tumbling downhill amidst billowing smoke. Distinguished by his expression of terror and a green-colored suit amidst a sea of red, the young boy at right clutches his nurse, who carries an infant while looking back with an expression of horror at the scene of battle, while his mother, arms upraised, looks heavenward as if for divine guidance. The young boy, said to be modeled after young John Copley, Jr., appeals to the viewer, the only figure in the painting so engaged.[78]

Had these vignettes comprised the full narrative action of the painting, none would detract from the central event of Peirson's martyrdom: Copley would have preserved

74. Longinus, chapter 40.

75. Shaftesbury 1714/1727, p. 353.

76. See, for example, Benjamin West to Copley, London, 4 August 1766, in which he praises Copley's *Boy playing with a Squirrel* (1765, Museum of Fine Arts, Boston) submitted to the Society of Artists exhibition, but found it "to liney, which was judgd to have arose from there being so much neetness in the lines;" one year later, West criticized Copley's *Young Lady with a Bird and Dog* (1767, Toledo Museum of Art) for lacking "Due Subordanation to the Principle Parts;" Copley's friend, Captain R.G. Bruce, reported from London the same day that Reynolds found the same painting had "a little Hardness in the Drawing, Coldness in the Shades, An over minuteness ...." (*Letters of Copley and Pelham* 1914/1972, pp. 44, 57, 42).

77. Algarotti 1764, p. 95.

78. Amory 1882, p. 23; Bayley 1915, pp. 16–7; and Prown 1966, II, p. 304. Bayley asserts that the woman with upraised arms represents Mrs. Copley, and the woman holding the baby the family nurse.

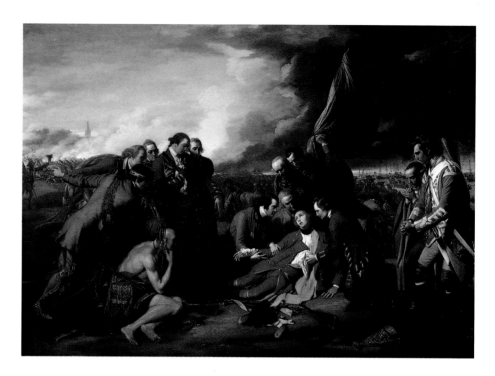

Fig. 57 Benjamin West
The Death of General Wolfe, 1770
Oil on canvas, 59¹/₂ × 84 in. (151 × 213.5 cm)
National Gallery of Canada, Ottawa

the sense of unity demanded by academic orthodoxy, in which all elements of the painting coalesced to form one general effect. But slightly behind Peirson, elegantly dressed in a navy-blue uniform with yellow facings and distinguished by a princely plumed hat, a figure, identified in the brochure as Peirson's black servant, leans into his musket and fires at the French marksman at the right. According to military practice of the period, an officer stands behind the marksman and points out the target, his finger an echo of the trigger below. By pushing two events to the foreground at once, Peirson's death and the servant's retaliation, Copley defies unity, cultivating a "noisiness" that Shaftesbury had found offensive when paintings conveyed multiple actions, "which must naturally have the same effect on the Eye, as such Conversation wou'd have upon the Ear were we in reality to hear it."[79] Reynolds and other academic theorists, of course, condoned some deviation of the rules once an artist achieved maturity, although in this painting Copley broke academic rules in ways unusual among his contemporaries as he endeavored to create a compelling and theatrical atmosphere within – and outside – the picture plane.

Copley's experiments with narrative multiplicity depended partly on the example of Benjamin West's *The Death of General Wolfe* (fig. 57), which offered a sophisticated and complex manner of representing temporal and spatial relationships. In West's painting, the background figures enact the events sequentially, reading from right to left.[80] The narrative sequence ends with the figure in the middle distance at the left, who brings news that the enemy is retreating, and who provides a temporal and spatial link between the background and foreground. The viewer assimilates the action by moving first from foreground to background, from present time to past time, and then forward again according to the narrative order West envisions for the viewer from past to present. In this manner, West constructs the death tableau so that the viewer exists in the literal present and completes the circle of mourners surrounding the dying Wolfe.

The American Indian at left, brilliantly arrayed in a costume which would have

79. Shaftesbury 1714/1727, p. 362. Interestingly, the Duke of Wellington mentioned to Copley's son, Lord Lyndhurst, that "it was the only picture of a battle that ever satisfied him or displayed the reality of the scene, inasmuch as the artist had only attempted to represent *one* incident ..." (Amory 1882, p. 92).

80. Montagna 1981.

Fig. 58 J. K. Sherwin after Thomas Stothard
The Death of Lord Robert Manners, 1786 (after
the painting of 1783)

Etching and engraving, 19⁹/₁₆ × 24³/₁₆ in. (49.7 ×
61.4 cm)

81. Just as the black seaman in Copley's *Watson and the Shark* has been the subject of extensive debate, so, too, has West's American Indian. Wind 1938–9, pp. 117–9, sees this figure as an example of the 18th-century fascination for *mirabilia* (the exotic), as the figure also serves as a 'repoussoir,' and offsets the viewer's purported shock at seeing heroes in modern dress. Solkin 1992, p. 212, finds the Indian's gaze "expressionless," a figure both "un-British and uncivilised" who serves as a foil to the mourners surrounding the dying hero, whose gestures of concern would have "confirm[ed] the propriety of their own reactions, of an admiration dominated by feelings of private grief." West's meticulous rendering of the wrinkled brow of the American Indian's forehead, a gesture of concern, refutes this idea that mars an otherwise compelling interpretation of the painting. See Fryd 1995 for a discussion of the historical significance of the combination of the Indian seated next to the figure of William Johnson.

82. In addition to the literary device of suspension, Copley's title for the painting shared with 18th-century novels a claim to truth: his painting, the title asserted, was "founded on fact." Thus painting shared a similar structure to the 18th-century Western novel, a genre which emerged in part from journalism. During the late 17th century, English writers attached truth claims to their stories, asserting their account was "founded on fact." The literary convention of truth claims in novels arose from earlier writers' need to avoid Puritan sanctions against writing fictions, perceived at the time as wasteful of human energy. See Davis 1983, pp. 106, 176. I have benefited by a discussion with Paul Staiti and Susan Rather regarding the suspenseful nature of *Watson and the Shark*.

connoted the exotic to an eighteenth-century London audience, sits poised in thought, as if he alone understands the deeper significance of the event.[81] He is cast as an outsider, a Rousseau-like noble savage whose foreign status provides a cultural innocence that allows him to receive the painting's messages of courage, loyalty, and patriotism. His wrinkled brow suggests his compassion, but his expression is more complex than those of the other mourners who merely express sympathy. An outsider looking in, he becomes the equivalent of the spectator: much like the mid-ground figure, who links past to present, he joins painting to audience, completing the ordered progression of time and space West constructs for the viewer.

Copley had already forced the viewer to become more immediately involved in the action in his earlier *Watson and the Shark*, though without yet breaking the rule of unity. In *Watson and the Shark* he freezes the action at the moment when the shark attacks Watson and the harpoonist aims his weapon; only the original title of the painting ("*A Boy attacked by a shark, and rescued by some seamen in a boat; founded on a fact which happened in the harbour of the Havannah*") conveys the outcome of the incident. The stable, pyramidal composition formed by the figures in the boat belies the true chaos and uncertainty of the outcome. Here Copley appears to adopt the literary device of suspense popularized by such novelists as Fanny Burney and Lawrence Sterne, who dropped narrative threads at perilous moments at the end of a chapter and picked them up again in the next installment or in later chapters.[82] Copley suspends the viewer above Watson and the attacking shark, and heightens the immediacy and danger of the story by keeping his audience in ignorance of its relatively happy ending, leaving his viewers supremely titillated. Like *Watson and the Shark*, *The Death of Major Peirson* is an anxious image. Here, however, Copley provides a satisfying ending by depicting two heroic actions – death and vengeance – simultaneously. While Peirson dies in the arms of his comrades, the viewer follows the imaginary line created by the musket in the hands of the black servant, which leads to Peirson's assassin himself lying in the arms of his comrades. The

Fig. 59 Simon Gribelin after Paolo de Matteis
Hercules Choosing Between Virtue and Vice, 1713
Engraving

avenging servant appears in gun-ready position: a puff of smoke above the hammer indicates he has just released the trigger, while a glance to the right demonstrates that the bullet has already struck its target. By this manipulation of temporal and spatial relationships, Copley forces the viewer's participation in the event. In the time taken for the viewer to move his eyes across the canvas, taking in the revenge sequence, he could assimilate the information and comprehend that the bullet would have met its mark. Copley thus plays with the device of depicted and real time and space to trap the viewer into the painting. Similarly, Thomas Stothard's *The Death of Lord Robert Manners* (fig. 58), painted and exhibited one year before Copley's painting, presents the death of a military hero surrounded by mourners, including a black figure at far left whose pointing fingers lead the viewer to the central action. Here, however, no secondary action pulls viewers into the fray, making them participants rather than merely observers. By contrast, Copley's keen sense of spectatorship endows his contemporary history paintings such as *Watson and the Shark* and *The Death of Major Peirson* with a special character of immediacy and danger that his contemporaries either did not aspire to or could not achieve.

As a further consequence, however, of its dramatic multiplicity, Copley's picture also compromised the moral example which, by long-standing tradition, history paintings provided. Where so many elements vie for the attention, how would viewers be able to glean the painting's messages? To avoid such confusion Shaftesbury had urged the artist to convey a single charged moment, from which attributes and expressive gestures might point to past or future events.[83] In his example, the well known story of the Choice of Hercules, he shows how the viewer is made to relate to the figure of Hercules, and, like Hercules, to make a moral choice between Virtue and Vice (fig. 59). In this manner, the artist would incite the viewer to act, composing the image so that the viewer made the morally appropriate choice. Equating aesthetics with ethics, Shaftesbury held that pictures of ordered clarity and harmony improved social skills and facilitated virtue. The thesis that art stood to benefit society found its most eloquent defender in Sir Joshua Reynolds, who argued in the *Discourses on Art*, delivered to the Academy, that the purpose of art and beauty was " ... to raise the thoughts, and extend the views of the spectator ... so ... that its effects may extend themselves imperceptibly into publick benefits, and be among the means of bestowing on whole nations refinements of taste: which, if it does not lead directly to purity of manners, obviates at least their greatest depravation, by disentangling the mind from appetite, and conducting the thoughts through successive stages of excellence, till that contemplation of universal rectitude and harmony which began by Taste ... may conclude in Virtue."[84]

Reynolds expressed the benefits of building a 'republic of taste' where art would lead its public through a series of ascending steps that led to the most exalted state of being, Virtue. The pursuit of art and beauty for Reynolds, in fact, operated like the "invisible hand" in Adam Smith's economic treatise *The Wealth of Nations* (1776), in which Smith argued that the pursuit of self-interest (paralleling the pursuit of art and beauty in Reynolds) simultaneously promoted the public good.[85] An earlier English theorist, Daniel Webb, had suggested this idea when he invoked the authority of the ancients, recounting the anecdote of the Athenian prostitute who looked at a painting across the room during a party and, catching the eye of a philosopher depicted in the painting, went home and became "ever after an example of temperance."[86] Webb's

83. Shaftesbury 1714/1727, pp. 353–4. It is worth mentioning that John Adams suggested to the Continental Congress that *Hercules Choosing between Virtue and Vice* represented a suitable seal for commemorating the British leaving Boston, testimony to the republican values asserted by the new country (Wood 1969, p. 49).

84. Reynolds 1769–90/1959/1975, *Discourse IX* (16 October 1780), lines 77–86, p. 171.

85. Jean-Jacques Rousseau's popular and influential *Emile, Or Education* (1762) used a similar analogy: the disciplinary *main cachée* of the tutor and parent.

86. Webb 1760, p. 33.

penitent prostitute was indisputable proof of the usefulness of painting to instruct the viewer, humanize the mind, and promote the public good, a point Copley would have understood and recognized as a key to success in London.

This belief system wielded a nationalist edge in eighteenth-century England, particularly in the work of Jonathan Richardson, who in 1715 appealed to the educative value of the arts as a means of bringing a cultural refinement to England commensurate with its status as a rising world-power. Reynolds responded to his call in the *Discourses on Art*, in which he detailed the prescriptions for making art and for leading an intellectual life, both of which were designed to create and nurture an "English School" of painting – of which Copley longed to be a part – that would equal if not surpass the longer established French Academy. The difficulty of creating a set of principles and persuading a body of artists to conform to them in the name of England helps to explain the note of urgency that underscores most eighteenth-century English treatises. Reynolds's use, in particular, of aesthetic terms such as "unity," "general effect," and "due subordination of the parts," were charged with political meaning: all implied a specific set of beliefs about republican virtue and order and the role artists would play in helping to maintain it. This was the exalted role the Academy envisioned for itself – as the protectors of British civilization, much as the growing eighteenth-century British military protected British economic interests. Adhering to academic orthodoxy signified not only personal refinement and taste but devotion to the creation of a national image.

The rigorous stoicism of Shaftesbury's aesthetic prescriptions had, however, evolved during the eighteenth century. Rather than the simple inculcation of virtue, paintings were expected to incite more emotional effects, and the exercise of feelings, such as sympathy, was believed to be beneficial and to maintain the social bonds of society.[87] Connected with this was the response to the 'sublime', an old – even ancient – idea that emerged with new life during the mid- to late eighteenth century.[88] Edmund Burke had theorized this fashionable notion, creating a complex system for understanding the effects of the physical world on the psyche in his influential *A Philosophical Enquiry into the Origin of Our Ideas of the Sublime and Beautiful* (1757). Burke's sensationist viewpoint, that the sublime formed a basis for knowledge through evincing specific passions and feelings, would eventually pave the way to a new type of English landscape painting; it also introduced new ways of conceiving and understanding history paintings. One of the characteristics of the sublime was that it was beyond rule, but Burke paradoxically systematized the unsystematic, building upon much of what had already been suggested by the ancient writer Longinus and the eighteenth-century theorist Richardson. He identified terror, obscurity, vastness, infinity, power, privation, darkness, variety, and suddenness, among architectural, geological, and atmospheric effects such as crenellated castles, rocky precipices, and stormy landscapes, as specific conditions that produce the sublime, an emotionally charged state that transports the viewer or audience. As Burke wrote, the source of the sublime was terror and the unknown: "Whatever is fitted in any sort to excite the ideas of pain, and danger, that is to say, whatever is in any sort terrible, or is conversant about terrible objects, or operates in a manner analogous to terror."[89]

Beyond the control of the viewer or reader, the effects of the sublime depended on the observer's actual safety: "the passions which turn on self-preservation are ... delightful when we have an idea of pain and danger without actually being in such

87. See 'Exhibitions of Sympathy' in Solkin 1992, pp. 157–213.

88. Earlier theorists such as Shaftesbury and Joseph Addison pointed to conditions that governed the sublime, but Richardson 1715/ 1725/1971 was the first writer to focus on the sublime as a category of painting.

89. Burke 1757/1958, p. 39.

circumstances."[90] Copley fully understood the psychological underpinnings of the sublime in *The Death of Major Peirson*, in which his elaboration of time and space carries the minds of viewers to their outer limits without upsetting a sense of personal safety. At least one viewer of his work, Abigail Adams, responded as if present at the scene of danger: "I never saw painting more expressive than this. I looked upon it until I was faint; you can scarcely believe but you hear the groans of the sergeant, who is wounded, and holding the handkerchief to his side, whilst the blood streams over his hand."[91] From the mid-eighteenth century onward, history paintings would engage the passions over reason, marking the transition from Shaftesbury's classical republic to a society tied together by social bonds of benevolence, affection, and sympathy – from the classical moralism of *The Judgment of Hercules* to the expressions of sympathy and admiration elicited by *The Death of Major Peirson*.[92]

The sublime would provoke a state of absorption on the part of the viewer, who, gripped by passion, exercised those bonds that maintained society. In order to enter, understand, and confirm the passions of their subjects, the artist would "feign a relish, till we find a relish come ... till we ... feel that what began in fiction, terminates in reality."[93] Artists would then capture such emotions in the sketch and transfer them to canvas. The subjects would serve as models for the viewer, who, in turn, would respond with the appropriate passions both felt and represented by the artist. As Leonardo da Vinci wrote, "That which is included in narrative paintings ought to move those who behold and admire them in the same way as the protagonist of the narrative is moved. So if the narrative shows terror, fear or flight ... or pleasure, joy and laughter ... the minds of the beholders should move their limbs in such a way as to make it seem that they are united in the same fate ...."[94] The painting, then, becomes an extension of the artist who has enacted all the parts played and captured them for the benefit of the viewer, who repeats the process. The reciprocity of such a process underscores the essential theatricality (or "artificiality," as Reynolds would have it) of history painting, its inherent sociability making it the perfect instrument for inculcating values perceived to be degenerating in the newly commercial society of eighteenth-century England.

West's presentation at the Royal Academy of *The Death of General Wolfe*, for example, elicited numerous comments regarding the expressions of the characters. One young woman felt the hero should be depicted responding rapturously to the news that the enemy fled, rather than enduring his private pain, and the famous actor David Garrick, in front of the painting and a small audience, reenacted the role of Wolfe according to the "correction" she offered.[95] The Earl of Chatham, likewise, believed that anyone who died for England should not look sad, as Wolfe does in the painting, but happy. In other words, the painting could provide models of behavior to be contested or condoned by its viewers. The atmosphere of reverent calm that the display of *The Death of the Earl of Chatham* elicited, in which one observer commented that "the room – whatever number of people it contains – is silent, or the company whispers as if at the bed of a sick person," was repeated before *The Death of Major Peirson*.[96] Contemporary history painting could retain moral urgency and reach a broader public, who had shared the history represented, than could classical or religious history painting.

Artists and theorists acknowledged that to understand the story, the viewer needed to recognize the figures' expressions. Here Charles Le Brun's *Conférence de M. Le Brun sur l'expression générale et particulière*, a seventeenth-century essay about the visual language of

90. *Ibid*, p. 51.

91. Abigail Adams to her sister Mrs. Cranch, London, 25 July 1784, in Adams 1841, pp. 31–2.

92. See 'A Republic of Taste' and 'Sir Joshua Reynolds' in Barrell 1986, pp. 1–163, and 'On Painting, Commerce and the "Public" in Eighteenth-Century Britain,' and 'Exhibitions of Sympathy' in Solkin 1992, pp. 1–26 and 157–213.

93. James Harris, "Rules Defended," in *Philological Inquiries* (1781) in Wind 1932/1986, p. 21. Johann Winckelmann offered a variant on the theme: "Sketch with fire; execute with phlegm," in Winckelmann 1765/1972, p. 269.

94. Leonardo da Vinci as quoted in Kemp 1989, p. 220.

95. Whitley 1928/1968, I, p. 282.

96. *St. James's Chronicle*, as quoted in Whitley 1928/1968, p. 358.

97. Le Brun 1698/1734, p. 12. See also Leonardo da Vinci as quoted in Kemp 1989, p. 144: "That figure is most praiseworthy which best expresses through its actions the passion of its mind." If it does not convey this expression, it is "twice dead, inasmuch as it is dead because it is a depiction, and dead yet again in not exhibiting motion either of the mind or of the body."

98. Reynolds 1769–90/1959/1979, *Discourse IV* (1771), lines 109–10, 115–20, p. 60.

99. *The Morning Chronicle, and London Advertiser*, 25 April 1778, as quoted in Miles 1994, p. 62 and Appendix, which reprints this and other critical reviews in full, pp. 70–1.

100. Miles 1994, p. 61. See Mitchell 1944, pp. 30–1, for references to West's appropriation of Le Brun's examples of the passions for *The Death of General Wolfe*.

101. Austin 1806/1966, p. 487.

102. Austin 1806/1966, p. 488.

103. This theatricality, appropriately, entered the language of the day, in which paintings were normally called "performances" and artists often called "composers." In both cases, the language employed emphasized a process unfolding in time. "Performance" did not refer exclusively to the presentation of plays or music, but included a literary or artistic piece, and the term "composer" emphasized the artist's play of mind as well as the manipulation of paint.

104. *V & A Cuttings*, vol. 1, p. 238; reprinted in *The Massachusetts Centinel*, 8 September 1784. The reviewer, after asserting that the painting was "inferior in point of honor to no transaction of the late war," and that of the fifteen principal figures, eleven were portraits, focused on its formal aspects: "*Mr. Copley* has *grouped* the figures with spirit, and in the whole *composition* has discovered great science. The scarlet drapery of a body of British soldiery would have produced a *fierceness*, had not the skill of a master softened the extreme, by a display of the *light-coloured* facings and linings. The blue drapery of the *black servant* and the uniform of the *Jersey officer*, gives also great relief to the picture. The accoutrements and arms are finished up to the highest effect, and the *lights* and *shades* throughout the picture is in *fine keeping*!" In *Peirson* 1784, Copley (presumably in conjunction with Boydell) wrote that the grenadier's countenance was intended to convey his feelings of sorrow upon seeing the dying major.

105. Winckelmann 1765/1972, pp. 30–9 See the recent studies of the subject in Richter 1990 and Potts 1994.

106. Copley to his wife, Florence, 9 June 1775 in Amory 1882, pp. 52–3. Copley writes that *The Laocoön* "is not only the best work of art in the world *now*, but it was esteemed by the ancients the first in point of merit that the chisel had ever produced." See Baretti 1781, p. 28, in which he

emotion, was particularly influential. Le Brun asserted that a painting "cannot be perfect without EXPRESSION: it is what stamps the true character of everything ... EXPRESSION is also a part that intimates the emotions of the Soul, and renders visible the effects of Passion."[97] As Reynolds, too, reminded artists, only by external appearance could passions or character be conveyed in painting: " ... a painter of history," he wrote, "shews the man by shewing his actions ... " and makes the figure correspond "with sentiment and situation".[98] The young woman observing Wolfe's death underscores the eighteenth-century viewer's recognition of the importance of appropriate expression. Eighteenth-century critics often referred to figures in a painting as "characters," as if they were in a novel or a play, and judged them by their effectiveness as "real" people responding to a specific situation. Spectators recognized that subjects in paintings enacted certain codified roles, such as Rage or Horror, and the substance of critical reviews often centered on their degree of success. In reviewing *Watson and the Shark* (cat. 4), for example, most critics remarked on the figures' expressions, and particularly noted that those of eagerness and concern, appropriately, were "strongly marked in every Countenance ..." – especially that of the black seaman who one critic identified as a "fine index of concern and horror."[99] Indeed Copley's figure of the old sailor in the boat in *Watson and the Shark*, with his opened mouth, wrinkled forehead, and undulating brow, corresponds to Le Brun's image of "Horror" (fig. 60).[100] Le Brun's treatise on the passions, not surprisingly, pervaded theatrical discourse as well; Gilbert Austin's influential *Chironomia; or a Treatise on Rhetorical Delivery* (1806), for example, demonstrates the degree to which the aesthetic theory of painting and theater treatises overlapped. Both included bibliographies featuring Baptiste Du Bos, Pliny, and Quintilian, and Austin even referred to Le Brun's series of the Battles of Alexander for fine examples of the expression of Terror (figs. 61, 64).[101] His accompanying illustrations for "complex significant gestures" borrow from verbal descriptions of antique sources as well as ancient and modern examples in painting (fig. 62). In *The Death of Major Peirson*, the figure of Captain Hemery, the figure in black at Peirson's feet who holds his hand out as if to deny Peirson's tragic fate, resembles the figure of no. 102 in "Complex Significant Gestures," which Austin describes as "Horror, which is aversion or astonishment mingled with terror ...".[102] Artists and actors thus shared a similar language, finding models to parlay mere nature into art, and circulating and repeating them with infinite variation.[103]

It is significant that a contemporary reviewer of *The Death of Major Peirson* commented on only two expressions, the frightened countenances of the women at right, and the dying sergeant of Grenadiers whose expression the viewer interpreted to mean that he "exhorts his companions to victory."[104] Perhaps the critic only commented on the most extreme cases, but by the eighteenth century artists had generally modified the exaggerated quality of Le Brun's expressions. This was, in part, a result of the influence of such Neoclassical theorists as the German art historian Johann Winckelmann, who believed that extreme expressions marred the beauty of the human figure.[105] Winckelmann praised the "noble calm and quiet grandeur" that he perceived in ancient Greco-Roman sculpture, admiring its relatively restrained emotion. The *Laocoön*, a sculpture specifically admired by Copley (who purchased a cast of it in Rome),[106] perfectly expressed Winckelmann's sense of moral rectitude conveyed through the beauty of the human figure (fig. 63). In the *Laocoön*, Winckelmann believed

Fig. 61 Charles Le Brun
The Passage of the Granicus, 1661-5

Oil on canvas, 185¹/₄ × 472³/₄ in. (470 × 1209 cm)
Musée du Louvre, Paris

Fig. 60 John Williams after Charles Le Brun
Horrour

From *A Method to Learn to Design the Passions, Proposed in a Conference on Their General and Particular Expression*, London 1734

John Singleton Copley, *Watson and the Shark* (detail of cat. 4)

Fig. 62 *Complex Significant Gestures, Aversion (No. 101) and Horror (No. 102)*

Plate 10 (detail) of *Chironomia; or A Treatise on Rhetorical Delivery* by Gilbert Austin, 1806

the tragedy of the event – serpents attacking a father and his sons – was heightened by the relative emotional restraint of the father, who struggles to maintain a spiritual calm at the height of human peril. Winckelmann admired the fact that Laocoön writhes in pain but does not appear to scream, as he does in Virgil's written account of the story. The German philosopher Johann Wolfgang von Goethe, like Winckelmann, recognized that the artist was required to convey the horror of the situation through the coiling serpents rather than through the doomed human figures whose heroic spirit necessitated a stoic demeanor.[107] In *The Death of Major Peirson*, Copley offers a parallel of the coiling serpents but uses human figures, as if to acknowledge Le Brun's remark that the eyes move wide open in "Fright" (fear) because "the Soul employs 'em to express the nature of the object that creates the Fright."[108] In *The Death of Major Peirson*, where the majority of figures appear remarkably impassive, it is through the women and children that Copley conveys horror, as Le Brun did, for example, in the foreground figure of *The Battle of Arbella* (fig. 64).[109]

Tempering his view of death and dying with heroic attitudes of stoicism, Copley deviated from older prescriptions. Leonardo, in the best known dictum on painting a battle, had instructed the painter to depict the uncontrollable tumult of war, the smoke of fire, the dust stirred up by the horses hooves, and the reddish tints of the combatants.[110] He continued: "Let the air be full of arrows of every kind, some shooting upwards, others falling, others flying straight ... You must make the foreground figures covered in dust ... Show the victors running ... Show the flared nostrils ... and the lips arched ... as if to wail in lamentation ... Show others shrieking, open-mouthed and in flight ... Show various kinds of weapons between the feet of the combatants such as broken shields and lances ... Show dead men ... and others in their death throes, grinding their teeth, rolling their eyes or clutching their crippled legs and bodies with their fists ... You would see the reserves poised full of hope and fear, their eyes sharpened and shaded with their hands ... likewise the Captain with his baton of command raised, as he hastens towards the reinforcements and points out to them the place where they are needed ... And do not depict a single level place that lacks a bloodied imprint."

The painting of *The Battle of Agincourt* (1779, fig. 65) by Copley's contemporary the British artist John Hamilton Mortimer demonstrates Leonardo's prescriptions at work more than two hundred and fifty year later.[111] But *The Death of Major Peirson* is remarkably different, with its orderly bayonets poised in diagonal unison, its pale and tranquil military faces above crisp, unsoiled military uniforms, and its vivid yet discreet passages

Fig. 64 Charles Le Brun
Fig. 64 Charles Le Brun
The Battle of Arbella, before 1689
Oil on canvas, 185¼ × 498½ in. (470 × 1265 cm)
Musée du Louvre, Paris

Fig. 63 Agesander, Athenodorus, and
Polydorus
Laocoön, 1st century AD
Marble
Vatican Museums, Vatican State

notes that Laocoön, instead of "roaring loud, like a
Bull wounded ... ," "expires here in such exquisite
anguish ...".

107. Richter 1990, pp. 16–20.

108. Le Brun 1698/1734, p. 32.

109. Copley's early colonial drawings include
sketches after Le Brun's *Battle of the River Granicus*
from the Alexander series (1753–58, British
Museum); see Prown 1966, II, p. 236, figs. 14–5.
He assuredly had access to an engraving of Le
Brun's series and in fact may have owned one: the
estate sale of Lord Lyndhurst's library included
"number 299. Le Brun's Battles, &c. 5 vols. –
strained and rolled" (Prown 1966, II, p. 398).

of dripping blood. All except the women and children respond with an unusually calm
reserve, with "noble calm and quiet grandeur," as Winckelmann might have called it.

Copley would have known, of course, that the military encouraged such calm yet
attentive behavior of its soldiers, particularly in its officers. One military treatise
remarked that "private Soldiers, when they are to go upon Action, form their notions
of the danger from the outward appearance of their officers ... to dissipate their fears,
and fortify their courage, the officers should assume a serene and cheerful air."[112] But
Copley would also have understood the moral side of such a statement, the belief that
such calm expressions asserted a stoic moral behavior appropriate for the English
people. Shaftesbury had already noted that martial paintings should express "the
several degrees of Valour, Magnamity, Cowardice, Terrour, Anger, according to the
several characters of Nations," as if a nation had a specific character that could be
identified and imprinted on a face.[113] Further, Shaftesbury noted of military scenes that
"'Tis here that we may see Heroes and Chiefs appear, even in the hottest of Actions,
with a Tranquility of Mind and Sedateness peculiar to themselves, which is indeed ... in
a direct and proper sense, profoundly Moral." This stoic ideal, recounted in
Shaftesbury and George Turnbull, and absorbed by Winckelmann, gave continued life
to the stoic ideal of behavior so carefully expressed, admired, and elaborated in *The
Death of Major Peirson*.[114] As in the *Laocoön*, Copley constructs an image so that terror,
confusion, and tragedy are conveyed without sacrificing the model behavior of its characters. For the benefit of those viewers who complained that West's *General Wolfe* died
appearing sad and in pain, rather than joyful at the news of British victory, Copley took
special note of Reynolds's advice to make the figure correspond with "sentiment and
situation," and eliminated any possibility of confusion over Peirson's sentiments about
his own death: in *The Death of Major Peirson*, the hero ignores his private pain and dies
with a slight smile on his face, content in the knowledge that he died for his country.

The Death of Major Peirson, like *Watson and the Shark* before it, attempted to absorb the
viewer's attention completely in the action represented, taking the spectators through a
series of emotions that exercised feelings of fear and sympathy. The artist still, however,
needed to ensure that his audience understood the painting's deeper meanings, as sacrificing unity and "making noise" potentially distracted the spectator from understanding
both the details of the narrative as well as its larger moral concerns. Copley's exhibition
brochure solved the problem of comprehension (fig. 66). The description of the painting offered in the brochure told the story of the event, already familiar in some fashion
to Copley's contemporaries. The brochure even instructed the viewer how to look at
the painting, so that what the viewer read would be illustrated in the painting, and

Fig. 65 Thomas Burke after John Hamilton Mortimer
The Battle of Agincourt, 1783
Engraving

22d of MAY, 1783

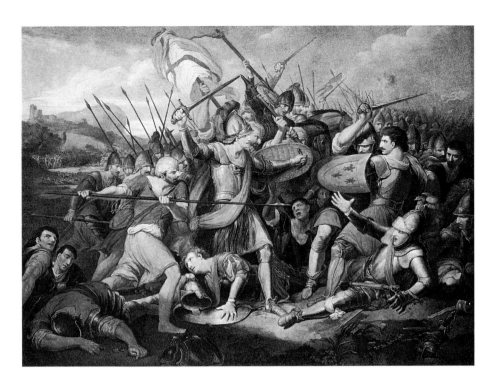

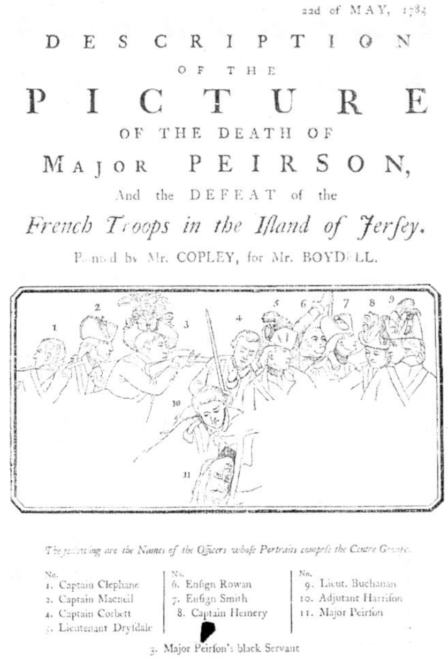

DESCRIPTION OF THE PICTURE OF THE DEATH OF MAJOR PEIRSON, And the DEFEAT of the *French Troops in the Iſland of Jerſey.*

Painted by Mr. COPLEY, for Mr. BOYDELL.

The following are the Names of the Officers whoſe Portraits compoſe the Centre Group.

No.	No.	No.
1. Captain Clephane	6. Enſign Rowan	9. Lieut. Buchanan
2. Captain Macneil	7. Enſign Smith	10. Adjutant Harriſon
4. Captain Corbett	8. Captain Hemery	11. Major Peirſon
5. Lieutenant Dryſdale		

3. Major Peirſon's black Servant

Fig. 66 Subscription Notice for *The Death of Major Peirson* by John Singleton Copley (details), 1781
Tate Gallery, London

what the viewer saw would be explained in the brochure. The reader learned that Major Peirson, "sensible to the invalidity of the capitulation made by the Lieutenant Governor ... with great valor and prudence, attacked and totally defeated the French Troops, and thereby rescued the Island, and gloriously maintained the honor of the British arms," and that his "death was instantly retaliated by his black servant on the man who shot the Major." The brochure also filled out parts of the story not depicted in the painting, notably Lieutenant-Governor Moses Corbet's cowardly capitulation to the French, the event that provoked Peirson's defiance of authority and led to his eventual death. By claiming that the "Picture is founded on ... Facts," and relating those purported facts, the brochure helped to convince the viewer that the painting represented the unvarnished truth.[115]

By academic tradition, specifically as prescribed in the seventeenth-century work of the French theorists Charles Le Brun and Roger de Piles, history paintings might combine fact with fiction. According to de Piles, the history painter should know the history represented but could deviate from the facts if the details of a story spoiled artistic harmony – what de Piles termed *vraisemblance* (or likelihood), resulting in what Benjamin West called the "Epic Composition."[116] So, while Copley probably knew Colley and Hedges's reportorial illustration of the event published in 1781 (fig. 67), borrowing its composition would have sacrificed the basic principles of academic theory, in which fancy offset the banality of facts. Peirson may have died while turning the corner of a house, as both the illustration and an account published in *The London Chronicle* of 6–9 January 1781 retell, but Copley would have recognized that Peirson's heroic character deserved a more glorious death. Copley does not so much fabricate the death as show the moment just after, when Peirson's comrades carry him away, Christ-like, from the scene of battle. Like West, whose *Death of General Wolfe* resembles a *Lamentation over Christ*, Copley understood the rhetorical power of casting contemporary heroes in the role of figures from the classical and biblical past. Such artistic borrowings, a basic

110. Leonardo da Vinci as quoted in Kemp 1989, pp. 228–33.

111. Mortimer exhibited this painting at the Royal Academy in 1779, and a print by Thomas Burke was published in 1783.

112. Bland 1727/1759, p. 170.

113. Shaftesbury 1714/1727, pp. 379–80.

114. Winckelmann's ideas emerged, in part, from earlier 18th-century British sources he read and quoted in his work, such as Shaftesbury 1714/1727, and Turnbull 1740, who cites Shaftesbury's comments on military painting *verbatim*.

115. Copley adds to the truth value of the painting when he assures the reader of the brochure that eleven of the principal figures are portraits. See cat. 18 for transcribed text.

116. Roger de Piles, *Art of Painting* (trans. of *Abrégé de la vie des peintres*, 1706) in, for example, Mitchell 1944, pp. 22–3; Peter Cannon-Brookes, 'From the "Death of General Wolfe" to the "Death of Lord Nelson": Benjamin West and the Epic Composition', in *Painted Word* 1991, pp. 15–22.

Fig. 67 *The Glorious Defeat of the French Invaders, on the Island of Jersey, Jany. 6, 1781 when the Valiant Major Francis Peirson was unfortunately Kill'd in the moment of Victory*, published by Thos. Gram. Colley and E. Hedges, 24 April 1781

Aquatint

British Museum, London

principle of aesthetic dogma, signalled the artist's visual erudition at the same time as it elevated the contemporary hero.

Many eighteenth-century observers and critics tested the veracity of pictures as a measure of value, often to absurd extremes; one observer of *Watson and the Shark*, for example, criticized Copley for not observing that two men leaning over a boat would cause it to heel.[117] Artists such as Copley and West recognized that fidelity to certain historical truths of costume and weaponry, architectural setting, or action, could offset the extremes of poetic license. So, even as Copley and West went to extraordinary lengths in their research to prove their mastery of the material, they could, and did, subsequently bend, distort, or reshape the facts of the event. Such attempts at mastering the subject and proving one's authority were key elements to becoming a reputable history painter, and such efforts at exactitude did not go unnoticed by the press. West, in fact, might even be chided for the macabre character of his historical precision when he conducted research for his series of paintings on King Edward IV: "When Edward IV's coffin was opened, Mr. West was present; and as far as the shrunk features will admit, it is his intention to transfer them to canvas."[118] Copley, too, attacked the subject matter of his paintings with the diligence of a research historian, including seeking out prints of Havana Harbor for *Watson and the Shark*; sending Pelham to reconnoiter and take sketches of the Jersey area, and interviewing officers present at the battle, for *The Death of Major Peirson*; traveling to Hanover to interview and to capture the likenesses of the German officers present at the scene for *The Siege of Gibraltar*; and visiting country homes throughout England, also soliciting the help of the well known author and critic Edward Malone, in his search for seventeenth-century portraits of the historical figures to be depicted in *Charles I Demanding in the House of Commons the Five Impeached Members*. Given the lengths Copley would go to master the facts of his subject, the extent to which he edited, reshaped, and even invented, his materials becomes particularly meaningful, especially in *The Death of Major Peirson*.[119]

In comparison to the report in *The London Chronicle* Copley considerably elaborated upon the events at St Helier. According to *The London Chronicle*, the capitulating Lieutenant-Governor Moses Corbet played an important role in the action, primarily

117. *V & A Press Cuttings*, vol. 1, p. 160, *General Advertiser*, dated in hand May 1778. See also Miles 1994, p. 71.

118. *V & A Press Cuttings*, vol. 2, unsourced, 1789, p. 498.

119. Saunders 1990, pp. 4–39, specifically pp. 30–2, notes that Copley downplayed the significant role the 78th Highlanders Regiment played in the event, substituting instead Peirson's 95th Regiment, perhaps believing the English regiment would be more appealing to his London audience.

as the French army's hostage against the British. When Peirson's regiment warned the French officers holding Corbet of their intention to attack, the French responded that Corbet would be placed on the front line of fire. The British regiments ignored the threat, the French placed Corbet on the front line, and Corbet suffered a musket ball shot through his hat. He also subsequently underwent a court martial for his cowardly behavior. Although Corbet might have made an excellent foil for the bravery of Peirson, Copley virtually ignores this element of the event, perhaps because Copley felt a British officer's cowardice was not worthy of immortalizing in paint. Instead, Copley focuses on Peirson's counter-attack, his death, and the purported revenge by his black servant, quite possibly a wholly fictitious figure.[120]

The only contemporary evidence for a black servant is an undated statement written by Peirson's father asserting that Peirson's black servant avenged his death. This statement, in turn, was based on information the father received from Adjutant Harrison, the figure in the painting who bends to lift Peirson's shoulder and head. But Harrison had already written a letter to Peirson's father on 10 January, only four days after the battle, in which he nowhere mentions revenge. *The London Chronicle* does not mention Peirson's death being so avenged, nor does the 16 January 1781 issue of *The London Gazette*, the account that Boydell, presumably, chose for reprinting in the leaflet that announced the final publication date for the engraving of *The Death of Major Peirson* in 1796.[121] Peirson's allowance as an officer did include a budget for a personal servant, although no record survives noting he employed one. In Colley and Hedges's etching of the event, a black figure does appear on the left, but his presence is not related to any retaliatory action. Finally, and most mysteriously, Copley's preparatory sketch identifies the avenging figure as "Captain Christie's Black Servant." A Captain Christie was indeed present at the battle but Copley chose not to represent him.[122]

If an avenging black servant did not exist, somewhere an allusion to a loyal black servant arose and spread. Or if he did exist, the fact did not become a matter of official record in news reports or subsequent historical accounts, but circulated by rumor or legend. Whether Copley himself originated the story or merely incorporated what he had heard, the corroboration of the loyal servant story appears to have occurred only after Copley completed the painting. Copley's deliberate exclusion of a known aspect of the battle (Moses Corbet's presence at the event), in order to include a possibly fictitious one (an avenging black servant), emphasizes the poetic truth, the higher moral dimension of the painting. But why was it important for the painting that Peirson's death should be avenged, particularly by a servant?[123]

By depicting the act of revenge, Copley satisfies as well as titillates the spectator, providing the narrative closure that could not be provided in *Watson and the Shark*, where the viewer learns the outcome of the event only by reading the title. The revenge sequence also imposes a greater degree of audience involvement, since the viewer participates in the painting's compression of narrative time. Such appeals to the viewer suggest Copley's heightened sensitivity to audience response, not just in terms of attracting attention or becoming, as he wrote, "conspecuous in the Croud," but in terms of challenging artistic conventions that he had labored so long to learn.[124] Like *Watson and the Shark*, in which Copley availed himself of devices of suspense common to the popular novel, *The Death of Major Peirson* demonstrates the artist's sensitivity to popular culture. By employing the trope of the faithful servant, Copley tapped into the best known

120. Saunders 1990, p. 33, includes the most comprehensive research on this aspect of the painting to date.

121. *Boydell Leaflet* 1796. I have been unable to find any contemporaneous account of the event that mentions a black servant.

122. Saunders 1990, pp. 34, 39 note 27. Using Copley's notation on one of the preparatory sketches, "Capt". Christies Black Serv'.", as evidence, Prown suggests that the figure of the black was modeled on the servant of Copley's neighbor the auctioneer James Christie (Prown 1966, II, p. 303; see cat. 21). Saunders notes that nine years after the battle an account of an indigent calling himself Major Peirson's servant was printed in a Yorkshire newspaper (Saunders 1990, pp. 34, 39 note 28).

123. In the context of heated debates about slavery during the period, the presence of the black servant also suggests the underlying anxiety about these issues, as well as the desire for a subordinate and faithful servant class during a time of changes in class structure.

124. Copley to Pelham, 17 August 1774, London, in *Letters of Copley and Pelham* 1914/1972, pp. 240–1.

character-type in eighteenth-century literature, one that, more than any other class of worker, dominated novels and plays of the period.[125] Copley, then, deviates from historical truth to broaden the painting's appeal by referring to a popular social type. He reinforced in the painting, and reasserted in the accompanying brochure, social attitudes about the duty of a servant to be loyal to the master. The faithful servant provided reassurance that in the midst of chaos, order can (and should) reign. In fact, the events as narrated and depicted by Copley reinforce attitudes about order, duty, and the observance of the rules of proper behavior. And yet both artist and protagonist essentially break the rules: Copley by defying unity, and Peirson by breaking the cardinal rule of military behavior, deference to a military superior.[126] Peirson defies his superior by ignoring the capitulation and rousing the troops, actions that no military manual or treatise would ever condone. Had Peirson's counter-attack been unsuccessful and he survived the battle, he might well have been a candidate for court-martial. Copley skirted these issues by downplaying the insubordination of Peirson to Corbet – eliminating the cowardly Corbet altogether – and by highlighting not only Peirson's heroic death but a revenge sequence involving the 'proper' behavior of a servant towards his master. Copley thus creates a system of checks and balances in *The Death of Major Peirson* in which the themes of duty and stoicism, control and submission, prevail.

Ultimately, despite its multiplicity of action, despite its vividness and its spectacle, Copley's painting instructs, telling the viewer how to move and act, how to arrange himself socially according to a prescribed ideal. One further means of doing this is through the figure of the boy, fleeing with his mother on the right, whose gaze confronts the spectator directly and who inducts her or him into the painting. Copley relied, like others, on this 'innocent' or outsider figure to underscore the pedagogical appeal of the painting. Like the American Indian in West's *The Death of General Wolfe*, and the black seaman in Copley's own *Watson and the Shark*, the boy is the touchstone for characters throughout who act properly, according to an idealized, or, in the case of the women, an expected norm. In eighteenth-century London these figures would be perceived as outsiders looking in, and therefore perfectly equipped to understand the painting's larger meanings because they were not already socially programmed. Like Rousseau's noble savages, they were uncorrupted innocents, compelling the viewer to consider the event through their eyes. As the American Indian in *The Death of General Wolfe* links the painting and the event to the audience, the boy in Copley's painting connects the public with the private. The boy seems to appeal to the viewer to recall those moments of childhood, to re-encounter society, to look at convention and tradition afresh; he encourages the viewer to play his part by sympathizing with the event and reflecting upon its larger messages of duty, patriotism, loyalty, deference, and the potential justification of insubordination.[127] It could be said that Copley himself appears in the painting through the child, a surrogate self-portrait. Having mastered the principles of art so fully, Copley could now re-enter the world of art through the eyes of a child, "uncorrupted . . . [and] free from all the fals notions and impertinant conceits that it is the result of a superficial knowledge of the principals of art."[128] Copley had not only mastered, he had surpassed the English artistic system.

125. See Perkins 1928, pp. 101–53. Perhaps thinking of Copley's grenadier and black servant in *The Death of Major Peirson*, which he would have seen in London, John Trumbull adopted similar devices in his *Death of General Warren in the Battle of Bunker's Hill, 17 June 1775* (1786, Yale University Art Gallery). In his "Explanation of the Two Prints Representing the Battle of Bunker's Hill, and the Attack on Quebec" [Museum of Fine Arts, Boston, Print Room files], Trumbull describes, "On the Right of the Print, a young American, wounded in the Sword Hand, and in the Breast, has begun to retire, attended by a faithful Negro;– but feeling his General fall, hesitates whether to save himself, or, wounded as he is, to return and assist in saving a Life, more precious to his Country than his own."

126. See Gruber 1980, pp. 23–41. Officers were expected to follow the "Rules and Discipline of War," which were "set forth in small printed books informally called the 'Articles of War'" which "made clear that an officer was to be loyal to his church and king and obedient to his commanding officer: blasphemy, and disrespect were punishable by court-martial; mutiny, sedition, disobedience, desertion, cowardice before the enemy, and plundering, by death" (p. 27).

127. It is not coincidental that insubordinate behavior was condoned only in 18th-century manuals of child-rearing, in which the child was allowed to reprove or ignore parents if they failed in their instructional duties. See Locke 1693/1913.

128. Copley to Thomas Ainslie, Boston, 25 February 1765, in *Letters of Copley and Pelham* 1914/1972, p. 33.

THE CATALOGUE

1.

The Copley Family, 1776–77

Oil on canvas, 72¹/₂ × 90¹/₄ in.
(184.1 × 229.2 cm)

National Gallery of Art, Washington, D.C.,
Andrew W. Mellon Fund, 1961.7.1

PROVENANCE: The artist, London, until 1815;
his son John Singleton Copley, Jr., Lord Lyndhurst
(1772–1863), London; (Lyndhurst sale Christie's,
London, 5 March 1864, no. 91); the artist's grand-
daughter, Martha Babcock Greene Amory (Mrs.
Charles Amory, 1812–1880), Boston; her husband
Charles Amory (1808–1898), Boston; their son
Edward Linzee Amory (1844–1911), New York;
his nephew Copley Amory (1866–1960),
Washington; his descendants Copley Amory, Jr.
(1890–1964), Cambridge, Massachusetts, Henry
Russell Amory (1892–1962), Santa Barbara,
California, Katharine Amory Smith (b. 1908),
Washington, Walter Amory (b. 1924), Duxbury,
Massachusetts, and Elizabeth Cole Amory (b.
1955), Princeton, New Jersey; National Gallery of
Art, Washington, D.C.

SELECTED EXHIBITIONS: London 1777, no.
61; London 1862, no. 51; Boston 1873, 1874, nos.
144, 130; Boston, Museum of Fine Arts, on long-
term loan 1888–1916, 1921–25; Boston 1938, no.
22; Washington, D.C., National Gallery of Art, on
long-term loan 1941–51; Washington, New York,
Boston 1965–6, no. 61; Washington 1974, no. 6;
Mexico City 1980–1, no. 1.

SELECTED REFERENCES: 'Exhibition of the
Royal Academy,' *The London Packet, or New Lloyd's
Evening Post* , 25–8 April 1777, p. 1; 'Exhibition of
the Royal Academy,' *The Morning Chronicle, and
London Advertiser*, 26 April 1777, p. 2; Cunningham
1831/1837/1868, V, pp. 178–9; Tuckerman 1867,
p. 79; Perkins 1873, pp. 20–1, 48–9, 134; Amory
1882, pp. 12, 23, 77–80, 106–7, 240, 262–3, 438;
Museum of Fine Arts, Boston 1892, p. 15, no. 140;
Museum of Fine Arts, Boston 1895, p. 17, no. 150;
Museum of Fine Arts, Boston Bulletin 18, 1903; Isham
1905/1907/1942, pp. 37–8; *Museum of Fine Arts,
Boston Handbook* 1906, p. 102; Bayley 1910, p. 35;
Bayley 1915, pp. 35–6, 79, 101–2; Addison 1924,
pp. 6–7; Bolton and Binsse 1930, p. 116; Parker
and Wheeler 1938, pp. 8–9; Prown 1966, I, p. 61;
II, pp. 262–3, 266, 275, 315, 363–4, 373n., 387,
403–4, 414–5, and fig. 344; Frankenstein 1970,
pp. 137–8, 1455, 147; Curwen 1972, I, p.132; II,
p. 701; Wilmerding 1980, p. 46; Williams 1981,
pp. 24, 30; Walker 1984, p. 384, no. 545; Prown
1986, pp. 281, 286 n. 32; Lovell 1987, p. 256;
Wilmerding 1988, p. 54.¹

RELATED WORKS: Sketch for *The Copley Family*,
1776, oil on canvas en grisaille, 15¹/₂ × 13³/₈ in.
(39.5 × 34 cm), National Gallery of Art,
Washington, D.C.; *The Copley Family*, 1789, oil on
canvas en grisaille, 20³/₄ × 26¹/₂ in. (52.7 × 67.3
cm), Museum of Fine Arts, Boston.

The Copley Family, exhibited to the Royal Academy in 1777, is the first – and only – public presentation of the artist in paint in his career of more than sixty years. As such, this monumental portrait should be understood as something more than a celebration of the artist's reunion with his
family, from whom he had been separated for about eighteen months; it reveals how the artist
wished to present himself, and his family, in the competitive art market of eighteenth-century
London.

In London, Copley worked on a larger scale than ever before, and adopted the British technique of applying paint in thin, transparent glazes. *The Copley Family* demonstrates both. Copley
successfully incorporated seven figures into a harmonious domestic setting, an ambitious multi-
figure grouping that he had not attempted since his portrait of *The Gore Children* of more than
twenty years before (*ca.* 1755, Winterthur Museum, Delaware).

The fictitious indoor/outdoor setting for *The Copley Family* is one of genteel splendor, breath-
takingly lush and sensuous in its rich tonalities of rose, gold, green, and blue, set off by vivid
passages of white. Members of the Copley family either pose self-consciously or frolic before a
verdant background landscape of gently rolling hills and crystal blue water. Dressed in a blue
brocade robe and wearing a powdered wig, his hair tied back with a neat bow, the artist at upper
left leans against a plinth, hovering over his seated family. He clutches a set of drawings, references to his artistic profession; behind him stands an antique urn with classical figures, identifiable as the famed Medici Vase (fig. 69).² Beside Copley, his father-in-law Richard Clarke
(1711–1795) holds in his lap the infant Susannah (1776–1785) who, clutching a coral whistle,
reaches to embrace him. He seems oblivious to the child's gesture, aloof and distant from the rest
of the family.³ At center, the eldest Copley daughter, Elizabeth (1770–1866), delicately holding
the transparent pink sash of her dress, gazes at the viewer with a slight smile upon her fleshy face.
Behind a brown hat with a blue plume, and tossed negligently to the floor at left, a doll echoes
the image of Elizabeth. On the other side of Elizabeth are three figures: John Singleton Copley,
Jr. (1772–1863), Copley's wife Susanna (1745–1836), and Mary (1773–1868). Susanna, elegantly
dressed in a voluminous blue dress with gold trim, sits upon a rose silk damask sofa. Wearing an
embroidered slipper, she rests her foot upon a matching ottoman. Her profile partially in shadow, she tenderly gazes into the eyes of her son and firmly holds him with long, tapering fingers
that gently press his flesh. Completing the graceful triad, Mary, at far right, playfully leans
against her mother's lap. Dressed in dark, rich colors, and assuming grave facial expressions, the
adults provide a stable counterpoint to the children, all of whom wear white or light-colored
clothing, and, in large part, display youthful exuberance in their faces and gestures.

As previous scholars have appropriately noted, *The Copley Family* represents the happy
reunion by October 1775 of the artist with his family, who had left revolutionary Boston for
London about one year after Copley embarked on the Grand Tour in 1774. Their separation
proved distressing, as borne out by the tender and anxious letters Copley sent to his wife, whom
he affectionately called Sukey. "I am very Ancious for you, my Dear, and our lovely Children,"
he wrote, "for I know not what state you are in, in Boston; but I pray God to preserve you and
them. ... give my blessing to my Dear Babys, and a thousand Kisses. tell my Dear Betsey
[Elizabeth] not to forget he[r] Papa."⁴ One can imagine the artist's distress when he later learned
that his wife left for England with three children rather than four: "My thoughts are constantly
on you and on our children. You tell me you brought *three*, but you do not say which you left
behind; I supppose it was the youngest, he being too delicate to bring."⁵ Indeed, their youngest
son Clarke Copley (1775–1776) was left behind in Boston, and he died after Copley had already
begun work on the painting. Presumably, the infant sitting on the grandfather's lap in the painting thus began as Clarke and evolved into Susannah, who was born only in October 1776.⁶
Given the trials and tribulations they experienced during this turbulent period, the joyful,
spirited, yet lovingly poignant image of domestic harmony in *The Copley Family* is, as Prown
noted, a "hymn of contentment."⁷

In addition to celebrating a family reunion, *The Copley Family* advertises the artist's virtuosity
to his new London market; the painting was only the second he presented to the Royal Academy
exhibition, and the first and only time he displayed an image of himself. Sumptuous furniture, an
elegant carpet, and fashionable clothing speak to his material success as an artist, and a dignified

NOTES

1. See Miles 1994, pp. 46–54, for the most comprehensive treatment of the painting to date and for full bibliographic citations.

2. See Haskell and Penny 1981, p. 316, for a discussion of the subject and for copies of the Medici Vase, popular in England during the 18th century particularly as garden ornaments. Copley perhaps worked from a print of the vase because he reversed the standing warrior whose foot rests on a pedestal, his arm stretched behind him. The uncompleted stipple engraving by Robert Thew (National Gallery of Art, Washington, D.C.) changes the details of the urn.

3. Indeed, a 19th-century writer believed that Copley delighted in depicting Clarke's "high narrow pride and dogmatism;" he also observed that the "contrast between him [Copley] and the rigid faced old man below is excellent," in *Art Interchange* 1889.

4. Copley to his wife, Lyons, 15 September 1774 in *Letters of Copley and Pelham* 1914/1972, pp. 259–60.

5. Copley to his wife, Parma, 28 July 1775, Amory 1882, p. 63.

6. Prown 1966, II, p. 262.

7. *Ibidem.*

8. Miles 1994 also cites the similarity between Copley's painting and *The West Family* and *Lady Cockburn and her Family*. Miles further notes that Copley may have seen Reynolds's painting in his studio in July 1774. *Mrs. Edward Lascelles and Child* was engraved *ca.* 1772. For discussions of the evolution and representation of the family in England, the Continent, and the colonies, see Duncan 1973, LeGates 1976, Lovell 1987, and Shawe-Taylor 1990, pp. 188–201. Also see cats. 3, 13 15, and 33.

9. Prown 1966, II, p. 260. See also Eleanor L. Jones in Boston, Cleveland, Houston 1992, pp. 156–8.

10. *The Morning Chronicle*, 26 April 1777, as quoted in Prown 1966, II, p. 263. The same review was printed in *The London Packet*, 25–28 April 1777.

11. Copley to Pelham, 17 August 1774, London, in *Letters of Copley and Pelham* 1914/1972, p. 241.

12. Amory 1882, p. 79.

wife surrounded by tumbling children attest to domestic tranquility and a stable home environment. The pose of his wife surrounded by children, loosely based on Renaissance images of the Holy Family with Saint John, demonstrates Copley's familiarity with the fashion for portraits celebrating motherhood, such as Benjamin West's *The West Family* (1772, Yale Center for British Art, New Haven) and Joshua Reynolds's *Mrs. Edward Lascelles and Child* (*ca.* 1762, Harewood House) and *Lady Cockburn and her Family* (1773, National Gallery, London).[8]

Copley also makes reference to his awareness of Grand Manner painting through subtle references to the Grand Tour. The Grand Tour, including travel in Italy, was necessary for the education of a serious painter and a gentleman, roles artists were eager to unite in the eighteenth century. Just one year before executing *The Copley Family*, Copley exhibited to the Royal Academy "*A Conversation*", probably the portrait of *Mr. and Mrs. Ralph Izard* (fig. 68), in which a number of props – Rome's Colosseum, a statue group identified as *Orestes and Electra*, and a fifth-century BC Greek vase – identify the sitters as connoisseurs of ancient art and architecture and testify to their sophisticated tastes.[9] Copley seems to overwhelm the viewer with these props, a reflection of both the sitters' and the artist's pretensions, as he appropriates the sort of ancient objects the Italian painter Pompeo Batoni (1708–1787) made popular in earlier portraits of English travelers. The portrait proclaims both the couple's and the artist's presence on the site of the ancient world. *The Copley Family* likewise incorporates Grand Tour themes, with the Medici Vase hovering above the drawings Copley clutches in his hand as he poses before a verdant Italianate landscape including, perhaps, a Romanesque church. The painting thus becomes a statement of Copley's civility and cultural sophistication.

The critic of *The Morning Chronicle* found the painting, in part, had "great merit," but that the surroundings were "so glaring" that it was "difficult for a beholder to guess which object the painter meant to make his main subject."[10] Despite this criticism, the painting succeeded in making Copley, as he once wrote, "conspecuous in the Croud":[11] the first item the critic noted was that "Mr. Copley, from the size of his family piece, is likely to be as much the subject of observation in the rooms as any artist who has exhibited ...".

According to the artist's granddaughter, the painting hung for nearly one hundred years over the fireplace in the Copley dining room in their George Street, London, home.[12]

2.
The Nativity, 1776–77

Oil on canvas, $24^{7}/_{8} \times 30^{1}/_{8}$ in. (63.2 × 76.5 cm)

The Museum of Fine Arts, Boston, Ernest Wadsworth Longfellow Fund, 1972.981

PROVENANCE: The artist, London, to 1815; his son, John Singleton Copley, Jr., Lord Lyndhurst, until 1863; (Lyndhurst sale, Christie's, London, 5 March 1864, no. 62); to Colonel Hawkesley; to Canon F.G. Brenchley; (Sotheby's, London, 17 November 1971, as Benjamin West, *The*

In 1971, this painting of the Madonna and the infant Christ, surrounded by Joseph, shepherds, a stableboy, and various animals, appeared at auction as a work by Benjamin West, testimony to the close relationships between the two artists' work at this moment in Copley's early career in England. On the basis of engravings of the subject and related drawings, Jules David Prown identified the painting as a work by Copley unlocated since the Lord Lyndhurst sale of 1864. Only the third of Copley's original history paintings, *The Nativity* shows remarkable artistic improvement from his first experimental attempt at grand subjects, *The Ascension*, painted in Italy just one year before (fig. 10 on p. 27). This composition has greater variety, the figures appear more convincing as human bodies in action, and the artist handles rich colors of green, blue, rose, gold, and vivid white with greater ease and subtlety.

The Nativity demonstrates Copley's rapid assimilation of the gestural language of history painting, through which the narrative might be conveyed with careful regard to compositional

Fig. 68 John Singleton Copley
Mr. and Mrs. Ralph Izard (Alice Delancey), 1775
Oil on canvas, 69 × 88^1/2 in (175.3 × 224.8 cm)
Courtesy Museum of Fine Arts, Boston, Edward Ingersoll
Browne Fund

Fig. 69 The Medici Vase, second half of 1st
century AD
Marble, height 68 in. (173 cm)
Uffizi, Florence

Adoration of the Shepherds, lot 38; Museum of Fine Arts, Boston, 1972.

SELECTED EXHIBITIONS: London 1777, no. 64; Los Angeles 1974, cat. 3.

SELECTED REFERENCES: Perkins 1873, pp. 129, 132; Bayley 1915, pp. 10, 31, 34, 183; Prown 1966, II, pp. 251, 262, 263–4 and n., 275, 387, 402, 444, fig. 347.

RELATED WORKS: Study, 1776, black and white chalk on buff paper, $8^7/_8 \times 10^7/_8$ in. (22.5 × 27.6 cm), Museum of Fine Arts, Boston; Study, 1776, black, white, and red chalk on blue-gray grounded white paper, $10^5/_8 \times 15^3/_8$ in. (27 × 39.1 cm), private collection.

NOTES
1. Prown 1966, II, p. 264.
2. As such, *The Nativity* provides another pictorial example of the cult of motherhood that pervaded the second half of the 18th century (see cats. 1 and 3). See also Fliegelman 1982, especially the chapters 'Educational Theory and Moral Indifference' and 'The Sealing of the Garden;' also see Prown 1986, pp. 269-86.
3. Pasquin 1796, p. 137.
4. Prown 1966, II, p. 444 lists three engravings: Henry Kingsbury, mezzotint, published 1 June, 1779; Jacob Hurd, mezzotint, published by R. Wilkinson, Boston, 1 August, 1785; Thouvenin, mezzotint, published by Tessari, Paris, n.d. Thomas Stothard also painted a *Holy Family* for the 1778 Royal Academy exhibition, but efforts to locate an image have been unsuccessful. Published in 1781–2, Stothard's illustration for *Cymon and Iphigenia* depicts Iphigenia in a pose almost identical to that of Copley's wife. Joshua Reynolds attempted the same subject in his *Nativity*, a cartoon for a stained-glass window at New College, Oxford, exhibited at the Royal Academy in 1779. According to Robert Rosenblum, Mrs. Brinsley Sheridan posed as the Virgin ('Reynolds in an International Milieu,' in London 1986, p. 45.)
5. Ribeiro 1984, pp. 174–8.
6. Von Erffa and Staley 1986, no. 419, p. 403.

unity. At center, the pyramid of deep folds of crisp white fabric of the Virgin's costume and the white pillow and blanket gives stability to the composition. Beams of divine light emanating from the left illuminate the bright whites of the coverlet, pillow, and clothing, helping to focus the spectator's gaze on the intimate scene of a mother and her newborn child. At left, Copley heightens the impression of commotion and excitement by posing Joseph (wrapped in green) glancing back toward the shepherds, all of whom react with gestures of adoration or surprise. The innkeeper or perhaps a shepherd, his back cast in shadow and his costume flapping somewhat awkwardly, helps to focus the viewer's attention toward the central pair, as if guiding followers to the divine scene with his pointing finger. This scene of activity at left, where even the dog appears alert and attentive, is balanced by the indifferent oxen at right, the donkey, and the stableboy in contemporary dress leaning forward to survey a scene whose mystery is conveyed by the moonlit vista at right.

Copley's carefully observed details lend immediacy to the scene: the piles of hay built up with thick lines of paint, the dense pattern of the foreground blanket, the pink-fleshed infant sucking his thumb while peacefully sleeping, and the mother tenderly holding her child and shading her eyes from blinding light, in a pensive gesture that suggests her understanding of the full impact of the moment. According to family tradition, Copley used his wife, Susanna, and her newborn namesake as models.[1] The painter often did incorporate his family in his paintings, but the appearance of them here as the archetypal mother and child is especially poignant.[2]

Copley submitted four paintings to the 1777 Royal Academy exhibition, where his large, grand painting of *The Copley Family* (cat. 1) was singled out by exhibition reviewers. *The Nativity*, Copley's first history painting to debut at the Royal Academy, was ambitious with its composition of eight figures and four animals worked into a relatively small canvas. The painting, however, apparently escaped printed notice, surely a disappointment for Copley, who wished to distinguish himself as a history painter. Years later, the perennially unkind Anthony Pasquin [John Williams] lampooned the painting, mentioning that "the immaculate mother reclines unconscious of her divinity, and is made to regard the *Salvator Mundi* with an air of despondence, rather than ineffable joy; and her white drapery is so inveterately modern, that it furnishes a lively notion of a female haberdasher in the third week of her *accouchement*. Had the Virgin never conceived more miraculously than Mr. *Copley*, I must apprehend the tribes of Christ would have been in a dolorous situation."[3] Writing sixteen years after the painting was first exhibited, Pasquin's criticism may reflect the then current taste for more grandiloquent depictions of biblical stories rather than the intimate representation of maternity represented here, more subtle in its references to the miracle depicted. Pasquin's review could not have reflected the majority of tastes; indeed, the painting must have found favor with some audiences as it was engraved three different times, in London, Boston, and Paris.[4]

The fact that, however satirical his intention, Pasquin saw the costume as befitting a pregnant haberdasher rather than the Virgin Mother suggests that the dress may have been perceived as something fashionable, something akin to the loose-fitting robes women often wore in portraits, which were often associated with dressing *à la turque*, as opposed to the more timeless blue robes associated with images of the Madonna.[5] Similar dresses appear in West's paintings, a probable source for Copley who, at this time in his career, relied on the senior artist's advice and encouragement. In the Royal Academy exhibition of 1776, West exhibited *The Golden Age* (1776, Tate Gallery, London), which depicts a seated Madonna-like figure – thought to be West's wife – wearing a voluminous white dress similar if not identical to the one worn by Copley's own wife one year later.[6] Copley may also have known the painting or print of West's *Una and the Lion*, the former included in the 1772 Royal Academy exhibition, and thought to be a portrait of Mary Hall in the guise of the character in Spenser's *The Faerie Queene* (fig. 70). Both Una and Copley's Virgin wear loose-fitting white robes and are posed partially reclined. Copley, perhaps relying on West's Una and the mother in *The Golden Age*, transforms them into something quite unusual: a reclining Virgin, rare if not unprecedented since medieval times in images of the Holy Family.

Such unusual combinations of models furthered the academic program of 'invention,' flattering the artist emulated, as well as the sitter. That Copley's wife posed as the Madonna, and Miss Hall as Una, suggests not (as some scholars have argued) the distance artists believed existed

7. For example, Robert Rosenblum's 'Reynolds in an International Milieu,' in London 1986, p. 45.

between mythical past and present, but rather the opposite: an effort among ambitious eighteenth-century artists to bring the past into the present.[7] Such strategies of making modern figures over into the descendants of grand figures from the past – mythological, biblical, political, or otherwise – helped to create an English artistic past, and were one way English artists could insert themselves into the long tradition of western art history of which they were becoming a part.

Fig. 70 Benjamin West
Una and the Lion (Mary Hall in the Character of Una), 1771
Oil on canvas, 65³/4 × 86¹/4 (167 × 219 cm)
Wadsworth Atheneum, Hartford, Connecticut, the Ella Gallup Sumner and Mary Catlin Sumner Collection Fund

3.

Sir William Pepperrell and his Family, 1778

Oil on canvas, 90 × 108 in. (228.6 × 274.3 cm)
Signed and dated lower left: *J.S. Copley P. 1778.*
North Carolina Museum of Art, Raleigh, purchased with funds from the State of North Carolina, 52.9.8

PROVENANCE: Sir William Pepperrell, Baronet, to 1816; his daughter, Harriot, wife of Sir Charles Thomas Palmer, 2nd Baronet, Wanlip Hall, Leicestershire; by descent in Palmer family until 1933; (J. Rochelle Thomas, Georgian Galleries, London, 1934); to William Randolph Hearst, St Donats, Wales, 1935; to Mallett and Son, London; (Thomas Agnew and Sons, Ltd., London, 1952); (sold to Scott and Fowles, New York, April 1952); to North Carolina Museum of Art, Raleigh, 1952.

A *tour de force* of Copley's early career in London, *Sir William Pepperrell and his Family* appeared in the 1778 Royal Academy show, the third in which the artist exhibited his work. Like *The Copley Family*, presented one year earlier but even larger in scale, the portrait of the Pepperrells reveals a fictitious and boldly colored interior and outdoor setting replete with gamboling children, games and toys, and solemn adults. The eldest child, Elizabeth (b. 1769), with a flirtatious toss of her head and beguiling glance, invites the spectator to enter this scene of domestic harmony. She leans against the lap of her mother Elizabeth ("Betsy," 1747–1775) and embraces her baby brother William (1775–1809), who clutches his mother's shoulder as he wriggles toward his father. Adopting a pose of casual elegance, Sir William (1746–1816) leans toward his seated wife and son, whose arm he gently squeezes; his wife echoes this gesture by holding the baby's foot. Linked together by tender gestures of touch, this intimate group provides a foil for the two middle daughters at right, Harriot (b. 1773) and Mary ("Polly," b. 1771), absorbed in their game of table skittles and oblivious to the activities of their siblings, parents, and the proud pets who provide their compositional counterparts.

The greens and golds visible in the patterned carpet create a kind of palette for the broad blocks of similar colors repeated throughout the composition: drapery drawn back with gold-fringed tassels, matched by the cloth thrown across a table, and Lady Pepperrell's silk dress spilling out of her seat. The greens and golds appear as well in the vertiginous patterning of the

SELECTED EXHIBITIONS: London 1778, no. 63; London 1934, no. 413; Minneapolis 1952, no. 26; Raleigh 1963, no. 9; Washington, New York, Boston 1965–6, no. 66; Los Angeles 1981–2, no. 16.

SELECTED REFERENCES: Amory 1882, p. 206; Howard 1894–5, vol. 31, pp. 54-65; Bayley 1915, p. 194; Rutledge 1957, pp. 195–203; Prown 1966, II, pp. 264–7, 315n., 318n., 363n., 428, fig. 356; Praz 1971, pp. 113, 116; Browne-Wilkinson 1982, p. 126; Bowron 1983, p. 18; Lovell 1987; Lovell 1991.

RELATED WORKS: Study, 1777, black and white chalk on blue-gray grounded paper, $11^{1}/_{4} \times 17^{1}/_{8}$ in. (28.6 × 43.9 cm), Museum of Fine Arts, Boston, The M. and M. Karolik Collection; Study, 1777–78, black, white, and red chalk on white paper, $17 \times 21^{1}/_{2}$ in. (43.2 × 54.6 cm), private collection; Study, 1777–8, black and white chalk on white paper, 17×21 in. (43.2 × 53.3 cm), private collection; Study, 1777–8, black and white chalk on pinkish buff paper, $17^{1}/_{4} \times 13^{1}/_{4}$ in (43.8 × 33.6 cm), Museum of Fine Arts, Boston, the M. and M. Karolik Collection; Study, 1777–8, black and white chalk on buff paper, $17^{3}/_{4} \times 10^{3}/_{8}$ in (45.1 × 27.3 cm), Victoria and Albert Museum, London.

NOTES

1. Browne-Wilkinson 1982, p. 126, writes that the portrait was commissioned when Lady Pepperrell was alive and before the remaining family left the colonies. But Copley had left the colonies in 1774, and no letters survive to suggest that Pepperrell wrote Copley to secure his services once abroad. Copley had painted members of the family before: Lady Pepperrell as a child in *Mary and Elizabeth Royall* (ca. 1758, Museum of Fine Arts, Boston), *Nathaniel Sparhawk*, William III's father (1764, Museum of Fine Arts, Boston), and Lady Pepperrell's mother and father, *Mrs. Isaac Royall* (Elizabeth MacIntosh, *ca.* 1769-80, Virginia Museum of Fine Arts, Richmond), and *Isaac Royall* (1769, Museum of Fine Arts, Boston). For more information on Pepperrell family portraits, see Howard 1894–5, pp. 54–67. General references for the Pepperrell family history include Browne-Wilkinson 1982, Shipton 1972, Rolde 1982, and Parsons 1855.

2. For example, see the spirited and affectionate letters written from Betsy to William when he traveled to England on business in 1768 in Browne-Wilkinson 1982, pp. 90–6.

3. Browne-Wilkinson 1982, pp. 112–3.

4. Sir William Pepperrell to Thomas Palmer, Pepperrell's cousin-in-law, quoted in Browne-Wilkinson 1982, pp. 114–5; and W.O. Raymond, *Winslow Papers* (New Brunswick Historical Society), p. 552, quoted in Shipton 1972, p. 403.

5. Prown agrees with Anna Wells Rutledge's suggestion that Copley's wife posed for Elizabeth Pepperrell's portrait in the painting (Prown 1966, II, p. 265).

landscape, flooded with beams of light. Passages of delicate pinks and whites in the linen or muslin dresses of the children, the bows, sashes, and plumes of Elizabeth's dress and the caps of the youngest and eldest daughters, Lady Pepperrell's hair trimming, the sunset sky, even the rosy glow of cheeks and baby's flesh link the family together, reiterating the image of domestic harmony through tonal unity.

The commission to paint Sir William's family probably occurred after the Pepperrells arrived as Loyalist exiles in London.[1] Pepperrell ancestors began as illiterate fishermen who emigrated from England in the seventeenth century, but they soon became a family of wealth and social position as merchants and landowners in Kittery, Maine, and the Boston area. Sir William Pepperrell II (1696–1759) was knighted in 1746 for his role in capturing the French garrison at Louisburg in Cape Breton, the first native colonial so honored. His only surviving child, Elizabeth Pepperrell (1723–1797), married Nathaniel Sparhawk (1715–1776), and bore William III (1746–1816), who succeeded to his grandfather's fortune upon the condition that he adopt his grandfather's surname at his majority. Educated at Harvard College, a man of means and promise, this William Pepperrell married Elizabeth ("Betsy") Royall, the daughter of Isaac and Elizabeth MacIntosh Royall, one of the most wealthy merchant families in New England. An apparently affectionate and happy couple, the Pepperrell's joint fortunes exponentially increased their social and political influence.[2]

In 1774, Pepperrell received word that his request to succeed to his grandfather's baronetcy was granted by the king. Political tensions, however, threw the steadfast Pepperrells into a tailspin. The York County Congress (near Kittery, Maine, the home of the Pepperrell family for three generations) passed a resolution declaring that Sir William, a Loyalist, should be "detested by all good men," and that the tenants who lived off his land should break all ties with his family.[3] Mounting political tensions forced the Pepperrell family from its Roxbury estate to Boston, where, despite the city's high-pitched revolutionary fervor, the Pepperrells and other Loyalists received protection from British troops. Pepperrell's son and heir, William, was born in 1775 (eventually predeceasing his father in 1809) and, three weeks later, Betsy succumbed to dysentery and died. "I still breathe – *live* I never shall again," Sir William wrote, a sentiment echoed years later by his friend Edward Winslow who wrote that Sir William's daughters were well married but that "the loss of his wife and son has imprinted strong marks of melancholy on his countenance which will never wear off."[4]

The most surprising fact surrounding the circumstances of the painting's commission is that at the time Copley conceived and painted the Pepperrells, the mother Elizabeth Royall Pepperrell had been dead for more than two years.[5] The image of domestic tranquillity in the painting, then, poignantly asserted a happy state of affairs that had not been and would not be – what the art historian Margaretta Lovell aptly has described as a painting in the "subjunctive mode."[6] She argues that the playing of skittles, a game in which the player aims and rolls the ball toward the placed pins, exercises order and control over chance and chaos, a metaphor for the function of the painting, which presents an image of domestic normalcy, order, and control in the face of family upheaval and tragedy. The artist's inclusion of table skittles reflects the fashion for including toys and games in family portraits. But depicting the game of skittles itself, a pictorial device unprecedented in eighteenth-century English portraiture, attests to Copley's inventiveness in devising and using props as an index of larger symbolic concerns.[7]

Pepperrell suffered a change of fortune but was not left without resources, buttressed by the return of his silver, income from a plantation in Surinam until the Dutch entered the war, and a yearly stipend from the royal government after his colonial properties were confiscated.[8] He became the president of the Loyalist Association and its Board of Agents, prosecuting claims for Loyalist losses of confiscated properties. In fact, the portrait was exhibited the very year the Pepperrells lost their colonial holdings, the genteel opulence and beatific family relationships represented in the painting publicly denying the true state of affairs.

Sir William Pepperrell and his Family received some notice by the critics, but most were focused instead on Copley's novel contemporary history painting, *Watson and the Shark* (cat. 4), exhibited at the Academy that same year. A reviewer for *The Morning Post* called Copley's family piece "a mere daubing," or a crudely painted picture, an opinion more vengeful than accurate. This

6. Lovell 1991 offers the most insightful reading of the painting to date.

7. For example, in *Mrs. Paul Richard* (1771, Bayou Bend Collection and Gardens, the Museum of Fine Arts, Houston), the sitter appears to be holding a deck of playing cards, a new (and never repeated) pictorial device in his career. Skittles do not appear in 18th-century portrait painting. Lawn skittles, however, prominently appeared in Francis Hayman's supper boxes at Vauxhall Gardens (see Allen 1987, p. 130), and were generally associated with taverns and the lower class. For histories of games that refer to skittles (also known as kayles, ninepens, and a variant of the game 'devil among the tailors'), see Strutt 1876, Hole 1948, and Taylor 1979.

8. Browne-Wilkinson 1982, p. 124, and Shipton 1972, p. 402. Accounts differ as to the exact amount of the stipend, but the point remains that William's contacts and network system enabled him to prosper.

9. *The Morning Post*, 25 April 1778, quoted in Prown 1966, II, p. 267. The letter to the editor of *The General Advertiser*, is in *V & A Press Cuttings*, vol. 1, p. 160.

10. The engraving of the image is reproduced in von Erffa and Staley 1986, no. 47, p. 187.

11. Reynolds suggests that "the painter has no other means of giving an idea of the dignity of the mind, but by that external appearance which grandeur of thought does generally, but not always, impress on the countenance" (Reynolds 1769–90/1959/1975, *Discourse IV* (10 December 1771) lines 115–8, p. 60).

Fig. 71 Joshua Reynolds
The Marlborough Family, 1778
Oil on canvas, 125^{1}/4 × 113^{7}/8 in. (318 × 289 cm)
Blenheim Palace, England, reproduced by kind permission of His Grace The Duke of Marlborough

criticism was redressed by a letter to the editor of *The General Advertiser*, who "beg[ged] leave to differ from this sage critic, as the figures have more expressive meaning than Sir Joshua's Marlborough family, and this is an excellence that even the great Mr. West falls short of, in not giving a strong picture of the mind in the visage."[9] The paintings the writer referred to were Joshua Reynolds's *The Marlborough Family* (fig. 71) and Benjamin West's history painting, *William de Albanac Presents his Three Daughters to Alfred III, King of Mercia* (ca. 1778, now destroyed).[10] The writer praises Copley for the "expressive meaning" of his figures and his ability to give a strong picture of the mind in the visage, a mark of high praise for Copley and censure for Reynolds considering that this fundamental principle of painting was promulgated by Reynolds himself in his *Discourses*.[11] Comparing *Sir William Pepperell and his Family* to Reynolds's likewise grand and ambitious portrait, the writer seems to commend the sense of character and intimacy Copley conveys in the Pepperells' both solemn and convivial expressions, and spirited and tender gestures, as opposed to the comparatively stagy and aloof demeanor of the Marlborough family. A review appearing in *The General Advertiser* sustains this notion of intimacy when it praises the picture for

12. *The General Advertiser*, in *V & A Press Cuttings*, vol. 1, p. 167. The reviewer goes on to criticize the landscape, however, suggesting the trees should have more "interstices" which would make the background less heavy; the "cold" flesh, and the "disunited and harsh" colors, although the "draperies are very fine."

13. See, for example, Locke 1693/1913 and Rousseau 1762/1979. See also here cat. 1, note 8.

14. Benjamin West, for example, posed his wife and children in the role of Madonna and Child in several paintings, notably *The West Family* (*ca.* 1772, Yale Center for British Art, New Haven, Paul Mellon Collection), and Copley's wife in *The Copley Family* suggests a similar association.

its "simplicity," and that the "gambols of the children, and the parental attention and comfort gives a beautiful idea."[12]

The similar pictorial conventions Copley and Reynolds adopt suggest the change in the structure and relationship of the eighteenth-century family, as children began to be recognized as separate creatures with specific needs of nurturing and care, and mothers as the guardian of the child's developing character.[13] Both artists picture children at play and the mother as the central, stabilizing force of the painting. Copley places the late Lady Pepperrell before a pillar, visual testimony to her guiding role in the family, and poses her in the attitude of the Madonna and Child appearing in countless Renaissance and Baroque paintings, the cherubic child sitting in the Virgin's voluminous lap.[14] If the mother takes on the role of blessed nurturer, the father upholds worldly concerns. In both paintings, the artist links the father to his eldest son and heir, the system of primogeniture made visible, as if, in one penetrating glance, the father transfers future family responsibility and social obligations to his son. This, like the survival of his wife, was a vain wish. The painting passed not to his son, but to his youngest daughter Harriot Pepperrell Palmer, and remained at the Palmer home at Wanlip, Leicestershire, until 1933.

4.

Watson and the Shark, 1778

Oil on canvas, 71³/₄ × 90¹/₂ in. (182.1 × 229.7 cm)

Signed center left, inside boat: *JS Copley. P. 1778–*

National Gallery of Art, Washington, D.C., Ferdinand Lammot Belin Fund, 1963.6.1

PROVENANCE: Brook Watson (1735–1807), London and East Sheen, Surrey; his wife, Helen Watson, London(?), bequeathed to Christ's Hospital, London; purchased by the National Gallery of Art in 1963.

SELECTED EXHIBITIONS: London 1778, no. 65; Manchester 1857; London 1946, no. 49; London 1951–2, no. 420; Washington, New York, Boston 1965–6, no. 68a; London 1968–9, no. 505; Berlin, Zurich 1988–9, no. 7; Washington, New York 1990; Boston, Detroit, Washington 1993.

SELECTED REFERENCES: Perkins 1873, pp. 128, 132, 188–9, supplement p. 9; Prown 1966, I, p. 18, II, pp. 264, 267–75, 459–61 and *passim*, fig. 371; Frankenstein 1970, pp. 11, 138–9, 146–9; Stein 1976, pp. 85–130; Jaffe 1970; Abrams 1979; Honour 1989, pp. 37–41; Boime 1990, pp. 20–26; Miles 1994, pp. 54–71.

RELATED WORKS: *Harpooner and Oarsman*, 1777–8, black and white chalk on green-gray paper, 13³/₈ × 15¹/₂ in. (34 × 39.5 cm), The Detroit Institute of Arts; *Head of a Figure on the Far Left*, 1777–8, black and white chalk on green-gray

Watson and the Shark depicts the dramatic rescue of fourteen-year-old Brook Watson from the attack of a shark in the harbor of Havana, Cuba, in 1749. Copley painted the episode almost thirty years after the event, exhibiting the large canvas at the Royal Academy in London in 1778. Since that time the work has been recognized as a highly important example of Anglo-American narrative painting.[1]

Who was Brook Watson? Born in Plymouth, England, in 1735, and orphaned in 1741, Watson was sent across the Atlantic to Boston to be cared for by a relative, Mr. Levens, a merchant who traded in the West Indies. In 1749 one of Levens's ships, with the fourteen-year-old Watson on the crew, docked in the Havana harbor. When Watson went swimming, a shark attacked him, tearing off his right leg below the knee. After he was rescued, he returned to Boston and was fitted with a wooden leg. Soon he settled in Canada and became a merchant, the career he continued in England after moving to London in 1759. Watson and Copley probably met through relatives of Copley's wife, Susanna Clarke Copley. Her uncle Joshua Winslow was Watson's employer in Canada in 1755. Her brother Jonathan Clarke was a London merchant. In 1773 he and Watson shipped a cargo of tea to several Boston merchants, including Mrs. Copley's father, Richard Clarke. This controversial shipment was dumped into Boston harbor during the Boston Tea Party that protested British colonial policies. Copley and Watson probably met in London during the summer of 1774, when Copley, who was traveling from Boston to Italy, contacted his brother-in-law Jonathan Clarke on his arrival in the British capital. On August 17 Copley wrote Henry Pelham in Boston: "To Morrow I ... Dine with a Mr. Watson."[2] Watson and Copley were both in London again in the early part of 1776, after Copley returned from Italy and before Watson returned to Canada with Jonathan Clarke.

Although there is no documentation, the painting was probably commissioned by Watson. As patron, he would have chosen its theme: individual salvation achieved by triumph over adversity. Such a theme is central to numerous religious autobiographies and autobiographical journals written in seventeenth- and eighteenth-century England and America. Early models of this genre include *Grace Abounding to the Chief of Sinners* (1666), which was the autobiography of John Bunyan (author of *The Pilgrim's Progress*, 1678), and the journal of Quaker leader George Fox

paper, 11⅞ × 9⁵⁄₁₆ in. (30 × 24 cm), The Detroit Institute of Arts; *Two Oarsmen*, 1777–8, black and white chalk on green-gray paper, 9¾ × 11¹¹⁄₁₆ in. (25 × 29.5 cm), The Detroit Institute of Arts; *Rescue Group (Eight Men)*, 1777–8, black and white chalk, squared and numbered in red chalk, on green-gray paper, 14³⁄₁₆ × 21¹¹⁄₁₆ in. (36 × 55 cm), The Detroit Institute of Arts; *Study of a Head (Brook Watson)*, 1777–8, pencil and white chalk on gray-blue paper, sheet 14³⁄₁₆ × 22⁹⁄₁₆ in. (36.5 × 57.5 cm), Museum of Fine Arts, Boston.

NOTES

1. For the most comprehensive discussion of this painting to date, and for full bibliographic references to earlier publications, see Miles 1995, pp. 54–71.
2. *Letters of Copley and Pelham* 1914/1972, p. 239.
3. On religious autobiography, see Morris 1966, pp. 89–168, and Starr 1971. Wilson 1989, pp. 33–4, discusses Bunyan's *Pilgrim's Progress* as a model for Benjamin Franklin's autobiography, begun in 1771 in England and published in 1790 after his death. Stein 1976, pp. 106–10, discusses similar sources, the narratives of deliverance from the sea, in relationship to this painting.
4. Watson died in 1807; his will is filed at the Public Record Office, London.
5. The narrative description of the event was published in *The Morning Chronicle, and London Advertiser*, 27 April 1778; it was sent by "a correspondent," presumably Watson.
6. Stein 1976, pp. 93–114 and Jaffe 1977, pp. 20–5, discuss the artistic sources for this painting, especially for its Christian imagery. In discussions about the painting, Charles Brock, Exhibitions Assistant, Department of American and British Painting, National Gallery of Art, focused my attention on the relevance of the story of Jonah to Watson's rescue.
7. The texts of all contemporary newspaper reviews have been published in Miles 1994, pp. 70–1.
8. Detroit 1991, pp. 2–64 (catalogue entry by Richard H. Saunders).

(1694). The recounting of a physical or emotional trial and a subsequent change of direction in life is central to these works, as it was to the equally influential fictional model of salvation, Daniel Defoe's *The Life and Strange Surprizing Adventures of Robinson Crusoe* (1719). The practice of writing personal stories of salvation and religious conversion continued throughout the eighteenth century.[3] Watson, a successful merchant, would have considered his life a triumph over adversity. Politically allied with the merchants in the City of London, he was elected in 1784 to Parliament. He was a director of the Bank of England, Lord Mayor of London in 1796–7 and chairman of the Corporation of Lloyds of London. He was made a baronet in 1803, the year that he bequeathed *Watson and the Shark* to Christ's Hospital, London, a boy's school established as a Royal Hospital in 1553 for the care and education of the poor. In his will he stated that he hoped "the said worthy Governors ... will allow it to be hung up in the Hall of their Hospital as holding out a most usefull Lesson to Youth."[4]

For *Watson and the Shark* Copley borrowed motifs from several artists. For the harbor, which he had never seen, he probably relied on the recent engraving by Peter Canot of *A View of the Entrance of the Harbour of the Havanna taken from within the Wrecks*, based on a drawing by Elias Durnford and published by Thomas Jeffreys in London in 1764. For the composition Copley turned to images of men in boats by the Renaissance and Baroque painters Raphael and Peter Paul Rubens, especially *The Miraculous Draft of the Fishes* and *Jonah and the Whale*, two appropriate sources for the theme of salvation. In Christian iconography the Old Testament narrative of Jonah was seen as a presage of the New Testament story of the resurrection of Christ, since both events involved the number three: Jonah was in the whale for three days, and Christ rose from the dead on the third day. According the account of Watson's accident, published in 1778 at the time of the exhibition, Watson was rescued as he came to the surface a third time.[5] Rubens's composition of *Jonah and the Whale*, which was engraved by Philippe Joseph Tassaert, was one of the lower panels of the altarpiece that he painted in 1618–19 for the Fishermen's Guild of Mechelen (Malines), present Belgium, for the church of Notre-Dame. The central image of the altarpiece, *The Miraculous Draft of the Fishes*, is described in the New Testament: arriving at the Sea of Galilee, Jesus instructed four fishermen to let their nets out again after an unsuccessful night of fishing. After they pulled in large numbers of fish, Jesus called the men to be his disciples, as "fishers of men." Copley owned an example of Schelte à Bolswert's engraving of this subject, although it is not known when he acquired it. A more stately, less dramatic image of the same subject is Raphael's *Miraculous Draught of the Fishes* (Collection of Her Majesty Queen Elizabeth II), one of the Renaissance master's cartoons for his Sistine Chapel tapestries, which Copley might have seen in the collection of King George III. Or he may have relied on an engraving, such as that by Nicholas Dorigny (see cat. 10). The use of these images is evidence that Watson and Copley saw the painting of *Watson and the Shark* as a modern tale of salvation.[6]

Copley exhibited *Watson and the Shark* at the Royal Academy in 1778 with the title "*A boy attacked by a shark, and rescued by some seamen in a boat; founded on a fact which happened in the harbour of the Havannah.*" Reviewers focused on many aspects of the work, including the type of boat, the setting, and the composition and novelty of the subject. The reviews indicate that the expressions and actions of the sailors were designed to represent a full range of human responses to the horror of the event. The reviewer for *The Public Advertiser* for April 28 noted this: "The Story is clearly told, and it scarce leaves any Thing for the *Amateur* to wish, or for the *Critic* to amend. The judicious Choice of the Characters, employed to rescue the Youth from the *Jaws of Death*; the Eagerness and the Concern so strongly marked in every Countenance; such Propriety in the different Actions and Attitudes of each, all concur to render it a very uncommon Production of Art."[7] *Watson and the Shark* established Copley's reputation in England. Copley made a same-size replica of the painting (Museum of Fine Arts, Boston), which he exhibited in his London studio. In 1779 Valentine Green made a mezzotint engraving of the composition with the title *A Youth Rescued from a Shark*, which further boosted the artist's reputation.

The prominence of a black sailor in the composition has attracted much attention. His identity is not known. When a portrait by Copley that may be of the same man (cat. 5) was sold in 1864 after the death of the artist's son, it was described as "HEAD OF A FAVOURITE NEGRO. Very fine. Introduced in the picture of 'The Boy saved from the Shark.'"[8] Copley

9. *Letters of Copley and Pelham* 1914/1972, p. 304.
10. Fryer 1984, pp. 67–77.
11. Stein 1976, pp. 122–3, recognized the crucial role of the seaman in the painting; Boime 1990, pp. 19–36, and McElroy in Washington 1990, p. 6, focused on the possible political and social meanings for his inclusion.
12. Boime 1990, pp. 34–6, and McElroy in Washington 1990, p. 6, agree with Abrams 1979, pp. 265–76, in this interpretation.
13. Dunlap 1834/1969, I, pp. 117–8.

discussed the practice of using familiar models in thematic paintings when he wrote Henry Pelham on 14 March 1775: "By making use of a Model for the heads you will naturally vary your faces agreable to your Models ... Chusing such Models as are most agreable to the several carracters you mean to paint, you will procure that variety in your Works that is so much admired in the first Works of Art."[9] Perhaps the man was a member of Copley's household, although there is no documentation that Copley had a black servant or slave. There were approximately 15,000 blacks living in England by the 1770s. At a time when slavery was legal in the British empire, slaves were brought to England and worked as servants, vendors, seamen, craftsmen and entertainers.[10]

Blacks frequently appear in eighteenth-century English paintings, usually in secondary roles. Very few painters give them the prominence that Copley has. We know that the inclusion of the black man in the painting was purposeful, since the central figure in the preparatory drawing *Rescue Group (Eight Men)* (1777–8, The Detroit Institute of Arts) is a white sailor. Perhaps the black sailor was included at Watson's insistence as one of the participants in the event, or perhaps Copley changed the sailor's race to indicate that the attack occurred in the West Indies, where many ships were manned by black seamen. Another possibility is that Copley included the black sailor to provide a reaction to the event that was different in some way from that of the other individual sailors. Reviewers believed this but disagreed on his exact role. The writer in *The Morning Chronicle, and London Advertiser* of 25 April 1778, for example, noted that "the Black's face is a fine index of concern and horror." However the writer in *The General Advertiser, and Morning Intelligencer* for 27 April criticized the fact that he seemed to be frozen in terror.

Recent analysis of the painting has given the black sailor's presence a political interpretation. This viewpoint sees the dominant position of the black as an image in support of the struggle of blacks for their freedom.[11] It assumes further that Copley and Watson were both opposed to the cause of American independence and used the dismemberment of Watson by the shark as a negative image for the Revolution.[12] This theory recognizes that Watson later took a pro-slavery stand in Parliament by suggesting that Watson changed his views as the possibility of abolition became a reality. The issue of Watson's political views had been raised by American artist William Dunlap, who was among the work's early admirers. He arrived in London in 1784 with a copy of *Watson and the Shark* that he had painted from the mezzotint to demonstrate his skill. However, he later became critical of Copley's English patronage, writing in his *History of the Rise and Progress of the Arts of Design in the United States* (1834): "Copley was, when removed to England, no longer an American painter in feeling; and his choice of subjects for historical composition, was decided by the circumstances of the time, or by employers." Dunlap introduced the subject of Watson's Tory allegiance and his opposition to the abolition of slavery in 1789–92. He characterized Watson as "an American adventurer from one of the New-England provinces," who "is memorable as arrayed with our enemies in opposition to our independence, and with the enemies of God and man in opposition to the abolitionists of the slave-trade in the English house of commons ... To immortalize such a man was the pencil of Copley employed."[13]

Although political interpretations of both Watson's and Copley's actions and opinions continue to be part of the discussion about *Watson and the Shark*, the idea of redemption and salvation seems to be the idea that was on Watson's mind when he willed the painting to Christ's Hospital. And it is Copley's startling rendition of the rescue that has remained fixed in the memory of many viewers from that time to today.

[Ellen G. Miles]

5.
Head of a Negro, 1777–78

Oil on canvas, 21 × 16¼ in. (53.3 × 41.3 cm.)
Detroit Institute of Arts, Founders Society Purchase, Gibbs-Williams Fund, 52.118

PROVENANCE: The artist, London, to 1815; his son, John Singleton Copley, Jr., Lord Lyndhurst, to 1863; (Lyndhurst sale, Christie's, London, 5 March 1864, no. 69); to Isaac J.W. Burnett, Rock Hall, Alnwick, Northumberland, England; (J.W. Burnett sale, Christie's, London, 23–4 May 1938, no. 217); to Mann; (Christie's, London, 24 Feb. 1951, no. 102); bought by Mason; (M. Knoedler & Co., New York, 1951); Detroit Institute of Arts, 1952.

SELECTED EXHIBITIONS: Washington, New York, Boston 1965–6, no. 69; Washington, New York 1990, pp. 4–5; Boston, Detroit, Washington 1993.

SELECTED REFERENCES: Perkins 1873, p. 132; Bayley 1915, pp. 34, 36, 184; Richardson 1952–3, pp. 68–70; Prown 1966, II, p. 274, fig. 381; Frankenstein 1970, p. 149; Honour 1989, pp. 10–1; Detroit 1991, pp. 62–4; Miles 1993, p. 168.

NOTES
1. Prown 1966, II, p. 402.
2. Prown 1966, II, p. 274.
3. Perkins 1873, p. 132; Detroit 1991, p. 64.
4. Amory 1882, p. 69.
5. Hecht 1954, p. 34.
6. London 1986, pp. 245–6, pl. 116. Some have suggested that the subject represents Reynolds's servant.
7. The subject of the black in *Watson and the Shark* has received continued attention since the painting's debut at the Royal Academy in 1778. For several theories, see Stein 1976, Boime 1989, and Miles 1994, pp. 62–5; here also cat. 4.

The estate sale of John Singleton Copley's son, Lord Lyndhurst, in 1864 included the following description for lot number 69: "HEAD OF A FAVOURITE NEGRO. Very fine. Introduced in the picture of 'The Boy saved from the Shark.'"[1] Although "very fine" does not adequately describe the compelling brilliance of this portrait, it has long been thought to be the "head" in question, as no other portrait of a black figure is known in Copley's œuvre.

As Prown has observed, *Head of a Negro* does not resemble the black figure in *Watson and the Shark* (cat. 4), whose facial features appear rounder, less defined, and, as befitting the action in the story, more sober.[2] Prown notes, however, that Copley may have wanted to focus the viewer's attention on the rescue operation of the harpoonist, and so deliberately played down the gesture and expression of the black seaman. The intimacy of the sketch has led several scholars to believe that the sitter was a servant in the Copley household.[3] A woman servant named Susan is known to have worked for the Copleys, but no other references to family servants survive.[4] Nonetheless, Copley would have found it easy to find models, for in the latter decades of the eighteenth century the population of blacks in England ranged from 15,000 to 20,000, many of whom had been freed from slavery in 1772, but still remained in England as servants.[5]

Perhaps the most famous servant in the eighteenth century was Francis (Frank) Barber, the servant and heir of the distinguished man of letters, Dr. Samuel Johnson, and the possible subject of Joshua Reynolds's *Study of a Black Man (Frank Barber?)* (fig. 72), painted *ca.* 1770.[6] Copley visited Reynolds's studio at least once, in July of 1774, and may have seen and been inspired by the closely observed and spontaneous sketch of the dignified sitter. The figure in Reynolds's portrait, gazing in the distance and enveloped in diaphanous clouds, appears otherworldly and ethereal in comparison to the stunning simplicity and directness of Copley's sitter, who returns the viewer's gaze with a gentle smile. Copley uses a limited palette of blacks, browns, whites, and tints of rose, allowing the warm flesh tones to stand out against a buff colored ground. The dash of white, suggesting the starched crispness of the collar, is picked up in the reflective enamel surface of the sitter's teeth, and glints across his illuminated lips, cheek, nose, and forehead. With tiny strokes of black, Copley suggests the tight curls of his hair, beard and moustache. This is one of the most immediate and engaging sketches of Copley's long career, similar in its intensity to the sketches of the Hanoverian officers for *The Siege of Gibraltar* (cats. 34, 35).

Black subjects figure prominently in Copley's history paintings, from the model viewer who forms the apex of the pyramidal composition of *Watson and the Shark* to the hero of *The Death of Major Peirson*, who avenges his master's death.[7] In both paintings, black figures play pivotal roles in the story depicted, a device that the French nineteenth-century painter Théodore Géricault surely would have recognized. He appropriated Copley's use of the black figure as a central character for *The Raft of the Medusa* (1819, Musée du Louvre, Paris), where a muscular black man seen from the back and waving a flag forms the apex of the pyramid suggested by the surviving soldiers and passengers of the shipwreck.

Fig. 72 Joshua Reynolds
Study of a Black Man (Frank Barber?), 1767
Oil on canvas, 21 × 25⅛ in. (78.7 × 65 cm)
The Menil Collection, Houston

6.
Mrs. Seymour Fort(?), ca. 1778

Oil on canvas, 49¹/₂ × 39⁵/₈ in.
(125.73 × 100.65 cm)
Wadsworth Atheneum, Hartford, Connecticut,
Gallery Fund, 1901.34

PROVENANCE: (Dowdeswell & Dowdeswell
Gallery, London, 1901); Wadsworth Atheneum,
Hartford, Connecticut, 1901.

SELECTED EXHIBITIONS: New York 1909, no.
13; Chicago 1933, no. 57; New York 1937, no. 37;
Boston 1938, no. 30; Paris 1938, no. 32; Pittsburgh
1940, no. 61; London 1946, no. 46; St. Louis
1947, no. 7; New York 1958, p. 112.

SELECTED REFERENCES: Bayley 1915, p. 108;
Bolton and Binsse 1930, p. 83; Prown 1966, II, pp.
264, 267, 420, fig. 363; Townsend 1966, pp.
12–23; Novak 1969, p. 35; Frankenstein 1970,
pp. 137, 146–7; Ahrens 1978, pp. 508-19.

NOTES
1. Townsend 1966, p. 12. See also object files,
Wadsworth Atheneum, Hartford.
2. Prown 1966, II, pp. 264, 267, proposes this
painting as the one submitted to the Royal
Academy exhibition. The painting is similar in
composition and costume to the portrait of *Mrs.
Isaac Royall* (*ca.* 1769-80, Virginia Museum of Fine
Arts, Richmond), which Copley began in the
colonies and completed in London.
3. Dinnerstein 1981, pp. 109-11.

Perched on the edge of a crimson-covered gilt armchair, this sitter addresses the viewer with a proud yet engaging stare. As befits her formidable demeanor, she has kept inquisitive spectators at a distance for over two hundred years, for her identity remains as elusive as ever. Traditionally identified as Mrs. Seymour Fort, the name written in a nineteenth-century hand on a label attached to the back of the stretcher, the portrait may not, in fact, represent her; a G. Seymour Fort, writing from London in 1909, claims she never existed.[1] Copley probably exhibited this portrait at the Royal Academy exhibition of 1778, as "number 64. Portrait of a lady; three quarters," although no known critical review of the exhibition provides a descriptive clue, for critics turned their attention to Copley's other contributions to the exhibition that year: the monumental and elegant full-length portrait of *Sir William Pepperrell and his Family* (cat. 3) and the even more striking and celebrated *Watson and the Shark* (cat. 4).[2]

The dramatic contrasts between illuminated spaces and dark shadows, vivid white and rich dark colors, soft fabrics and starched trimming, and carefully observed details combined with broad handling, create a bravura performance that was sure to engage the exhibition visitor. Copley displays his virtuosity in the layering of whites upon whites, loading his brush and dragging it over the canvas to create the illusion of ruffles and embroidered surfaces. The satin sash, tied in the front, includes stripes of transparent gauze that contrast with the dotted sheer ruffles of the black mantle the sitter wears around her shoulders and lets fall to the floor, the perfect counterpoint to the white and buff colors of her dress. Peeking out of a ruffled *dormeuse*, posed before crimson folds of drapery and a panelled wall, the sitter seems to pause in her activity as she catches the eye of the beholder. Engaged in knotting, a popular pastime for elegant women in eighteenth-century England, she holds a gold shuttle, or *navette*, in her right hand, and silk or linen thread in her left, the thread dangling from her fingers and disappearing in the folds of the working bag hanging from her wrist.

This image of patrician industry recalls the portrait of *Mr. and Mrs. Thomas Mifflin* (1773, Historical Society of Pennsylvania) Copley had painted just before leaving the colonies, in which Mrs. Mifflin sits at her loom making fringe, an ornate trim similar to this sitter's knotted threads (fig. 73). Mrs. Mifflin's activity signifies her genteel status but also, in the context of a boycott on English luxury items during the revolutionary period, her willingness and even desire to do her part as a patriot; instead of importing luxury goods, she makes her own.[3] Several thousand miles

Fig. 73 John Singleton Copley
*Mr. and Mrs. Thomas Mifflin
(Sarah Morris)*, 1773
Oil on ticking, 60¹/₂ × 48 in. (153.7 ×
121.9 cm)
Courtesy Historical Society of
Pennsylvania

4. William L. Pressly discusses such portrayals in his essay in this catalogue (pp. 23–59).

5. Printed in *The Spectator*, 14 November 1712, quoted in Townsend 1966, pp. 17–8.

away, the sitter of this portrait, seated in an English armchair like a flounced, puffed cushion, could not be more different from the stoic Mrs. Mifflin, a sign of Copley's changing technique as well as a measure of the different cultural aspirations of his patrons.

Knotting was an appropriate activity for genteel women young and old, and women were frequently portrayed engaged in such activities.[4] As one eighteenth-century observer remarked, "it shews a white hand and a Diamond ring to great advantage."[5] This same observer, perhaps satirically, encouraged young "beaux" to take up knotting as a cure for idleness, "for want of Business," she wrote, men "are often as much in Vapours as the Ladies." Despite such encouragement, knotting remained a woman's occupation, serving a practical end and, as the observer noted, advertising the industriousness of the sitter and the finer physical qualities of her hands. Indeed, among the most sensitively observed details in the portrait are the sitter's hand movements. She holds the shuttle as if it were a teacup, with her little finger outstretched – a sign of her civility and grace. But her left hand, where a ring would be shown "to great advantage," is cast partially in shadow, illuminating, instead, the veins of her aging hands. It is in such details that the vulnerability of Copley's sitters is revealed despite the sumptuous stuffs that might otherwise overwhelm them.

7.

Mrs. Clark Gayton (ca. 1748–1809), 1779

Oil on canvas, 50 × 40 in. (127 × 101.6 cm)

Signed and dated center right.: *J S Copley. Fec. 1779.*

The Detroit Institute of Arts, Gift of Mr. D.J. Healy, 27.556

PROVENANCE: The sitter, Mrs. Clark Gayton, née Legge (afterwards Mrs. James Pigott) until 1809;[1] her husband, the Reverend James Pigott, 1809-22; his daughter Lydia Pigott (Mrs. William Thresher), Fareham, Hampshire; Captain W. Thresher, R.N., Fareham, Hampshire; his niece, Lucy Mabel Thresher; (O'Hagan sale, Christie's, 24 November 1922, no. 106); (M. Knoedler, London); (Woolworth sale, American Art Association, 5–6 January 1927, no. 87); (Metropolitan Galleries, New York, 1927); Detroit Institute of Arts, gift of D.J. Healy, 1927.

SELECTED EXHIBITIONS: Detroit 1934; Grand Rapids 1943.

SELECTED REFERENCES: Bolton and Binsse 1930, p. 116; Prown 1966, II, pp. 275, 420, fig. 384.

It is not always clear how Copley and his sitters came to be united or under what specific circumstances the commission came about. In the case of the splendid portraits of Admiral and Mrs. Clark Gayton, little is known – not even the given name of Mrs. Gayton – but enough evidence survives to make it likely that Copley conceived these portraits as pendants, as the images face one another and the sitters hung them together in their home in Fareham, in Hampshire. Clark Gayton was promoted from Rear-Admiral of the Blue to Vice-Admiral of the White (the English fleet was divided into squadrons identified by colors) when stationed in Jamaica in 1776. Perhaps in response to such an honor, he commissioned the portraits upon his final return to England in 1778, after more than thirty-five years of naval service in North America, the West Indies, and the Mediterranean, among other places. It is certain that Copley regarded the Gayton commission an important one, for both paintings are bravura performances in terms of coloristic effects, composition, and the animated contrast between the sitters' poses and surroundings.

Seated on the corner of a crimson patterned damask sofa and posed against a matching swath of drapery pulled back to reveal a wall, Mrs. Gayton assumes a thoughtful pose. Her hair is piled high according to the fashion of the day, and she wears a sumptuous grey and silver silk robe, replete with pearl and jewel trim, and a light yellow underskirt. Her pose and props – the chalk-holder she holds and the portfolio of drawings on the floor by her side – identify her as a woman of leisure, making good use of her time by cultivating the genteel pursuit of drawing. In portraits of women in the eighteenth century, drawing-tool props appeared in paintings by Thomas Hudson in the 1740s, by Joshua Reynolds in the 1760s, and, with some frequency, by other British artists, such as Copley, in the late 1770s and 1780s. While the props may identify Mrs. Gayton's hobbies, they also indicates her privileged social status, and her role in the tradition of women depicted as Muses of Art.[2]

Movement and fluidity characterize her portrait, both in pose and execution. Depicted in a three-quarter profile pose, Mrs. Gayton leans toward the ledge where even the pot of geraniums appears precariously balanced. The sharp tilt of her pose makes the lush folds of her skirt seem to spill out of the picture plane. Such compositional movement is underscored by the loose, fluid manner in which the artist brushes pigments across the canvas in thin, transparent glazes. No Copley portrait of this period demonstrates so vividly the artist's mastery of English and Continental technique.

8.

Clark Gayton (1712–1797), Admiral of the White, 1779

Oil on canvas, 50½ × 40½ in. (128.3 × 102.9 cm)

Signed and dated lower left.: *J S Copley P./1779*.

National Maritime Museum, Greenwich, BHC2705

PROVENANCE: Mrs. Dockray, a descendant of the sitter; purchased by Sir James Caird, 1949, for the National Maritime Museum, Greenwich.

SELECTED EXHIBITIONS: San Diego 1992, p. 5.

SELECTED REFERENCES: Prown 1966, II, pp. 275, 352, 420, fig. 385.

NOTES

1. See object file, Detroit Institute of Arts. One description of the painting, presumably supplied by Metropolitan Galleries, New York, mentions that Mrs. Pigott was the daughter of a Captain Legge (perhaps Captain Edward Legge (1710–1747), who would have died before she was born).

2. In the American colonies, Copley used drawings as a prop in women's portraits as early as *ca.* 1764, when he painted *Mrs. Daniel Hubbard* (Art Institute of Chicago), although in her portrait he eliminated the chalk-holder. Also, in that portrait, drawings are visible rather than hidden in a portfolio. For a discussion of drawing implements as props in portraits of women in the 18th century, see Shelley M. Bennett, 'A Muse of Art in the Huntington Collection,' in Sutherland 1992, pp. 57–80.

3. Roche 1989/1994, pp. 221–56.

4. Richardson 1715/1725/1971, p. 188.

5. Reynolds 1769–90/1959/1975, *Discourse XI*, (10 December 1782) lines 306–18, p. 200.

6. Wind 1932/1986, pp. 31–2; also London 1986, p. 38. See also cat. 9.

7. According to *The Times* (London), 26 September 1782 the Admiral died Saturday "at Portsmouth", but it listed his rank as "Rear-Admiral" rather than Admiral of the Blue. Genealogical records list his christening date in Portsmouth as 18 April 1712.

The sense of flow and movement in Mrs. Gayton's portrait, however, is not matched in its pendant of the Admiral. His frontal, upright stance, piercing gaze, and right hand which firmly grips the maps and rests on a table, mark him as a man of action and, befitting his profession, of command. Whereas Mrs. Gayton is depicted indoors, framed by a protective wall that provides a window onto the world outside, the Admiral, posed against high seas and billowing storm clouds, stands proud and tall, a man who cannot – or will not – be overwhelmed by the cruelty of nature. In the background, Gayton's ship, the *Antelope*, flies his standard, a white flag showing one ball in the upper left quadrant, the sign of his rank as Vice-Admiral of the White. Copley brings out with great care the highlights of gold lace on Gayton's full-dress uniform; his navy jacket and buff-colored waistcoat show impasto surfaces of gold and yellow, picked up in the hilt of his sword and the braid of his hat.

To some degree, *Admiral Clark Gayton* is a portrait of this uniform. During the eighteenth century, the military uniform in England and in France witnessed a sharp rise in the specificity of its details – the numbers and arrangements of epaulets, cuffs, and buttons that recorded its wearer's 'signs of discipline."[3] The uniform established *esprit de corps*, for standardization enhanced the soldier's sense of being a part of a greater whole. Signs of rank distinguished the soldier within the corps, serving the practical end of instantly establishing a chain of command. The portrait, in a way, served the same function as Gayton's naval uniform: to announce and celebrate his rise in the ranks, and to distinguish him from his subordinates.

Such careful delineation of specific details designed to allude to the sitter's character and profession, however, threatened to compromise the portrait as it was understood by English theorists. Jonathan Richardson, England's first author of an aesthetic treatise, asserted that the job of a face painter was more difficult than the history painter, because the "Additional Grace, and Greatness he is to give above what is to be found in the Life, must not be thrown in too profusely, the Resemblance must be preserv'd, and appear with Vigour; the Picture must have Both."[4] In other words, the portraitist needed to capture the specific details that constituted a likeness without sacrificing the air of dignity demanded of a portrait. By 1782, Reynolds reminded the portraitist that "the excellence of Portrait-Painting, and we may add even the likeness, the character, and countenance ... depend more upon the general effect produced by the painter, than on the exact expression of the peculiarities, or minute discrimination of the parts ... let him not forget continually to examine, whether in finishing the parts he is not destroying the general effect."[5] With the attention Copley lavishes on capturing the illumined role of papers and maps on the table and the surface splendor of Gayton's uniform, the painter comes dangerously close to giving too much "discrimination of the parts" – especially in comparison to Reynolds's portraits of military men, such as Admiral Keppel (fig. 29 on p. 48), or Lord Heathfield (1788, National Gallery, London), where little of the uniform is noticeable or, at least, stands out among other features. Reynolds finds other methods of distinguishing these figures among the rank-and-file – with commanding strides, stormy skies, off-center compositions designed to suggest movement rather than stasis, and narrative elements.[6] Here, Copley strives to combine his fascination with physical and textural details and a sense of epic grandeur, a hallmark of the more fluid and fashionable portrait style that he experimented with and developed in England.

Gayton's ill health eventually forced him to remain in England after his return in 1778, although he ultimately achieved the rank of Admiral of the Blue. He returned to Fareham in Hampshire, at the northwest branch of Portsmouth harbor, a small port town known as a popular retirement spot for service officers (although in the case of Gayton, his family had lived there for at least two generations). After his death in 1797, his wife, at least thirty years his junior, married twice more, to a Mr. Newnham, and to a Reverend James P. Pigott, vicar of Wigston, County Leicester, himself a widower with three daughters, one of whom inherited the portrait of her stepmother and passed it to her descendants, still living in Fareham.[7] The portrait of the Admiral descended through his line, but it is not known when the portraits were separated; they may have remained together until the death of the former Mrs. Gayton in 1809.

9.

Major Hugh Montgomerie (1739–1819), 1780

Oil on canvas, 94$\frac{1}{2}$ × 59$\frac{3}{4}$ in. (240 × 151.8 cm)

Signed and dated lower right: *JS Copley/1780*

Los Angeles County Museum of Art, Gift of Andrew Norman Foundation and Museum Acquisitions Fund, M.68.74

PROVENANCE: The sitter, Ayrshire, Scotland, to 1819; his daughter, Lady Jane Montgomerie (Mrs. Edward Archibald Hamilton), to 1860; Lt. Commander John Hamilton, R.N., by descent, to 1967; (sale, Christie's, London, July 7, 1967, no. 109); (M. Knoedler & Co., New York, 1967–8); Los Angeles County Museum of Art, 1968.

SELECTED EXHIBITIONS: London 1780, no. 172, as *"Portrait of an Highland Officer;"* Washington 1968, p. 7; Oakland 1969; Los Angeles 1975, no. 116, pp. 215–6.

SELECTED REFERENCES: Bayley 1915, p. 179; Prown 1966, II, pp. 275–6, 276n., 282, 328, 387, 427; Simon 1987, pp. 68–9; Fort and Quick 1991.[1]

RELATED WORKS: Study, *ca.* 1779–80, black and white chalk on pink buff paper, 12 × 17 in. (30.5 × 43.1 cm), Bennett H. Stayman; Study, *ca.* 1779–80, black and white chalk on blue-gray paper, 12 × 23$\frac{3}{8}$ in. (30.5 × 59.3 cm), University of Virginia Art Museum, Charlottesville, Virginia.

NOTES

1. See full bibliographic citation in Fort and Quick 1991, pp. 97-8.
2. Hugh Montgomerie was the son of Alexander Montgomerie and Lilias, daughter of Sir Robert Montgomerie, 11th baronet of Skelmorlie. The family home, Coilsfield, was located about 90 miles southwest of Edinburgh in Ayrshire. Montgomerie was elected to Parliament in 1780, 1784, and 1796. In 1789, he was appointed Inspector of Military Roads, and in 1793, rose to the rank of Colonel. He succeeded to his title, as 12th Earl of Eglinton, in 1796, and, according to biographical sketches, refurbished the modern castellated family home (cited as the "Castle o' Montgomery" in the Scottish Robert Burns's poem *My Highland Lassie*) and made local improvements in agriculture and infrastructure. In 1806, he was made a peer of the realm under the title Baron Ardrossan of Ardrossan, and in 1812 received the Order of the Thistle. He married his cousin, Eleanora Hamilton, in 1772, had six children, and was succeeded by his grandson, Archibald William Montgomerie. According to Robert Burns, Montgomerie's public-speaking skills were not as great as his military accomplishments: "I ken if that your sword were wanted,/Ye'd lend a hand;/But when there's ought to say anent it,/Ye're at a stand." See Paul 1906, pp. 448–9, 460–3, and Stephen and Lee 1917–, XIII, pp. 54–5.

Shortly before Major Hugh Montgomerie was first elected to Parliament in 1780, Copley painted him in the role of an officer whose swagger matched the brio of the artist's brush.[2] Montgomerie possibly met Copley during the years 1779–80 when the artist made studies of English lords for his monumental contemporary history painting, *The Death of the Earl of Chatham* (fig. 18 on p. 39), which included a portrait in the background of Montgomerie's uncle Archibald, 11th Earl of Eglinton.

Montgomerie entered the army in 1756 and served in the 77th Regiment (Montgomerie's Highlanders) raised by his uncle Archibald during the French and Indian War (1754–63). The regiment saw action at Fort Ticonderoga, Fort Duquesne, War-Woman's Creek, Etchoé, and the West Indies, among other places, and it is a generic scene of combat against the Cherokee nation, possibly from the 77th's 1760 expedition to the southern colonies, that Copley represents in the background at lower left and right.[3] Copley accurately represents the sitter's full-dress uniform of Montgomerie's Highlanders, the same uniform as that worn by the Black Watch or 42nd Regiment, consisting of a red jacket, a waistcoat, pistol and dirk (knife), basket-hilted broadsword, animal-skin sporran (purse), and diced bonnet and hose.[4] The Black Watch tartan included an additional twelve feet of cloth wrapped around the body and attached at the left shoulder, a detail of the uniform of which Copley makes artistic use. The billowing movement of Montgomerie's drapery echoes the circular formation of storm clouds, shaping the dramatic background and helping to create an atmosphere of turbulent energy.

One of only two full-length portraits of military officers painted during Copley's career in England, *Major Hugh Montgomerie* fulfills the academic prescription popularized by Reynolds that lower genres of painting, such as portraiture, may be elevated by borrowing elements of history painting. Or, as Reynolds wrote, "the lower may be improved by borrowing from the grand."[5] This formula for historical portraiture in the grand manner included dramatic background elements intended to indicate the sitter's character and achievements, as well as poses that made reference to venerated art of the past. Here, the sitter's pose recalls the revered ancient sculpture of the *Apollo* Belvedere (Vatican Museums, Vatican City), which Allan Ramsay had similarly appropriated for his *ca.* 1747 portrait of *Norman, 22nd Chief of MacLeod* (Skye, Dunvegan Castle, Collection of MacLeod of MacLeod), from which, and in turn, Joshua Reynolds borrowed for his *ca.* 1753 portrait of *Commodore Augustus Keppel* (fig. 29 on p. 48).[6] All three portraits feature figures set against a dramatic sky as they boldly stride forward with an outstretched arm. A recent scholar has noted a closer similarity of the pose to ancient sculptures of Roman toga-clad magistrates in which the figure walks forward with an open hand, a gesture known as *adlocutio* (signifying greeting, clemency, or both).[7] This gesture asserted the public-spiritedness and civic duty of the sitter, a particularly meaningful reference for images of public servants. The pose also recalls sixteenth- and seventeenth-century Italian and Flemish portraits which feature similar hand gestures. Copley does not precisely replicate either ancient source but, rather, offers a variant of the pose.

In an earlier preparatory drawing, Copley positioned Montgomerie closer to the stance of the *Apollo* Belvedere, with an arm gesturing back into space, as if to display the background action.[8] In a subsequent drawing and the finished painting, Copley sprang the figure into action by depicting him with his left arm stretched in front of him.[9] Copley allows the pose to operate in both a narrative and symbolic sense. Officers typically did not engage in combat but rather pointed out targets and directed assaults, and so, in one sense, Copley demonstrates the sitter's duty of commanding his regiment with his outstretched arm. At the same time, the pose's allusion to historic models makes Montgomerie a British descendant of august figures of the antique world, a reference that would not have been lost on eighteenth-century viewers of Copley's paintings.

The background figures in combat increase the history-painting quotient of the picture in ways unprecedented in eighteenth-century British portraiture. Background views of marching soldiers were a common element of seventeenth-century French and English portraits of military officers, and the device had been adopted by colonial American artists, including Copley, who used it as early as 1768 in his portrait of *General Thomas Gage* (New Haven, Yale University Art Gallery).[10] Departing from those polite views of soldiering, Copley made combat visceral in *Major*

3. MacLean 1900, pp. 254, 265, 279, 284–7. See also Knox 1916/1968, I, pp. 163, 510; II, pp. 484, 520.

4. Adam 1970, p. 448. The bonnet was cocked over the right ear, over which feathers were attached, as noted in MacLean 1900, p. 255. Possibly for aesthetic reasons, Copley placed the feathers, a modern feature of Highlander dress, over the left ear.

5. Reynolds 1769–90/1959/1975, *Discourse IV* (10 December 1771), lines 460–1, p. 72. At this point, Reynolds appears to be emphasizing style rather than composition, although the concept is entirely consistent with his portrait practice. Copley's other full-length military portrait represents *Colonel William Fitch and his Sisters Sarah and Ann Fitch* (1800–1, National Gallery of Art, Washington, D.C.)

6. Reynolds probably knew the MacLeod portrait through Joseph Vaerhaecken's *ca.* 1747 drawing after Ramsay. See Smart 1992, p. 82. For additional information about the currency of antique sculpture and the *Apollo* Belvedere in 18th-century England, see Haskell and Penny 1981, pp. 148–50.

7. Solkin 1986, pp. 429.

8. See Prown 1966, II, fig. 390.

9. See Prown 1966, II, fig. 390a (University of Virginia Museum of Fine Arts, Charlottesville).

10. For example, John Smibert's portrait of *William Pepperrell*, 1746 (Essex Institute, Salem, Massachusetts) and Charles Willson Peale's *George Washington at Princeton*, 1779 (Pennsylvania Academy of Fine Arts, Philadelphia).

11. I thank Joe Fronek, John Twilley, and Shelley Svoboda, Department of Paintings Conservation, Los Angeles County Museum of Art, for generously sharing their expertise during a full technical study of the picture. Many accounts of the French and Indian War reflect an avid interest as well as revulsion toward war atrocities such as scalping. For example, one account that circulated described Scottish heads impaled on stakes wrapped with their kilts. See MacLean 1900, pp. 267–78.

12. Copley exhibited the portrait at the 1780 Royal Academy exhibition with the title, "*Portrait of an Highland Officer*". The critic remarked: "A fine whole length of Major Montgomery [*sic*], who signalized himself in the destruction of the Cherokee Settlements last war. He is dressed in his Highland dress, which is most accurately described. There is great animation and expression in the figures of the background, and the Officer is relieved by the burning of the town" (Artist 1780, no. 172, p. 26).

13. Henry Raeburn's copy dates 1821, and belongs to the Town Hall, Ayr, Ayrshire, Scotland; the date, dimensions, and location of Angelica Kauffmann's copy are unknown. The collection of the National Portrait Gallery of Scotland, Edinburgh, also includes an undated copy after the portrait by an unknown artist (87 × 56½ in., 220.9 × 143.5 cm). See Prown 1966, II, p. 427.

Hugh Montgomerie by pushing the action closer to the foreground, heightening the emotional effect by showing hand-to-hand combat, expressions of wide-eyed determination or fear, weapons such as raised tomahawks and levelled pistols, as well as fleeing and dying figures (see detail). An examination of the detail using infrared reflectography shows that Copley originally depicted the dying figure at left with his foreshortened head turned to the left. He ultimately changed the position of the head by tilting it back toward the viewer, a pose that heightens the gruesomeness of the event. This change reveals the extent to which Copley aimed to make the vignette dramatic, if not sensationalist. The detail is, however, consistent with contemporary accounts of violent combat during the French and Indian War, and in keeping with the eighteenth-century fascination with American Indians, whom many perceived were sometimes noble but always 'savage'.[11] The drama of the scene, which presages the expressive actions of *The Death of Major Peirson*, was not lost on contemporary viewers, one critic specifically noting the "great animation and expression of the background figures."[12]

Testimony to the painting's success and importance, both the Swiss Neoclassical artist Angelica Kauffmann and the Scottish portraitist Henry Raeburn made copies after Copley's painting.[13]

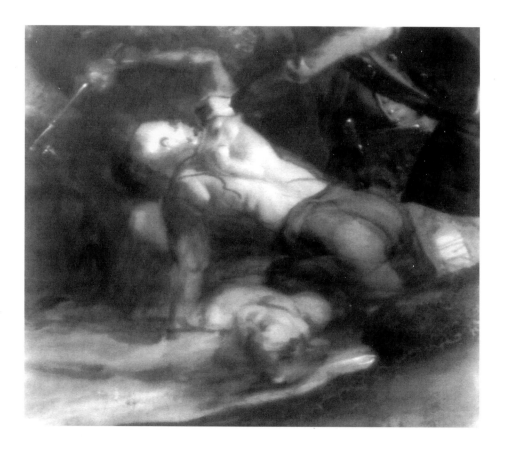

Infrared reflectograph showing detail of cat. 9, courtesy Los Angeles County Museum of Art

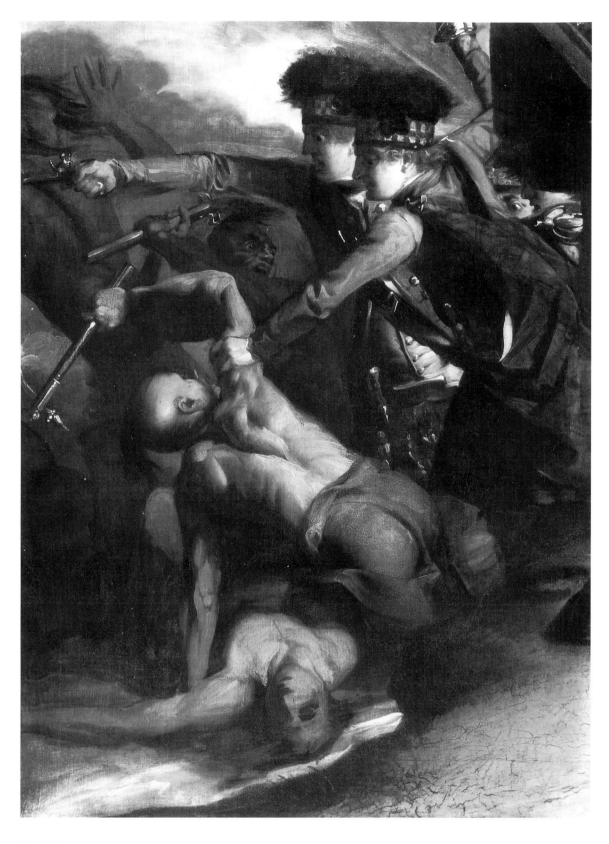

Detail of cat. 9

10.

Samuel Relating to Eli the Judgments of God upon Eli's House, 1780

Oil on canvas, 77½ × 59⅞ in. (197 × 152.5 cm)

Signed and dated lower left: *J S Copley Pinx./1780.*

Wadsworth Atheneum, Hartford, Connecticut, The Ella Gallup Sumner and Mary Catlin Sumner Collection, 1941.590

PROVENANCE: (Leger Galleries, London, 1936); Sidney Clark, London; G.M. Cherry, London; Wadsworth Atheneum, Hartford, Connecticut, The Ella Gallup Sumner and Mary Catlin Sumner Collection, 1941.

SELECTED EXHIBITIONS: Hartford 1952.

SELECTED REFERENCES: Perkins 1873, pp. 127, 133; Bayley 1915, pp. 35, 36, 213; Prown 1966, II, pp. 276 and n. 4, 382 n. 29, 388, 446, fig. 391.

NOTES
1. 1 Samuel 33:16-8.
2. *Hannah Presenting Samuel to Eli* (ca. 1778-80, His Grace the Duke of Rutland). See von Erffa and Staley 1986, no. 271, pp. 309-10, which notes West's other versions of the theme. West painted the theme again in 1800 in a version more closely allied with Copley's 1780 painting, even using Copley's ornate breastplate (a prop he used in several later paintings as well). Thomas Stothard also painted a *Samuel and Eli* (Getty Provenance Index), as did John Opie, who painted several images on the Samuel and Eli theme, one of which was reproduced in the Macklin Bible (1791–1800). See Prown 1966, II, p. 446, which states that *The Times* report on the Lord Lyndhurst sale mentioned that Copley's *Samuel and Eli* was "engraved by Valentine Green for Macklin's Bible." It was Opie's composition, not Copley's, that appeared in Macklin. See Boase 1963, p. 177 and Earland 1911, p. 332, and pl. facing p. 239.
3. See von Erffa and Staley 1986, no. 350–1, pp. 356–8, for a fuller discussion of the different versions of this painting, and the copy of St. Peter after West, ascribed to Copley.
4. *Letters of Copley and Pelham* 1914/1972, Copley to Henry Pelham, Rome, 14 March 1775, p. 299.
5. Prown 1966, II, pp. 392–3, transcribes nos. 131 and 132 of the Copley print sale at Sotheby's, 15 and 17 February 1820, respectively "The Cartoons, after Raphael by Dorigny – 7," and a small set by Tardieu. As only seven of the original ten cartoons for the Sistine Chapel survived, Copley must have owned a full set of engravings after them.
6. Reynolds 1769–90/1959/1975, *Discourse II* (11 December 1769), lines 83–6, p. 27.
7. *Letters of Copley and Pelham* 1914/1972, Copley to Henry Pelham, Rome, 14 March 1775, p. 302.
8. See Prown 1966, II, p. 387; see also here cat. 9. *The Morning Post*, undated, in *V & A Press Cuttings*, vol. 1, p. 191, is the source for the painting's

The third of only seven paintings of religious subjects Copley painted during his career in Italy and London, this work depicts the Old Testament story of the young boy Samuel, who relates to the priest Eli God's intention to punish Eli's family for the sins of his sons.[1] This event marks the first time Samuel heard the voice of God, a sign of his new role as a prophet and leader of Israel. Copley's dramatic rendering of this story manages to capture the seriousness of the event itself, and the tender and affectionate relationship between Eli and Samuel, even as Eli responds to the startling news of the tragic fate of his family and Samuel's blessedness.

Copley heightens the dramatic effect of the story by incorporating two enormous columns at right atop a pedestal sharply angled back into space. Light lends a narrative intensity by spotlighting faces, hands, and arms. Rich tones of gold in the altar cloth and vessels and Eli's elaborate breastplate are picked up in fringe and embroidered details which set off the blue and aubergine of Eli's vestments. The simplicity of Samuel's dress and the severity of the columns nearby provide counterpoints to the lavishness of Eli's material goods, which form a still life enlivened by mysterious rising smoke.

Benjamin West had interpreted an earlier moment in Samuel's story in *Hannah Presenting Samuel to Eli,* of *ca.* 1778-80, and his portrayal possibly inspired Copley to tackle a similar subject shortly thereafter.[2] Even so, Copley did not emulate its composition but, rather, that of West's *St. Peter Denying Christ* (1778–9, St. John's Church, Perlethorpe, Nottinghamshire; a variant version is illustrated in fig. 14 on p. 31), from which Copley borrowed West's head of St. Peter for Eli, repeating its precise turn, and its wizened face, bald pate, and grey beard.[3] Copley includes the dramatic lights and shadows and mysterious background of West's painting, but there the similarities end. Copley's composition, in fact, owes a greater debt to two of the modern giants in the eighteenth-century's pantheon of artistic heroes, Michelangelo and Raphael. The enormous seated figure of Eli, one foot resting on a footstool, the other pulled back to his side, recalls

Fig. 76 Nicolas Dorigny after Raphael
The Blinding of Elymas, ca. 1719

Engraving
The Royal Collection © Her Majesty Queen Elizabeth II

location during the exhibition. Joseph Baretti described the Lecture Room (also known as the Council Room) in 1781, mentioning that "the walls of it are hung round with *Frames*, that are in time to contain Pictures by the Academicians." He mentions only four portraits, two of which were Reynolds's King George III and Queen Charlotte. It may be that Copley's *Samuel and Eli* was intended as his diploma picture for the Royal Academy (as first suggested by Prown), and would have stayed there, had it not (presumably) found a buyer. Helen Valentine, Curator of Paintings and Drawings at the Royal Academy, mentions that it was not uncommon for artists recently elected to the Royal Academy to deposit a painting with the institution until their diploma painting was completed; this may also explain why the painting was present in the Lecture Room, although not a part of the Royal Academy exhibition that year. See Prown 1966, II, p. 276, and Baretti 1781, p. 25, also Hutchison 1968, p. 65.

9. *Morning Post*, undated, 1780, in *V & A Press Cuttings*, I, p. 191.

10. See Boase 1966. Copley also made a replica of the painting in 1810, subsequently destroyed, and exhibited it with the British Institution in 1811. See Prown 1966, II, pp. 446, 388.

Michelangelo's ample and athletic figures of the Prophets and Sibyls in the vaults of the Sistine Chapel, or his monumental marble sculpture of Moses (*ca.* 1513-15, S. Pietro in Vincoli, Rome). The dramatic gestures of Eli's arms and hands to indicate the condition of being startled may have had a source closer to home: Copley's own set of engravings by Nicolas Dorigny (1658-1746) after Raphael's cartoons for the Sistine Chapel tapestries, which Copley esteemed to be the master's "best compositions."[4] Raphael's cartoon of *The Blinding of Elymas* shows the Proconsul Paul similarly enthroned with hand gestures like Eli's, and shares the same gestural language of divinely provoked surprise (fig. 76).[5]

Reynolds encouraged Royal Academy students to make quotations from venerated art of the past. "Invention, strictly speaking," he wrote, "is little more than a new combination of those images which have been previously gathered and deposited in the memory; nothing can come of nothing."[6] Appropriating a model from the past, Copley reinvented his sources in order to create an image that, as he wrote to his half-brother Henry Pelham in 1775, was "no more than a remembrance of what we have seen."[7]

The 1780 Royal Academy exhibition was Copley's first exhibition since 1778 and the first exhibition to unveil the new headquarters of the Royal Academy at Somerset House. Although not officially a part of the exhibition (Copley submitted four others that year), *Samuel Relating to Eli the Judgments of God upon Eli's House* hung in the Lecture Room, surrounded by antique casts, historical paintings by West, allegorical pictures by Angelica Kauffmann, and Reynolds's grand portraits of the Royal Academy's patrons King George III and Queen Charlotte (figs. 51, 53 and 54 on p. 73).[8] The space made visible the aims of the Academy: to respect and emulate the masters of the past in order to create an English school of art, a goal fulfilled spectacularly in Copley's painting. Perhaps not all Royal Academy visitors absorbed the message inherent in the Academy's display – one critic took note of "that masterly picture of Eli and Samuel by Copley," but wryly castigated the Academy for exposing nude sculptures to female visitors.[9] A mark of the high esteem accorded this painting, it was engraved by Valentine Green, and published in September of 1780, and again in mezzotint form in 1805 by James Daniell during the revival of biblical illustration in English art.[10]

11.
Elkanah Watson (1758–1842), 1782

Oil on canvas, 58¹¹/₁₆ × 47⅝ in. (149 × 121 cm)

Inscribed on papers, lower left: *John Brown Esq / President* and *Mess[ieurs] Watson & Cossoul, Nant[e]s.*

The Art Museum, Princeton University, presented by the Estate of Josephine Thomson Swann, 1964–181

PROVENANCE: The sitter, Elkanah Watson; his daughter, Mary Lucia Watson (Mrs. Aaron Ward); her daughter, Josephine Ward (Mrs. John R. Thomson); presented to The Art Museum, Princeton University, by the Estate of Josephine Thomson Swann, 1964.

SELECTED EXHIBITIONS: New York, The American Academy of The Fine Arts, on loan 1822–9;[1] New-York Historical Society, *ca.* 1862;[2] New York 1936, no. 97; New York, Metropolitan Museum of Art, on deposit, 1963; Washington, New York, Boston 1965–6, no. 73; Montreal 1967, no. 121; Washington 1979, no. 17.

In 1781, Elkanah Watson commissioned Patience Wright, the celebrated wax portraitist and American spy abroad, to mold his portrait.[3] Just one year later, celebrating his rising fortune and having received an insurance claim of one hundred guineas (presumably upon goods he lost during the siege of Gibraltar), Watson "determined to devote the sum to a splendid portrait of myself" and engaged the painter Copley to produce a likeness with all the dash and glamour that the medium of wax precluded.[4] A young man of twenty-four when Copley painted his portrait, Watson was a merchant of recent success whose entrepreneurial spirit, enthusiasm, and devilish sense of humor characterized his years abroad during the Revolutionary War. He seemed to be especially fascinated by art that fooled the eye, inviting guests to visit his friend Benjamin Franklin, only to deceive them with the wax head of Franklin that Wright had supplied him, enlivened by puppeteering rigs Watson constructed to give movement to the clothed figure.[5]

When he agreed to a long-term loan of his portrait to the American Academy of Fine Arts, Watson specifically pointed out its lively and lifelike qualities and how the aid of a looking glass enhanced the effect. He wrote to Academy President John Trumbull that "it would be superfluous to add to you – the importance of placing it in a Strong Light, peculiarly important to give full effect to Copley's deep shades. In such a light and Viewed thro' a looking glass, it gives it perfect animation."[6] *Elkanah Watson*, indeed, displays the hallmark features of a Copley portrait, with its high-style props and costume combined with the artist's convincing realism. Fluted and plain columns, billowing green draperies, a sailing vessel in the background brightly lit by the morning sun, combined with bold colors and dramatic contrasts of light and shadow add visual swank to an otherwise ordinary portrait formula. Further, the artist's precise method of conveying the

SELECTED REFERENCES: Perkins 1873, pp. 21, 118–9; Bayley 1915, p. 254; Prown 1966, II, pp. 293–4, 300, 352, 434, fig. 419; Hollander 1978, p. 124.

RELATED WORKS: Study, 1782, pencil, black and white chalk on blue-gray paper, 12¼ × 19¾ in. (31.12 × 50.17 cm), The Metropolitan Museum of Art, New York, Harris Brisbane Dick Fund, 1960.

NOTES

1. See The Art Museum, Princeton University object files; letter from Carrie Rebora dated 19 September 1988, to Robert Guy, in which she reconstructs the transaction between Academy President John Trumbull and Elkanah Watson, who offered to lend the painting, as well as the waistcoat he wore for the portrait, to the Academy until his death. Trumbull's efforts to purchase the portrait for the Academy collection were unsuccessful.

2. See The Art Museum, Princeton University object files; letter from Stephen R. Edidin, New-York Historical Society, dated 3 February 1992, to John Wilmerding, in which he states that New-York Historical Society archives include a note from Aaron Ward to George H. Moore, the librarian of the Historical Society, requesting him to send the portrait to Pfeiffer and Co. for reframing. The picture may have been on deposit at the New-York Historical Society as early as June 1858. See also the letter from Howard Merrit dated 30 September 1966, in which he mentions notices of the painting at the Historical Society in the June 1858 and July 1859 issues of *The Home Journal*.

3. Watson 1856, pp. 118–9; Watson saw Wright often in Paris in 1781, and again in England between 1782 and 1784. See Sellers 1976, pp. 156, 167, 233, in which he mentions that Thomas Hutchinson's *Diary and Letters* (London, 1883–6, II, p. 367) notes Elisha Hutchinson's diary account of seeing the portrait head, probably in 1783. Sellers notes that the wax head was probably commissioned in 1781 in Paris, when Watson also commissioned a wax head of Franklin.

4. "Soon after my arrival in England, having won at the insurance office one hundred guineas, on the event of Lord Howe's relieving Gibraltar, and dining the same day with Copley, the distinguished painter, who was a Bostonian by birth, I determined to devote the sum to a splendid portrait of myself," in Watson 1856, p. 176.

5. See Watson 1856, pp. 122–3; Sellers 1976, pp. 184–7; Reynolds 1826, I, pp. 246–9, in which Watson is mistakenly identified as "Watkins," and the chronology of events is misstated.

6. The Art Museum, Princeton University object files; letter from Carrie Rebora to Betty Rosasco dated 9 November 1988 provides a transcript of a letter from Elkanah Watson to John Trumbull dated 7 September 1821 (New York Historical Society, American Academy of Fine Arts papers, vol. 1, item 60), regarding the loan of *Elkanah Watson* to the American Academy of Fine Arts.

conveying the sheen of satin, the texture of embroidery on a brilliant buff waistcoat, the crispness of a white jabot, the softness of the feather on a quill pen, and loose sheets of crumpled paper – including legible bits of writing – appealed to sitters like Watson who appreciated realistically rendered details that added to the portrait's illusionism. The fragments of writing and the background sailing vessel refer to Watson's recent maritime business success as well as to his patriotic spirit concerning the newly formed United States of America. .

Watson's commission occurred during the summer of 1782, when he left France for England to recover from influenza and to seek possible business opportunities there. Carrying introductions from Franklin (then American envoy to Paris) to the scientist Joseph Priestly and the philosopher Edmund Burke, Watson gained access to the intellectual elite of England. He may have met Copley through his friend the former President of the Continental Congress Henry Laurens, whom Copley had recently painted (fig. 31 on p. 49) and whose engraved portrait by Valentine Green after Copley had recently been published.[7] He may have also known the artist already since he shared distant relatives with Copley's wife, Susanna Farnum Clarke.[8] Later, he described the historic circumstances of the commission in detail: "The painting was finished in most admirable style, except the back-ground, which Copley and I designed to represent a ship, bearing to America the intelligence of the acknowledgment of independence, with a sun just rising upon the stripes of the Union, streaming from her gaff. All was complete save the flag, which Copley did not deem prudent to hoist under present circumstances, as his gallery is a constant resort of the royal family and the nobility. I dined with the artist, on the glorious 5th of December, 1782, after listening with him to the speech of the King, formally recognizing the United States of America as in the rank of nations. Previous to dining, and immediately after our return from the House of Lords, he invited me into his studio, and there with a bold hand, a master's touch, and I believe an American heart, attached to the ship the Stars and Stripes. This was, I imagine, the first American flag hoisted in old England."[9]

This anecdote concerning the ship may mark Watson's desire to allude to his participating role in the American Revolution as a courier of dispatches to Franklin. When he first traveled abroad in 1779, he was acting as agent to the successful merchant John Brown, whose family was a founder of Brown University, and with whom he had apprenticed at the age of fifteen when he moved from his native Plymouth, Massachusetts, to Providence, Rhode Island.[10] He traveled in France and England over the course of the war, delivering dispatches to Ben Franklin, and circulating in polite French circles. In 1779, he established a partnership in a mercantile house in Nantes called Watson and Cossoul even though he was, he wrote, "sustained by few advantages, either of connection or capital, and almost ignorant of the French language."[11] Within three years, at the time his portrait was painted, Watson's French-American enterprise was enormously successful, earning 40,000 guineas in profits that year, employing seven clerks, and owning six ships and brigs for their commercial ventures.[12] The letters in the portrait that include the names "John Brown, Esq." and "Watson and Cossoul" refer to his former business credentials as well as his recent success. During this time abroad Watson acquired more genteel habits, making a point of hiring a "respectable servant" who procured clothing for him more appropriate for a portly Continental gentleman than a provincial rustic, and Watson's apparel in the portrait vouches for his recent transformation.[13] The portrait, therefore, announces Watson's gentlemanly comportment and successful business venture in the context of new international relations symbolized by the rising sun on the American flag.

The optimism that informs the portrait was short-lived, however; Watson's business venture soured by 1783. His indefatigable spirit survived nonetheless. When he returned to the United States, settling in Albany, New York, he promoted the first canal system built in the United States, and, after retiring to Pittsfield, Massachusetts, he sponsored the country's first agricultural fair. Copley's portrait of Watson, one of the few ardent Whigs that Copley painted abroad, is testimony to the artist's effort to give the appearance of a neutral stance in politics by painting sitters from various backgrounds and point of views – "Political contests," he wrote, "being neighther pleasing to an artist or advantageous to the Art itself."[14]

Watson was proud of Copley's portrait, continuing with Trumbull that "as this painting can never be replaced and as Copley assured me it was his Chief d'ouvre [sic] – I request it may be a standing order to the Keeper in case of imminent danger by fire to make it a point to save this in preference to any other object." The portrait was exhibited at the American Academy of Fine Arts from 1822 until 1829, according to Rebora, who asserts the portrait represented Trumbull's desire to fill the Academy with works by masters rather than new artists. Rebora also supplied two transcripts of reviews to the Princeton object files, one of which noted: "He [Copley] is one of those artists who seem to have laboured con amore to polish a boot or button; but that he could do more, his pictures of Major Pierson [sic], at Jersey, and Lord Chatham, in the British Parliament, fully prove." (*The Daily Advertiser*, 'Brief Remarks on the Exhibition of the American Academy of Fine Arts,' 8 June 1824 [concluded], no. 94). See also Rebora 1990, pp. 364–5.

7. Henry Laurens's portrait belongs to the National Portrait Gallery, Washington, D.C. (Mellon Collection), although there is some question that

the portrait may, in fact, be a replica. Valentine Green made an engraving of the portrait that was published 1 October 1782 by J. Stockdale. It was intended to be a pendant to a published engraving of George Washington. See Prown 1966, II, p. 293, fig. 416. Watson mentioned that he originally planned to travel with Henry Laurens to England in 1782, but that he traveled alone instead (Watson 1856, pp. 138–9).

8. Susanna Farnum Clarke Copley's mother was a Winslow, a descendant of John Winslow (1597–1674), whose brother Edward Winslow (1585–1655) was the ancestor of Elkanah's mother Patience Marston (1733/4–1767). Edward and John Winslow traveled to the colonies on the *Mayflower* (Sherman 1978, pp. 3–11, 16–7, 40–1, 98–9; McGuyre and Wakefield 1988, pp. 1–17).

9. Watson 1856, p. 176. In a footnote, Elkanah Watson states that the painting was "pronounced by artists, second to no painting in America. ... Copley assured me that it would not, in his own language – 'ripen in forty years' – and now, after an interval of more than half a century, its colors appear clearer and more brilliant than on the day

they left the painter's palette" (1821). Copley's remark as told by Watson suggests Copley's fascination with pigments of a lasting quality, such as eluded Joshua Reynolds, known for his fugitive pigments.

10. Brown University was known as Rhode Island College until its name was changed in 1804. The Browns' merchant house was established by John's father, who imported English manufactured goods. They also distilled rum, made iron products, and engaged in the slave trade.

11. Watson 1856, p. 97.

12. *Ibid.*, p. 136.

13. *Ibid.* p. 89; Anne Hollander notes he is wearing fashionable masculine dress of the time, its construction omitting the darts and tucks that would have given a more shapely appearance. Potbellies were not concealed but revealed by this construction, flaring at the hip as in Copley's portrait of Watson (Hollander 1978, pp. 123–4).

14. *Letters of Copley and Pelham* 1914/1972, Copley to [Benjamin West], Boston, 24 November 1770, p. 98.

12.

Midshipman Augustus Brine (1769–1840), 1782

Oil on canvas, 49¹/₂ × 39¹/₂ in. (125.7 × 100.3 cm)

Signed and dated lower left.: *J.S. Copley Pin[xit]/1782*.

The Metropolitan Museum of Art, Bequest of Richard De Wolfe Brixey, 43.86.4

PROVENANCE: The sitter, Boldre House, Lymington, Hampshire; his son, the Rev. Augustus James Brine (assumed name of Knapton in 1860), Boldre House, Lymington, Hampshire, to 1879; his son, Augustus L.K. Knapton, Rope Hill, Lymington; Mrs. Knapton, Stanwell House, Lymington; to Lord Duveen, London; (sale, Christie's, London, 12 December 1924, no. 111); to Frank T. Sabin, London, 1924; (Duveen Brothers, London, 1924); to Richard De Wolfe Brixey, by 1930–43; Metropolitan Museum of Art, New York, Bequest of Richard De Wolfe Brixey, 1943.

SELECTED EXHIBITIONS: New York 1929; Chicago 1933, no. 413; Montreal 1950, no. 2; New York 1958–9; Washington, New York, Boston 1965–6, no. 75; Boston 1970, p. 103; Washington 1970–1, no. 12; New York 1975–7, no. 9.

Standing in three-quarter profile, his right hand resting on an out-thrust hip, his left hand gripping his tricorn, his arm outstretched and resting on a vaguely detailed small boat with ropes spilling over its sides, the thirteen-year-old subject of this portrait conveys enormous confidence. In contrast with Copley's portrait of *Admiral Clark Gayton* (cat. 8) of three years before, *Midshipman Augustus Brine* could not be called a portrait of a uniform, even though Copley has carefully observed the correct details of this midshipman's costume – white cuffs with a blue slash set with three buttons.[1] Indeed, Copley appears to have mastered Reynolds's advice concerning portrait painting, in which he recommended that specific details of the face and the setting be modified so as not to mar the "general effect" so esteemed in academic orthodoxy (see cat. 8). By the early 1780s, Copley proved that he understood and had mastered Reynolds's rules, for in *Midshipman Augustus Brine*, minutiae do not detract from nor destroy the effect of almost insolent swagger the sitter conveys and the stormy seascape echoes.[2]

Bright light illuminates the left side of the sitter; in the vague background, a cliff, rough seas rendered with loosely applied, thick strokes of paint, and a large, ominous anchor pitched toward the sitter allude to sublime effects that an eighteenth-century spectator would have understood as terror and awe. Copley thus composes the portrait so that this youth of thirteen, coolly staring at the viewer, indicates his early skill and natural promise in his elected profession, unperturbed by the forces of nature gathering behind him.

Eighteenth-century naval portraits often include background seascapes filled with sailing or burning ships, smooth or stormy seas as a visual reference to the sitter's profession or to a specific naval event.[3] Anchors, cannons, and ships had been standard props in naval portraiture since the seventeenth century, when Sir Anthony Van Dyck painted *Algernon Percy, 10th Earl of Northumberland* (*ca.* 1636, Duke of Northumberland, Alnwick Castle) with his right elbow perched on the fluke of an anchor.[4] Likewise, Sir Godfrey Kneller depicted *Prince George of Denmark* standing behind an anchor (1704, National Maritime Museum, Greenwich Hospital Collection), and Thomas Gainsborough had more recently used a carefully delineated anchor to form a sort of

SELECTED REFERENCES: Allen 1944, pp. 260–2; Metropolitan Museum of Art 1965, pp. 48–9; Prown 1966, II, pp. 294–5, 345, fig. 423; Frankenstein 1970, p. 150; Metropolitan Museum of Art 1994, pp. 105–6.

NOTES
1. The midshipman uniform was created in 1748, at the same time as those of other naval officers. I thank Mrs. P.M. Plackett Barber, Curator of Uniforms, Medals and Weapons at the National Maritime Museum, Greenwich, for providing commentary on Brine's uniform.
2. The term 'swagger,' used in the 18th century, although not to refer to a portrait type (as it currently is), is nonetheless descriptive, implying grandeur, insolence, and pretension. The art historian Andrew Wilton notes (London 1992–3, p. 17) that glamour and 'sex appeal' form a part of the term. It applies not only to *Midshipman Augustus Brine*, but also *Richard Heber* (cat. 13), *Mrs. Daniel Denison Rogers* (cat. 16), and *The Three Youngest Daughters of George III* (cat. 33).
3. The same year Copley painted Brine, George Romney depicted the fourteen-year-old *Midshipman Joseph Yorke* (private collection) posed with his right hand tucked in his shirt, and burning ships in the background, perhaps a reference to the Battle of the Saints in the West Indies. See Greenwich 1976, no. 565, p. 209.
4. London 1992–3, p. 142.
5. *Ibid.*, pp. 142–3, 112–3. Metropolitan Museum of Art 1994, pp. 104–5, notes that Gainsborough's *Augustus John, 3rd Earl of Bristol* was engraved in 1773. This entry for the painting also compares *Midshipman Augustus Brine* to Adriaen Hannemann's portrait of Henry, Duke of Gloucester (National Gallery of Art, Washington, D.C.), once thought to represent William of Orange, painted by Van Dyck.
6. Metropolitan Museum of Art 1994, p. 106, mentions that the art historian T.J. Fairbrother suggested that Copley here represents night-time. The indication of time of day could also increase the dramatic effect.
7. Richardson 1715/1725/1971, p. 166.
8. I am grateful to Dorothy Mahon, Paintings Conservation, and Carrie Rebora, American Art, at the Metropolitan Museum of Art, New York, for arranging to study the painting using infrared reflectography.
9. I thank Stuart Feld for bringing this painting to my attention.
10. Metropolitan Museum of Art 1994, pp. 105–6.
11. *Ibidem.* Brine served as Commander of the ship *Medway* during the War of 1812, and captured the American ship *Syren*.

ledge against which *Augustus John, 3rd Earl of Bristol* (1768, Ickworth, the Bristol Collection) could lean.[5] In these portraits, the anchor serves as an obvious symbol of the sitter's profession. In Copley's portrait of *Midshipman Augustus Brine*, however, the anchor's obscure detail and vague position, as it rushes in from the right and becomes almost indistinguishable from the cliff, heightens the dramatic effect of the painting.[6] Thus, such subtleties should not be viewed as a lack of clarity but as a controlled effort to conform to the "general effect" and to create high drama.

Such a development in the artist's style suggests his ability to tailor his brushwork according to the sensation he wished to provoke in the viewer. As the theorist Jonathan Richardson had once encouraged, "if the Character of the Picture is Greatness, Terrible, or Savage, as Battels, Robberies, Witchcrafts, Apparitions, or even the portraits of Men of such Characters there ought to be employ'd a Rough, Bold Pencil; and contrarily, if the Character is Grace, Beauty, Love, Innocence, &c. a Softer Pencil, and more finishing is proper."[7] Consistent with this view is the fluid handling of the portrait and even the pentimento visible to the left of Brine's coat, which suggests that Copley originally intended the coat to be shorter, with its tail shown flapping by a gust of wind.[8] Copley had earlier cultivated rough handling in a portrait probably exhibited to the Royal Academy of 1780 of a lieutenant in the Navy, John Loring (fig. 77), in which fluid applications of paint throughout convey a similar sense of naval swagger.[9]

Brine came from a service background; his father, James Brine served with the British Navy during the American Revolution, commanding the ship *Belliqueux* at Yorktown.[10] Eight years after Copley painted his portrait, Brine rose to the rank of lieutenant, and was eventually promoted to commander, post-captain (1802), and ultimately rear-admiral (1822), retiring shortly before his death in 1840.[11] The family estate in Lymington was not Brine's own but that of his wife, Maria Martha Dansey, whom he married in 1803. His name died in 1860, for in that year his son, by royal license, was granted his great grandfather's surname Knapton, of Lymington, Hampshire, twenty years after his father's death.

Fig. 77 John Singleton Copley
John Loring, ca. 1780

Oil on canvas, 29½ × 24 in. (74.9 × 61 cm)
Private collection, courtesy Hirschl and Adler Galleries, New York

13.
Richard Heber (1774–1833), 1782

Oil on canvas, 65¼ × 51³⁄₁₆ in. (165.8 × 130 cm)

Yale Center for British Art, Paul Mellon Collection, B1981.25.745

PROVENANCE: The sitter; his half-sister Mrs. Charles Cholmondeley (Mary Heber), Yeovil, Somerset; Cholmondeley family, by descent; (Thomas Agnew and Sons, London, 1979); to Paul Mellon Collection, 1979; Yale Center for British Art, Paul Mellon Collection, 1981.

SELECTED EXHIBITIONS: London 1865, no. 122; Leeds 1868, no. 3188; Wrexham 1876, no. 224.

SELECTED REFERENCES: Bayley 1915, pp. 140–1; Cholmondeley 1950; Prown 1966, II, pp. 294–5 and n., 422, fig. 424; Frankenstein 1970, p. 151.

RELATED WORKS: Study, 1782, black and white chalk on blue-gray paper, 11¼ × 14⅛ in. (28.6 × 35.9 cm), Winterthur Museum, Delaware.

NOTES
1. Prown 1966, II, p. 295; Copley to Reginald Heber, 7 September 1782. Prown also includes a letter from Copley to Heber dated earlier, 9 August 1782, in which he first mentions that the "Picture is intirely finished and framed," awaiting the framer to provide a crate.
2. Rose 1989, pp. 45–50.
3. *Journal des Luxus und der Moden*, 1787, in the print collection of the Victoria and Albert Museum, quoted in Rose 1989, p. 50.
4. For the evolution in child-rearing philosophies, see Locke 1693/1913 and Rousseau 1762/1979. See also cat. 1, note 8.
5. Green 1988, *passim*. Heber is shown with the long cricket bat and double-stump wicket in use until the 1770s, when the straight blade bat and three-stump wicket used today was introduced.
6. See Johnson 1976, figs. 70, 72.
7. See Nicolson 1968, II, plates 279–80.
8. A preparatory drawing for the painting belongs to the Winterthur Museum, Wilmington, Delaware, and is illustrated in Prown 1966, II, fig. 425.
9. Information about the Heber family derives from Cholmondeley 1950.
10. Richard's half-siblings were Reginald (1783–1826), Thomas Cathbert (1785–1816), and Mary (1787–1846). Mary married Charles Cholmondeley, and the portrait descended in the Cholmondeley family.
11. Cholmondeley 1950, pp. 32, 52.
12. *Ibid.*, p. 59.

In September of 1782, Copley wrote Reverend Reginald Heber, Rector of Malpas in Cheshire, that his "... son's portrait goes off tomorrow morning in the Waggon for Whitchurch [near Malpas], where I hope it will arrive safe ..."[1] He was referring to this full-length portrait of Reginald Heber's son, Richard Heber, aged eight, posed against a verdant landscape punctuated by a flowing stream. Dressed in a white ruffled shirt, maroon silk sash, buttoned gold-colored breeches, and blue jacket tossed over his arm, young Heber averts his gaze from the viewer, as if glancing toward some unseen occurrence outside the picture plane. Holding a ball, he leans against a cricket bat, its curved edge pointing to a double-stump forked wicket at his feet. Areas of loose brushwork and exaggerated chiaroscuro highlight Heber's face and create abstract patterns on the sitter's brilliant white shirt and parts of his hands, thighs, and shins, adding a dash of glamour and verve to this young subject.

Richard Heber's activity and costume in the painting illustrate the 'natural' ideal for children's behavior and appearance that became voguish in the late eighteenth century. During the 1770s and 1780s, young boys wore their hair long and loose with their shirt collars open to the shoulder, abandoning the miniature version of adult clothing (sometimes including a powdered wig) worn in earlier decades.[2] Such reforms in children's clothing came to be associated with England, one German fashion magazine in 1787 terming the style "comfortable and functional clothing for children based on the theories of John Locke."[3] John Locke was credited with revolutionizing the eighteenth-century family through his encouragement of more affectionate means of disciplining children and, parallel with the philosophy of Jean-Jacques Rousseau, of outdoor play as a means of promoting health and vigor.[4] That Richard Heber appears in this functional clothing at play out-of-doors indicates that he is among the fashionably 'natural' children of upper-class England.

Eighteenth-century portraits of children often include props associated with the playing of cricket. The game's popularity increased exponentially during this period.[5] As early as 1766, Francis Cotes included a cricket bat in his portrait of Charles Collyer and, three years later, exhibited at the Royal Academy his portrait of Lewis Cage, which featured a full-length sitter, looking slightly disheveled, holding a bat and standing beside a wicket.[6] Joseph Wright of Derby, the artist whose mid-century portraits were confused with Copley's own, included the cricket portrait device in his *ca.* 1789–90 portrait of the Thornhill children, as well as his portrait of the Wood children of the same date, which shows a young girl throwing the ball in the air, a reminder that both sexes played the sport.[7]

Neither Cotes nor Wright of Derby in their portraits conveyed the degree of elegance that Copley establishes for young Heber through his studied nonchalant pose and sparkling clothes. Copley suggests the actual activity of the sport by showing Heber with his jacket slung over his arm, as if picking it up after playing (a change he made from a preparatory drawing that shows Heber fully dressed), and by the detail of the wicket with its bail dislodged, one of the goals of the game.[8] By including this subtle detail, not found in other eighteenth-century portraits of cricket players, Copley asserts the sitter's athletic prowess at the same time as he claims his nonchalance.

The circumstances for the portrait's commission are unknown, and no evidence in the Heber family letters suggests any special relationship between cricket, the Hebers, or the Heber property in Shropshire.[9] The summer Copley painted this portrait, Richard's father had remarried; his first wife Mary Baylie had died three and a half weeks after Richard was born, leaving the widower with an infant son. In July of 1782, Reginald married Mary Allanson, with whom he had two sons and a daughter.[10]

The Heber family letters, in fact, disclose young Richard's early taste for book collecting rather than cricket. In 1786, Heber's father wrote, "Tell Dicky I will have no more debts contracted with book-sellers or bookbinders," an indication of a life-long passion for book collecting that his father had once said should be "nipt in the bud."[11] In addition to books, Heber aspired to study music, until his father persuaded him to wait until he attended university where he could play the "German flute or forte piano, which are the fittest instruments for a gentleman ...".[12] According to the bills of which his father complained when Richard attended his *alma mater*, Brasenose College at Oxford University, Heber studied music, bought wine, and continued to

13. I thank Kimberly A. Kneeland at the Yale Center for British Art for supplying file information from Thomas Agnew and Sons, Ltd., 1979.

collect books. Following a period of travel abroad after graduation, including visits to fashionable salons such as Mme Récamier's in Paris, Richard settled on the family estates he inherited at his father's death in 1803. He befriended the novelist Sir Walter Scott, and served in the House of Commons, from which he resigned in 1826, whereupon he moved to the Continent to be closer to the foreign book market. At his death, his library had grown to 200,000 volumes. He is credited with the saying: "No gentleman can be without three copies of a book: one for show, one for use and one for borrowers."[13]

14.
The Tribute Money, 1782

Oil on canvas, 50¹/₂ × 60¹/₂ in. (128.3 × 153.7 cm)

Royal Academy of Art, London

PROVENANCE: Painted for the Royal Academy, London, 1782.

SELECTED EXHIBITIONS: London 1817, no. 42; Manchester 1857, no. 108; Leeds 1868, no. 1267; Washington, New York, Boston 1965–6, no. 74.

SELECTED REFERENCES: Perkins 1873, p. 127; Prown 1966, II, pp. 293–4, 313, 340, 350–1, 457–8, fig. 420; Frankenstein 1970, p. 140; London 1991, p. 43.

RELATED WORKS: Study, 1782, black and white chalk on blue-gray paper, 12¹/₄ × 19³/₄ in. (31.1 × 50.2 cm), The Metropolitan Museum of Art, New York, Harris Brisbane Dick Fund, 1960.

NOTES
1. Assembly Minutes and Council Minutes of the Royal Academy, cited in Prown 1966, II, pp. 293–4.
2. *Ear-Wig* 1781, p. 4.
3. Prown 1966, II, p. 294 and n. 7. Prown suggests that Copley may have chosen a biblical subject based on the Royal Society of Arts' suggestion that a prize would be awarded for a religious painting suitable for a church, although the competition did not occur and Copley's painting did not conform in all respects to their original specification. Notable examples of paintings of this biblical story include Masaccio's *The Tribute Money* (ca. 1423–8, Brancacci Chapel, S. Maria del Carmine, Florence) and Rembrandt's two paintings of *The Tribute Money* (1629, National Gallery of Canada, Ottawa, and 1655, Viscount Allendale, Bywell, Northumberland).
4. Prown 1966, II, p. 294, in which he also suggests Guercino's *The Betrayal* (Fitzwilliam Museum, Cambridge) as a prototype for *The Tribute Money*.
5. Copley to Pelham, 14 March 1775, Rome, in

Following his grand success in the 1778 Royal Academy exhibition, Copley was elected to its membership in February of 1779. He neglected, however, to fulfill one condition of membership – to present his 'diploma piece' to the Royal Academy's collection in a timely manner – possibly because of the extraordinary amount of time *The Death of the Earl of Chatham* had taken to complete (fig. 18 on p. 39). As other artists were likewise late in submitting their works to the Academy, its General Assembly voted in 1782 to dismiss potential members if their diploma works were not presented within a year after the invitation to join the august group; Copley consequently presented *The Tribute Money* to the Academy as a "Specimen of his Abilities" in December 1782, and in February 1783 he formally became an academician.[1] Valentine Green engraved and published the painting only five months later, a mark of the esteem held for the artist as well as the commercial possibilities of the painting. Dilatory artists in the Academy were not unusual, but in view of his controversial exhibition of *The Death of the Earl of Chatham* outside the Academy in 1781, Copley could hardly afford to neglect the institution that had given him such early success. Suggesting the hotly contested subject of the exhibiting artist outside the Academy, one satirical reviewer of the 1781 exhibition wrote: "Hey-day! How comes it that we see here no pictures of Loutherbourg, Copley or Humphreys. ... Copley was made an Academician; and, as soon as he had reaped such advantageous honors, he no longer chose to contribute to their show; but he deserted his standard, and levies contributions on the public, for the first work he produced of any real consequence – and the partial, illiberal conduct of the Academicians, by exciting parties and factions, has disgusted and driven from them ... artists of established, and others of promising genius."[2] Copley could blame Academy factionalism for his reluctance to participate fully, but doing so would risk his rapidly established reputation. The Academy for its part could not exclude an artist whose name might add so much luster to its roll. Both artist and institution probably uttered a collective sigh of relief when Copley at last fulfilled his obligation.

The event pictured is described in the New Testament account of St. Matthew 22:15–22 (also in St. Mark 12:13–7, and St. Luke 20:20–6). As the Gospel authors relate, Jews in Jerusalem were required to pay taxes to Rome; the Pharisees, attempting to entrap Jesus, asked him to render an opinion about whether taxation was lawful. Pointing to the head of Caesar on a coin, he replied, "Render therefore unto Caesar the things which are Caesar's; and unto God the things that are God's." Recognizing the double sense of the word 'tribute' as meaning both a tax and honor or praise, Prown has suggested that *The Tribute Money* offered a nod of approval to the Academy itself, which Copley needed to appease. Copley likely recognized the double meaning of the word also and tweaked authority by thus alluding to the diploma painting as a 'tax' an artist was obliged to pay to maintain membership. This may help to explain Copley's choice of a subject relatively obscure in the history of Western art.[3] As Prown observed, Copley's composition appears to be based on an engraving after Rubens's *Christ Giving the Keys to St. Peter*, which features Christ, one arm upraised, surrounded by several bearded apostles including a stooping St. Peter.[4] Appropriately for a diploma painting for the Royal Academy, Copley's *The Tribute Money* conveys an 'Old Master' sensibility, recalling the cropped compositions, saturated colors,

Letters of Copley and Pelham 1914/1972, p. 302.

6. Masaccio's *The Tribute Money*, likewise, has been interpreted as a religious painting with contemporary overtones – the issue of tax reform in Florence during the 16th century. The emergence of the taxation theme in 16th-century art has also been interpreted within the context of the contemporaneous political struggle between the Holy Roman Emperor Charles V and the pope. See Roberts 1993, especially p. 60, for a succinct summary of the various interpretations; also Baldini and Casazza 1992, pp. 39–45. I have not discovered which, if any, of these sorts of interpretations could have been accessible to 18th-century audiences. I thank A. Thereza Crowe for her insightful comments about this painting and its possible political implications.

7. Von Erffa and Staley 1986, no. 330, pp. 343–4, discusses *Christ Blessing Little Children* which, like Reynolds's *Self-Portrait*, was painted for the Royal Academy in honor of its new headquarters. Von Erffa and Staley mention that Royal Academy exhibition catalogues, beginning in 1811, cite the permanent paintings in the lecture room, with Matthew 22:21 cited next to West's painting. The catalogue writers must have confused the chapter and verse appropriate to Copley's *The Tribute Money* with West's painting in the same room.

and chiaroscuro effects of seventeenth-century Italian and Flemish paintings. Copley highlights the importance of Christ by placing him in full light in front of a vague architectural background, depicting him in vivid red and blue, positioning his body frontally to give the figure fuller volume, and turning his head in profile to look downward at his followers as if to convey his role as wise teacher. The four figures at left illustrate the artist's understanding of aesthetic rules concerning multi-figure subjects. The painter should, he wrote to his half-brother Henry Pelham, "give Carracter to the figures that compose the Picture. this consists chiefly in making that variety which we find in the life; and making the heads to think agreable to the subject that is before them and ingages their attention and agreable to their attitudes."[5] Each of the four figures at left suggest such variety. His bald pate dramatically lit, St. Peter wrinkles his forehead, alert to Christ's response as he stoops and reaches toward Christ with the coin, his neck displaying the sinewy features of the strained posture. Other followers respond in various ways: crouching to examine the coin, lifting the hand to the chin in a gesture of thought, craning the neck to see above the crowd. The elegantly turbaned Matthew gazes directly at Christ with an expression of respect.

Copley's selection of the theme of taxation appears provocative at most, and odd at the very least, for an artist born in the colonies where rebellion over this very issue delivered a critical blow to England's rising empire.[6] No known evidence survives that suggests Copley's colleagues recognized his chosen subject matter as a reference to the artist's colonial background or his desire to impose a contemporary political interpretation on a religious subject. He had already publicly engaged the issue of taxation in 1781 with his *The Death of the Earl of Chatham*, but there, much of the controversy arose from the manner in which Copley presented the painting to the public, or the manner in which he arranged the various lords. If any academician did view Copley's painting as politically volatile, and if any detected a note of impropriety in the subject, it must have dissipated sometime before 1793, when Henry Singleton painted *The Royal Academicians Gathered in their Council Room, 1793, to Judge the Work of the Students* (fig. 53 on p. 73). This painting, engraved by C. Bestland and published in 1802, shows *The Tribute Money* in an honored position in the Lecture Room. It is displayed at upper right, beside Reynolds's *Self-Portrait* (in the guise of Rembrandt with his hand resting on a bust of Michelangelo), and in the company of Benjamin West's *Christ Blessing Little Children* (fig. 15 on p. 33), Reynolds's portraits of King George III and Queen Charlotte (figs. 53 and 54), and the exquisite flower still lifes of Mary Moser, a founding member of the Academy.[7] In this engraving, Copley himself occupies a privileged position; he is the standing dark-suited figure on the front row carrying a walking stick.

15.

Charles Callis Western (1767–1844) and his Brother Shirley Western (1769–1824), 1783

Oil on canvas, 49 × 61 in. (124.5 × 154.9 cm)

Henry E. Huntington Library and Art Gallery, 14.7

PROVENANCE: Mrs. Charles Western of Rivenhall (Frances Shirley); Lord Western, the sitter; his cousin, Sir Thomas Burch Western, Bart. (d. 1873), Felix Hall, Kelvedon, Essex; (sale of the property of Sir Thomas Charles Callis Western, Bart., Christie's, London, 13 June 1913, no. 102); (Scott and Fowles, New York); to Mr. and Mrs. Henry E. Huntington, 1914.

SELECTED EXHIBITIONS: London, 1783, no. 227; London 1868, no. 880.

SELECTED REFERENCES: Perkins 1873, p. 128; Bayley 1915, pp. 31, 262 [as two pictures]; Baker 1936, pp. 35–6; Whitley 1928/1968, II, p. 376; Prown 1966, II, pp. 297, 299, 387, fig. 436.

NOTES

1. I thank my colleague, Elizabeth Ann Coleman, Curator of Textiles and Costume at the Museum of Fine Arts, Houston, for her valuable comments regarding features of dress.
2. In 18th-century England, drawing was taught to both young men and women privately or in school, and numbered among the 'polite accomplishments' children were expected to achieve. See Sloan 1982, pp. 217–40.
3. For example, John H. Mortimer's painting, *Joseph Wilton, R.A., and John H. Mortimer, A.R.A.* (ca. 1765, Royal Academy of Art). shows Mortimer seated with a portfolio of drawings in his lap; the sketch he is working on is of an antique cast.
4. See 'The State and Estate of Nature' and 'The Picturesque Decade' in Bermingham 1986, pp. 9–83.

This unusual portrait of the Western brothers prefigures the youthful exuberance and high spirits of *The Three Youngest Daughters of George III* (cat. 33), as well as recalling the swagger of Copley's previous portraits of the young sitters *Midshipman Augustus Brine* (cat. 12) and *Richard Heber* (cat. 13). In the portrait of Brine, Copley had given the sitter a serious demeanor far beyond his thirteen years. The Westerns, by contrast, appear with carefree attitudes associated with youth; they enjoy the country pleasures of the landed gentry, looking over a view that suggests or represents the property that the eldest Western would one day inherit and manage.

Copley poses two youthful figures and a leaping dog before a balustrade, and frames them with a stone building on the right, and, on the left, trees swaying on a hill in the distant background. At the center, the fourteen-year-old Shirley Western wears a large black hat and, befitting his age, a crisp white shirt with its collars open to the shoulder, striped vest, and double-breasted brown waistcoat (see cat. 13). He wears a fob-chain suspended from his breeches with a ribbon, which possibly holds a seal and watch key.[1] His face flushed by exercise, and his hair blown by the wind, the boy catches the attention of his brother and dog by gesturing toward some unseen prospect outside the composition, his outstretched arm and pointing finger set against the sky and given visual weight by subtle highlights. His older brother Charles, at right, sits in front of the balustrade, wearing a white jabot, yellow double-breasted vest, and blue coat, his loose hair falling about his shoulders and blown by the wind. To his left, a black hat is perched upon the balustrade and an elephant-headed walking stick leans against it. With his left hand, he clutches a drawing portfolio, its marbled paper cover described by loose scribbles of paint. With his right, he holds a chalk-holder, red and black chalk carefully rendered on either end of the implement. Illuminated by bright light, a sheet of paper showing Charles's energetic landscape sketch in red chalk flaps in the wind, a vivid sign of Western's genteel status and proper upbringing.[2]

In its attention to detail, this painting recalls *Mrs. and Mrs. Ralph Izard* (fig. 68 on p. 95), *The Copley Family* (cat.1), and *Sir William Pepperrell and His Family* (cat. 3). As in those portraits, the accessory elements point to larger, symbolic concerns. The fanciful walking stick and hats call attention to the Westerns' outdoor activity, as if the brothers had been strolling their property in the county of Essex. Charles sketches the landscape vista until Shirley interrupts, pointing to something that appears over the spectator's left shoulder. Here, as in Copley's *Watson and the Shark* (cat. 4) and *The Death of Major Peirson* (cat. 18), the artist elicits viewers' participation, inviting them into this domestic tableau by making them wonder what Shirley wants his brother to see. Taking into account the freely handled landscape sketch in Charles's lap – its large and small windblown trees perhaps the very ones the viewer sees in the background at left – one may imagine that Shirley points out to Charles a more picturesque prospect to sketch, one that is behind rather than in front of the viewer. This, of course, is conjecture, but it is an indication of the consistency of Copley's strategy in contemporary history painting and portraiture to heighten the dramatic impact of the scene by eclipsing the space between sitter and spectator, and embracing the space occupied by his audience.

Sketches and sketching tools were not uncommon props in eighteenth-century portraiture, whether in portraits of women (as in cat. 7) or of young artists showing their skill and progress in drawing. The inclusion of a freely sketched landscape, however, is unusual if not unprecedented in English eighteenth-century portraiture, as it was more usual for the artist – amateur or otherwise – to be seen drawing an antique cast, the first step in the academic training system.[3] The fact that Copley pictures Charles sketching a landscape suggests that he and, by extension, the sitter were culturally *au courant*: Western's sketch testifies to the growing idealization of the English landscape at the very moment in which it was radically changing as a result of enclosure and other agricultural improvements designed to increase productivity.[4] A new-found spiritual reverence for the English countryside accompanied its scientific improvement, as landscape became the locus of nationalist and aesthetic values.

Beginning in the latter decades of the eighteenth century, aestheticians such as Edmund Burke, William Gilpin, Uvedale Price, and Richard Payne Knight classified the English countryside by such categories as the Sublime, the Beautiful, and the Picturesque: rough and varied terrain became associated with the sublime, cultivated rolling hillsides were beautiful, and

5. Gilpin 1809, p. 87.

6. *Ibid.*, p. 89. In 1788, Joshua Reynolds, delivering his yearly discourse, discussed this feature of Gainsborough's working method. Since he was not formally trained and studied nature directly, Reynolds suggests, his style "did not require that he should go out of his own country for the objects of his study; for they were everywhere about him; he found them in the streets, and in the fields" (Reynolds 1769–90/1959/1975, *Discourse XIV* (10 December 1788), lines 191–4, pp. 252–3).

7. Baker 1936, pp. 35–6.

8. *The Times* (London), 7 January 1833, mentions that "Mr. Western, the late member for Essex, is to be immediately raised to the peerage. We hail this as an additional proof of the cordial good wishes of His Majesty to all those who, like Mr. Western, have been the stanch [*sic*] advocates of the principles and opinions of Ministers. The Tories of Essex will perceive in this mark of His Majesty's favour to Mr. Western, that their attachment to the inveterate foes of the Government finds no sympathy in the highest quarter of the State."

the quality of the landscape as something worthy of being a picture was picturesque. If Copley invokes the sublime in *Midshipman Augustus Brine*, it is the beautiful and the picturesque that he engages in the portrait of the Westerns, with its background of a cleared, rolling hillside gracefully combined with a distant forest. These are the very features, in fact, that Reverend William Gilpin, the enormously popular guidebook writer and proponent of the Picturesque, celebrated in his tour of the county of Essex, the home of the Westerns. Gilpin made reference to the trees of Essex, remarking on the "noble oaks, and elms; many of which, even single, had dignity enough to grace a scene."[5] After passing through Kelvedon, a "sweet village," in which the Westerns lived, he remarked on the "noble continuation of woods."[6] Copley, and by extension the Westerns, then, appear to be investing the English landscape with the very values Gilpin and others were promoting: the cultivated landscape as a sign of order, stability, and balance.

Copley's portrait of the Westerns offers a counterpoint to *Sir William Pepperrell and his Family* (cat. 3), in which the artist presents a scene of domestic bliss that was not to be. In the case of the Westerns, Charles eventually became the owner of the land he ostensibly pictured as a youth. He bought Felix (or Filiols) Hall in 1793, and inherited the family estate, Rivenhall, in Kelvedon.[7] He served as a Member of Parliament for Maldon and for Essex, and was known for taking up the cause of agricultural interests. He was created a baron in 1833, but died unmarried eleven years later, and the peerage became extinct.[8] His brother Shirley entered the clergy, serving as rector of Hemingstone, Suffolk, and of Rivenhall.

16.

Mrs. Daniel Denison Rogers (Abigail Bromfield, 1753–1791), ca. 1784

Oil on canvas, 50 × 40 in. (127 × 101.6 cm)

Fogg Art Museum, Harvard University Art Museums, Gift of Paul C. Cabot, Treasurer of Harvard University, 1948–1965, and Mrs. Cabot, 1977.179

PROVENANCE: The sitter; her son, Henry B. Rogers; descended in the family to Mrs. W.C. Cabot (1915); Miss A.P. Rogers; Henry B. Cabot; Mrs. Henry B. Cabot; Paul Codman Cabot; Fogg Art Museum, Harvard University Art Museums, Gift of Paul C. Cabot, Treasurer of Harvard University, 1948–1965, and Mrs. Cabot, 1977.

SELECTED EXHIBITIONS: Boston 1828, no. 9; Boston 1938, pp. 12, 27, cat. no. 66; Washington, New York, Boston 1965–6, no. 81; Boston 1976, no. 7.

SELECTED REFERENCES: Perkins 1873, pp. 99–100; Bayley 1915, p. 209; Bolton and Binsse 1930, p. 118; Prown 1966, II, pp. 296, 430, fig. 428; Shank 1984, pp. 141–3.

NOTES
1. Roberts 1985, I, p. 332.
2. *Samuel Fayerweather* (*ca.* 1758–60, Yale University Art Gallery) and *Hannah Fayerweather Winthrop* (1773, Metropolitan Museum of Art).
3. Private collection. The Rogers married in October 1781. See McClenen 1977, p. 319.
4. Copley often depicted women sitters with one hand gloved, the other bare. Here the artist emphasizes the moment of pulling or taking it off; a difference which gives the portrait a sense of immediacy and vitality.
5. For example, Thomas Gainsborough's *Giovanna Bacelli* (1782, Tate Gallery, London), and Joshua Reynolds's *Mrs. Musters as Hebe* (1785, The Iveagh Bequest, Kenwood, London) and *Lady Jane Halliday* (1779, National Trust, Waddesdon Manor). See London 1992–3, p. 134.
6. Private collection. See Prown 1966, II, p. 430.

In the fall of 1791, a Boston newspaper reported the death of "Mrs. Abigail Rogers, the amiable consort of Mr. D.D. Rogers, merchant, and daughter of Henry Bromfield, Esq. The exemplary patience, resignation and cheerfulness with which she supported a long and very painful illness, demonstrate the importance even to the present life, of that exalted piety, which is founded in a firm belief in the truths of Christianity."[1] Little is known about Abigail Rogers but, considering two other references to her that also refer to her ill health, it appears that this portrait maintained a fiction of health and exuberance in the face of her pain and suffering.

The portrait may in fact have been occasioned by the sitter's ill health. In October 1784, Susanna Copley wrote to Daniel Denison Rogers in London that his wife Abigail was staying with the Copleys at Windsor while she recovered from an illness; at the time, Copley was presumably working on *The Three Youngest Daughters of George III* (cat. 33). The similar painterly qualities of Abigail's portrait and of that of the three princesses suggests that Windsor, with its collection of lush portraits by Sir Anthony Van Dyck (1599–1641), Sir Peter Lely (1618–1680), and Sir Godfrey Kneller (1646 or 1649–1723), provided Copley with a heady atmosphere for experimenting with new color combinations, bravura brushwork, and unusual compositional formats.

Abigail Bromfield Rogers was not the first member of her extended family whom Copley painted. She was Copley's step-niece through his sister-in-law Hannah Clarke, the second wife of Henry Bromfield. Abigail was a daughter from Bromfield's earlier marriage to Margaret Fayerweather (1732–1762), whose nephew, Samuel Fayerweather, and niece, Hannah Fayerweather Winthrop (Abigail's older cousins), were painted by Copley in the late 1750s and early 1770s.[2] After Abigail's mother's death by smallpox at age thirty, her father almost immediately married Hannah Clarke, who helped to raise the four Bromfield children from the earlier marriage. In 1781, Abigail married the Bostonian Daniel Denison Rogers in Stow, Massachusetts; Copley had painted the groom's father, the merchant Daniel Rogers, in 1767.[3]

Around the age of thirty-one when Copley painted her, Abigail appears to be a fashionable young matron whose large rolled and powdered curls fall underneath an enormous lace-trimmed and ostrich-plumed silk hat that almost overwhelms her delicate, pale face. Standing in profile, her face inclined toward the viewer, she toys with her gloves, a beguiling gesture Copley had not used since his portrait of *Mrs. Nathaniel Allen* (*ca.* 1763, Minneapolis Institute of Arts).[4] Swirls of diaphanous drapery blend almost imperceptibly with the dramatic clouds of white, blue, pink, yellow, and red that comprise the background. If the top two-thirds of the portrait have a painterly sweep and grandeur, the bottom third appears somewhat hard, not unlike the vibrant folds of silk painted by the colonial painters John Wollaston, Joseph Blackburn, and even Copley at an earlier stage in his career, as in his famous portrait of *Mary and Elizabeth Royall* (*ca.* 1758, Museum of Fine Arts, Boston). This almost nostalgic feature adds a note of tension to the composition, the metallic quality of the lower register competing with the gossamer qualities of the upper, as if to fuse the hard-edged realism of Copley's colonial career with the painterliness of his London style.

Copley's portrait of Abigail Bromfield Rogers is contemporary with Thomas Gainsborough's pursuit of painterly effects through skittering brushwork, and with Joshua Reynolds's depiction of women in windblown environments which added to the ethereal quality of his paintings.[5] Here, Copley makes high fashion compete with the breezy effects of almost gale force winds, a combination that, like the hard contrasts between opaque and transparent fabrics, appears improbable. These tensions subvert the social portrait type that aimed to make the sitter look 'naturally' genteel. Nonetheless, *Mrs. Daniel Denison Rogers* testifies to Copley's technical virtuosity, experimental attitude, and desire to try his hand at high-fashion portraiture. The family must have been pleased with the results, for Copley produced a miniature based on the portrait at the same time.[6]

17.
John Singleton Copley, 1780–84

Oil on canvas, 17³/₄ in. diam. (45.1 cm)

National Portrait Gallery, Smithsonian Institution, Washington, D.C., Gift of the Morris and Gwendolyn Cafritz Foundation with matching funds from the Smithsonian Institution, NPG.77.22

PROVENANCE: The artist, London, to 1815; his son John Singleton Copley, Jr., Lord Lyndhurst (1772–1863), London; (probably Lyndhurst sale, Christie's, London, 5 March 1864, no. 75); to Mrs. Caspar C. Crowninshield, the artist's great grand-daughter, 1873–82; to Mrs. Gardiner Green Hammond (Esther Fiske), 1915–38; private collection, 1938–77; to National Portrait Gallery, purchased in 1977, gift of the Morris and Gwendolyn Cafritz Foundation with matching funds from the Smithsonian Institution, Washington, D.C., 1977.

SELECTED EXHIBITIONS: New York 1937; Boston 1938, p. 21, no. 19; Washington, New York, Boston 1965–6, pp. 89, 139, no. 64.

SELECTED REFERENCES: Perkins 1873, pp 47, 132; Bayley 1915, p. 84; Bolton and Binsse 1930, p. 116; Christman 1978, pp. 23–8.

NOTES
1. In 1769, the year of his marriage to Susanna Farnum Clarke, Copley made pastels of his wife and himself (Winterthur Museum and Gardens, Wilmington, Delaware). That same year he made a self-portrait miniature, presumably for his wife (Gloria Manney Collection). See Prown 1966, II, pp. 66, 212, figs. 226–7, 250.
2. Cunningham 1831/1837/1868, p. 144. Carter's account reflects a bit of pique that Copley himself felt no less. Regarding Carter, Copley described him as "a sort of snail which crawled over a man in his sleep, and left its slime and no more."
3. See *Letters of Copley and Pelham* 1914/1972, Copley to Pelham, 3 August 1771, New York, pp. 131, 136, *passim*. See also Poesch 1988.
4. Public Record Office, London, C.O.5/39, 191, 10 June 1774, 'Memorandum of sundries to be purchased by Mr. Copley in London.'
5. Copley to his wife, 8 October 1774, Genoa, in Amory 1882, p. 33.

Copley made few self-portraits: a pastel and miniature dating from his career in the colonies, his image in the grand *Copley Family* (cat. 1), and this self-portrait of 1780–84.[1] In comparison to Benjamin West or to Joshua Reynolds, who frequently painted themselves in various guises and poses, Copley left little visual evidence of the way he saw himself and wished himself to be seen by others; but, combined with written records, these few self-portraits demonstrate the effort of the eighteenth-century British artist to elevate his social and intellectual status.

By all accounts, including his own, Copley cultivated a genteel, if not flamboyant, appearance. The English history painter George Carter, Copley's traveling companion to Italy in 1774, offered the most vivid account of the artist's physical appearance and style of dress: "He had on one of those white French bonnets, which, turned on one side, admit of being pulled over the ears: under this was a yellow and red silk handkerchief, with a large Catherine wheel flambeaued upon it ... this flowed half way down his back. He wore a red-brown, or rather cinnamon, great coat, with a friar's cape, and worsted binding of a yellowish white; it hung near his heels, out of which peeped his boots: under his arm he carried the sword which he bought in Paris, and a hickory stick with an ivory head. Joined to this dress, he was very thin, pale, a little pock-marked, prominent eyebrows, small eyes, which, after fatigue, seemed a day's march in his head."[2] Carter was clearly unfavorably disposed toward his companion. His 'portrait' of the artist describes a tiny figure overwhelmed by accessories and fantastic fabrics 'joined' to his body. In Carter's view, Copley's clothes wore him, rather than the reverse. Carter was correct in stressing Copley's acute concern with presentation, which had shown itself long before the artist left the colonies, and embraced both his person and his surroundings. In his first self-portrait, an exquisite pastel (*ca.* 1769, Winterthur Museum and Gardens, Wilmington, Delaware), he focused on his elegant costume – blue silk brocade dressing gown with an embroidered red vest, white lace-trimmed shirt, and powdered wig – thus emphasizing his status as a well-to-do gentleman. After marrying one of the more eligible heiresses in Boston and acquiring property on Beacon Hill, Copley proceeded to build a grand house next door to John Hancock's, making sure that it featured the latest details, such as a 'peaza,' a fashionable porch he had admired on his 1771 trip to New York.[3]

Abroad, Copley consciously made himself over once again to accommodate London and Continental standards of fashionable dress. The very day, in fact, he set sail for England he, or perhaps his half-brother Henry Pelham, wrote a memorandum regarding the sundries he would need from London, including "A Suit of Cloathes: Coat Jacket and Breeches to be made in a genteel neat manner of the best and finest broad Cloth ... Scarlet Whitney Coat a printed Velvet Jacket and a Crimson pair of Breeches."[4] By the time Copley reached Genoa, he admitted to his wife that "I believe you will think I have become a 'beau' to dress in so rich a suit of clothes, and truly I am a little tinctured ...," for Copley had just purchased in Genoa "as much black velvet as will make a suit of clothes; for this I gave about five guineas, and about two more for as much crimson satin as will line it. This is the taste throughout Tuscany, and today I bought some lace ruffles and silk stockings ... You see how I spend my money, but it is necessary to attend to dress, and not unpleasing when business does not interfere. I hope ere long to see some returns for the money I now spend."[5]

Copley clearly had a taste for fine and fashionable costume. But he must have also recognized the need to project a gentlemanly demeanor, to "see some returns" in the clients a gentleman would attract. Both the pastel portrait and the image of himself in *The Copley Family* proclaim his attention to dress, fashion, and the belief that in order to be successful, one needed to look the part.

The self-portrait here expresses a different set of concerns, as it embraces themes of thought, mood, and characterization. Copley presents a more private self – striking because the usually 'materialist' Copley is not painting stuffs with his habitual flair. He still appears in a fashionable powdered wig with his hair tied back in a black bow, and a vivid red jacket, but in order to maintain the painting's general effect, these allusions to dress are suggested rather than carefully rendered.

Turned to the side in a three-quarter view, Copley emerges from a dark background and looms in the viewer's space. Compared with the tighter manner of his pastel portrait and the more loosely painted image of himself in *The Copley Family*, this self-portrait is built from thick

6. See 'Representing Genius: Fragonard's Portraits de Fantaisie,' in Sheriff 1990, pp. 153–84, for a discussion of 18-century French execution. English artists such as Reynolds disdained technical verve, particularly Gainsborough's, as a sign of the mechanical side of the artist's profession. In France, artists such as Fragonard used loose brushwork as a sign of the artist's (required) enthusiasm and inspiration.

7. As Ellen G. Miles has suggested, Copley likely used two mirrors or 'looking glasses,' standard props of the artist's studio, to help produce the three-quarter angle of the pose. See Gustafson 1978, p. 1256. Reynolds used mirrors to exaggerate the distance between artist and sitter, thereby helping him to generalize rather than particularize the sitter's features. See Simon 1987, p. 112.

8. The German philosopher Johann Caspar Lavater popularized physiognomy, the study of the relationship between exterior features and inner character, in his *Essays on Physiognomy*, translated into English by the late 1780s. Copley's portrait, while it predates the English translation of Lavater's popular essay, nonetheless engages similar issues.

strokes of fluid paint, which add expressiveness and denote dash, spontaneity, and energy, as if the artist were seized with a fiery spirit, a moment of artistic inspiration.[6] His small eyes, set off by prominent eyebrows seem indeed to be a "day's march in his head." A strong jaw, high cheekbones, and aquiline nose indicate his fine features, while the trace of his beard and moustache make him appear brilliantly alive. Pools of light illuminate his white jabot, lips, nose, powdered wig, eyelids, even his earlobe. His high forehead, emphasized even more by the receding hairline and the lift created by his wig, is his most prominent, and most dramatically lit, facial feature.

Copley appears completely absorbed and deep in thought.[7] The painter's emphasis on his forehead, in fact, implies the process of thinking, the very faculty that eighteenth-century artists claimed distinguished them from artisans. Whether or not Copley possessed a high, pronounced forehead, the fact that he emphasizes it here indicates his effort to bring the mental – rather than material – to the foreground.[8] While Copley's other self-portraits assert his social position and advertise his gentlemanly status, this painting embraces the spectator's space by looming forward, presenting a seemingly spontaneous and thoughtful view of the artist. Thus, in spite of their compositional and stylistic differences, the range of Copley's self-portraits indicates the manner in which eighteenth-century English artists wished to present themselves, as polite and learned gentlemen.

Detail of cat. 18

18.
The Death of Major Peirson, 1782–84

Oil on canvas, 97 × 144 in. (246.4 × 365.8 cm)

Tate Gallery, London, N00733

PROVENANCE: John Boydell, until 1805; (Boydell sale, Christie's, London, 8 March 1805, no. 98, bought in); to John Singleton Copley, until 1815; his son; Lord Lyndhurst, until 1863; (Lyndhurst sale, Christie's, London, 5 March 1864, no. 90); to National Gallery, London; transferred to the Tate Gallery, London, 1954.

SELECTED EXHIBITIONS: Manchester 1857, no. 112; London 1862, no. 128; New York 1937, no. 40; Boston 1938, no. 19; London 1946, no. 48; Washington, New York, Boston 1965–6, no. 77.

SELECTED REFERENCES: Cunningham 1831/ 1837/1868, pp. 138, 149–50; Dunlap 1834/1969, I, pp. 106, 116, 118, 119, 127, 357; Tuckerman 1867, pp. 8, 79, 81; Perkins 1873, pp. 127, 134; Amory 1882, pp. 11, 23, 91–3; Isham 1905/1907/1942, p. 29; Bayley 1915, pp. 16–7, 35, 92–3; Hartmann 1901, I, p. 18; La Follette 1929, p. 50; London 1934, no. 733, p. 71; Hagen 1940, p. 138; *Connoisseur* 1946, p. 57; Larkin 1949, p. 66; Barker 1950, p. 218; Prown 1966, II, pp. 275, 278, 289, 296, 298, 302, and *passim*, fig. 442; Frankenstein 1970, pp. 10, 140, 154–5; Mayne 1981, pp. 89–90; Allard 1983, pp. 411–2; Harris 1990; Honour 1989, pp. 41–4; Saunders 1990; Harrington 1993, p. 41.

See further in this catalogue 'The History Theater: Production and Spectatorship in John Singleton Copley's *The Death of Major Peirson*,' pp. 60–90.

The brochure provided *gratis* to the visitor to the picture's exhibition at 28 Haymarket in 1784 included a description of the painting, a key to the portraits of the officers of the central group, and a subscription proposal. The description of the painting read as follows: "22d of MAY, 1784. DESCRIPTION OF THE PICTURE OF *The Death of Major Peirson*, and the DEFEAT of the French Troops in the Island of Jersey. Painted by Mr. COPLEY, for Mr. BOYDELL. This PIC-TURE is founded on the following FACTS: A Body of French Troops having invaded the Island of Jersey in the year 1781, and having possessed themselves of the Town of St. Heiller's, and taken the Lieutenant-Governor prisoner, obliged him in that situation, to sign a capitulation to surrender the Island; Major PEIRSON, a gallant young Officer, under the age of twenty-four years, sensible of the invalidity of the capitulation made by the Lieutenant-Governor, whilst he was a prisoner, with great valor and prudence, attacked and totally defeated the French Troops, and thereby rescued the Island, and gloriously maintained the honor of the British arms; but unfortunately for his Country, this brave Officer fell in the moment of Victory, not by chance shot, but by a ball levelled at him, with a design by his death, to check the ardor of the British Troops. The Major's death was instantly retalliated by his black servant on the man that shot the Major.

The Picture exhibits in the centre, a groupe bearing off the dead body from the field of battle, and the black servant shooting the man who killed his master. This groupe consists entirely of the portraits of Officers of the 95th Regiment, an Officer of the Jersey Militia, and of the said black servant.

On one side is represented a Captain of Grenadiers, leading on a body of Troops to charge the Enemy, who are seen in the back-ground, some in disorder, giving way, and others in flight; an English Serjeant mortally wounded on the ground, and endeavouring with his handkerchief to stop the effusion of blood, but greatly affected at the sight of the body of Major PEIRSON.

On the other side of the Picture are Women and Children flying with terror and distress from this scene of blood; near them a Highland Serjeant lays dead, and a party of Highlanders are seen attacking the Enemy, who are flying for refuge into the Court-house.

The background is an exact view of that part of the town of St. Heiller's where the battle was fought; and at a distance, a hill is seen over the houses, on which some companys posted themselves, and kept up a brisk fire on the Enemy."

19.

Sketch for *The Death of Major Peirson*, 1782–84

Oil on canvas sketch, 27¼ × 35¼ in.
(69.2 × 89.5 cm)

Yale University Art Gallery,. Lelia A. and John
Hill Morgan Collection. 1943.67

PROVENANCE: The artist, until 1815; his son,
John Singleton Copley, Jr., Lord Lyndhurst, until
1863; (Lyndhurst Sale, Christie's, London, 5
March 1864, probably no. 71); to Cox; (Christie's,
London, 14 January 1888, probably no. 51); to
Horace Buttery; to C. Newton Robinson; (Leggatt
Bros., London); bequest of John Hill Morgan,
Farmington, Connecticut; to Yale University Art
Gallery, New Haven, Connecticut, bequest of
Lelia A. and John Hill Morgan Collection, 1943.

SELECTED EXHIBITIONS: Boston 1938, no. 28.

SELECTED REFERENCES: Perkins 1873, p. 132;
Bayley 1915, p. 35; Bolton and Binsse 1930, p. 76;
Prown 1966, II, pp. 304, 403, 441, fig.450;
Saunders 1990, p. 14.

20.

The Battle over Patroclus's Body, formerly called *Roman Conquest*, 1774–75

Chalk and crayon on wove paper, 13¹⁵⁄₁₆ ×
30³⁄₁₆ in. (35.4 × 76.7 cm)

Addison Gallery of American Art, Phillips
Academy, Andover, Massachusetts, 1935.23

PROVENANCE: The artist, until 1815; his son,
John Singleton Copley, Jr., Lord Lyndhurst, until
1863; (probably Lyndhurst Library sale, Christie's,
London, 26 and 27 February 1864, no. 669 or
676); to Albert Rosenthal, Philadelphia; (Macbeth
Gallery, New York, 1935); to Addison Gallery of
American Art, 1935.

SELECTED EXHIBITIONS: Washington, New
York, Boston 1965–6, no. 57.

SELECTED REFERENCES: Prown 1966, II,
pp. 250, 458, fig. 336; Saunders 1990, pp. 34–5.

NOTES

1. For the chronology of the drawings, see Prown
1966, II, pp. 303–6, and Saunders 1990, pp. 14–30.

2. Saunders 1990, p. 34.

3. See Quincy 1879, p. 25, for Eliza Quincy's
description of John Trumbull's working method
for enlarging, using silk thread and chalk.

Brought together for this exhibition from seven collections and reproduced here in color for the first time, this suite of seventeen preparatory drawings and an oil sketch reveals Copley's development of the theme of *The Death of Major Peirson*. While the exact order in which Copley produced these drawings is unknown, it is likely that he began with a pencil-and-ink sketch of nude figures in battle (cat. 23a) which shows the key elements that, from the very beginning, Copley intended to represent: a central group surrounding the fallen Peirson; fleeing figures at right; a revenge sequence, here represented at left; all set against a background hill, city buildings, and swirling smoke.[1] As Saunders has observed, Copley took a dying figure supported by comrades from a drawing of *ca.* 1774–5, now identified as *The Battle over Patroclus's Body* (cat. 20), as a model for the pose of the dying Peirson.[2] In the study for the central group (cat. 23a), Copley emphasizes disorder and chaos, and heightens the event's sensational value by including a bound figure, perhaps a woman, kneeling below the avenging figure. In another early drawing (cat. 22a), the bound figure remains at far left, but the avenger moves to the right of the central group, and Copley includes for the first time a figure who stands behind the marksman, pointing to the target at right. In this drawing, the fleeing figures are more defined, but include only one adult female, with two children. It seems likely that Copley then began refining the central group, adding costume details, and indicating passages of shadow and bright light. Copley found a graceful solution to the painting's composition by moving the revenge sequence from the right of the central group (cat. 24) once again to the left, where he originally intended it (cat. 22b). The next sketch (cat. 25) shows continued refinements to this central grouping: Copley switches the pointing arm of the officer aiding the marksman from his right to his left, which makes him appear more firmly in control. By the time Copley prepared an oil sketch (cat. 19), to indicate passages of light and shade, and to suggest the sharp angles of the building that will help to compress the space, the principal group was well defined (cat. 21); he had prepared a drawing that indicated the names of the most important figures, uniform details, and specific facial features. For the first time, Copley indicates the race of the avenging figure who, in earlier drawings, appears to be Caucasian.

In subsequent drawings, Copley elaborated the other groupings, concentrating on specific figures such as the ensign (cat. 26); the leader of marching soldiers, with arms outstretched and bayonet held high, a figure that remained relatively unchanged from the very beginning (cat.27); the dying French officer (cats. 28b, 29); the dying drummer who seems to have replaced the bound figure from earlier drawings, and whose position was continuously shifted (cats. 30a, 27), as were the dead figures lying on the ground (cats. 28a, 29). The studies for the fleeing figures, among the most exquisite drawings of the suite, show Copley's decision to expand the female group to two adults; on one of these sheets is the only surviving portrait study for any figure in the painting, the boy – thought to be young John Singleton Copley, Jr. – the one figure who looks directly at the viewer (cats. 23b, 30b, 31, 32).

Two drawings show Copley's notes on the identification of the officers and on uniform colors and details, indicating his effort to emphasize the portrait aspect of the painting and to record faithfully certain elements of dress (cats. 29, 21). Others display Copley's system of scales and measures for transferring the prepatory drawings to the larger canvas (cats. 21, 26, 30, 27, 28a, 29, 30, 32). While the exact process by which Copley transferred his sketches to the canvas remains obscure, it may be that he created a grid on the canvas and squared the drawings for transfer, or that, like John Trumbull, he created a grid on the canvas using string.[3] He may not have used a grid at all; several of the drawings include measurements for certain features, such as the sixteen inches designated for Ensign Rowan's elbow to hand (cat.26), suggesting that Copley may have simply worked the canvas somewhat freely, using the measurements indicated on the drawings as guides for scaling the larger canvas.

21.
Study for the central group of *The Death of Major Peirson*, 1782–83

Black and white chalk on gray-green paper,
14 × 22⅝ in. (35.6 × 57.5 cm)

Inscribed as follows: figures labeled left to right,
Captain Macneil, Captn Christie's Black Servt, Mr. Hemer, Captn Clephene, Lieutt Drysdale, Enn Rowan/bearing the Colours, Adjutant Harrison; lower left, scaled, *2 feet 11½ inches* with marks of *16* and *20½*; upper left, *Highd* [?].

Tate Gallery, London, NO4984

PROVENANCE: The artist, until 1815; his son, John Singleton Copley, Jr., Lord Lyndhurst, until 1863; (Lyndhurst Library sale [?], 26–7 Feb. 1864, no. 666); to Mrs. Jessie Colin Campbell until 1939; to National Gallery, London, 1939; transferred to the Tate Gallery, London, 1954.

SELECTED REFERENCES: Prown 1966, II, pp. 303, 441, fig. 447; Saunders 1990, p. 14.

22a.
Study for the central group of *The Death of Major Peirson* (recto, 1939.268a)

22b.
Study for *The Death of Major Peirson* (verso, 1939.268b), 1782–83

Graphite on cream laid paper with watermark GR crowned in circle, 7⅞ × 12⅞ in. (20 × 32.7 cm)

Museum of Fine Arts, Boston, M. and M. Karolik Collection, 1939.268a,b

PROVENANCE: The artist, until 1815; his son, John Singleton Copley, Jr., Lord Lyndhurst, until 1863; (probably Lyndhurst Library sale, 26–7 Feb. 1864, no. 666); to Graves; to Lord Aberdare, London, 1915; (Weyhe Galleries, New York, *ca.* 1929); to Maxim Karolik; Museum of Fine Arts, Boston, 1939.

SELECTED EXHIBITIONS: Boston 1938, no. 106.

SELECTED REFERENCES: Bayley 1915, p. 93; Hipkiss 1941, pp. 18–9, no. 249; Prown 1966, II, p. 304, figs. 448, 452; Saunders 1990, p. 14.

23a.
Study for *The Death of Major Peirson* (recto, 1939.267a)

23b.
Study for the fleeing woman and child in *The Death of Major Peirson* (verso 1939.267b), 1782–83

Recto: pen and ink with graphite underdrawing on cream laid paper with watermark GR crowned in circle; verso: graphite, 8 × 12¾ in. (20.3 × 32.4 cm)

Museum of Fine Arts, Boston, M. and M. Karolik Collection, 1939.267a,b

PROVENANCE: The artist, until 1815; his son, John Singleton Copley, Jr., Lord Lyndhurst, until 1863; (Lyndhurst Library sale, Christie's London, 26–7 Feb. 1864, no. 666); to Graves; (Weyhe Galleries, New York, *ca.* 1929); to Maxim Karolik; Museum of Fine Arts, Boston, 1939.

SELECTED REFERENCES: Hipkiss 1941, pp. 320-1; Prown 1966, II, pp. 304, 441–2, figs. 449, 461; Saunders 1990, p. 14.

SELECTED EXHIBITIONS: Boston 1938, no. 105.

24.
Study for the central group of *The Death of Major Peirson*, 1782–83

Black and white chalk on blue-gray paper, 11 × 14 in. (27.9 × 35.6 cm)

Courtauld Institute Galleries, London (Witt Collection) 553

PROVENANCE: The artist, until 1815; his son, John Singleton Copley, Jr., Lord Lyndhurst, until 1863; (Lyndhurst Library sale, 26–7 Feb. 1864, no. 666); to Graves [?]; Frank Sabin, London, *ca.* 1924; to Sir Robert Witt; Courtauld Institute Galleries.

SELECTED EXHIBITIONS: Boston 1938, no. 111.

SELECTED REFERENCES: Prown 1966, II, p. 442, fig. 451; Saunders 1990, p. 14.25.

25.

Study for the central group and the fleeing woman and child of *The Death of Major Peirson*, 1782–83

Black chalk with white chalk highlights on blue laid paper, faded to pale blue/green, 13³/₄ × 12¹/₄ in. (34.9 × 31.1 cm)

Museum of Fine Arts, Boston, M. and M. Karolik Collection, 1939.269

PROVENANCE: The artist, until 1815; his son, John Singleton Copley, Jr., Lord Lyndhurst, until 1863; (Lyndhurst Library sale, 26–7 Feb. 1864, no. 666); to Graves; (Weyhe Galleries, New York, *ca.* 1929); to Maxim Karolik; Museum of Fine Arts, Boston, 1939.

SELECTED EXHIBITIONS: Boston 1938, no. 107.

SELECTED REFERENCES: Hipkiss 1941, pp. 320-1, no. 252; Slatkin and Shoolman 1947, p. xii; Comstock 1942, pp. 151-2; Prown 1966, II, p. 442, fig. 453; Saunders 1990, p. 14.

26.

Study for the figure with the flag (Ensign Rowan) in *The Death of Major Peirson* (verso, 1947.38b), 1782–83

Study for *The Death of the Earl of Chatham*(?) (recto, 1947.38a), *ca.* 1779–80 [not illus.]

Verso: black and white chalk on gray-blue paper; recto: charcoal, pencil, and white chalk, 13⁷/₈ × 12³/₄ in. (35.2 × 32.4 cm)

Mead Art Museum, Amherst College, Museum Purchase

PROVENANCE: The artist, until 1815; his son, John Singleton Copley, Jr., Lord Lyndhurst, until 1863; (Lyndhurst Library sale, 26–7 Feb. 1864); to Edward Basil Jupp, London; to Amory family, Boston; to Linzee Amory, Boston; (Charles D. Childs Gallery, Boston); (The Old Print Shop, New York); to Mead Art Museum, 1947.

SELECTED REFERENCES: Prown 1966, II, p. 443, figs. 415, 459; Saunders 1990, p. 14.

27.

Study for the officer and wounded drummer in *The Death of Major Peirson* (recto, 1939.262a), 1782–83

Sketch of robed figure and two geometric torsos (verso, 1939.262b)[1] [not illus.]

Black and white chalk with highlights on blue laid paper, 13⁷/₈ × 22¹/₂ in. (35.2 × 57.2 cm)

Museum of Fine Arts, Boston, M. and M. Karolik Collection, 1939.262a,b

PROVENANCE: The artist, until 1815; his son, John Singleton Copley, Jr., Lord Lyndhurst, until 1863; (Lyndhurst Library sale, no. 666); to Graves; (Weyhe Galleries, New York, *ca.* 1929); to Maxim Karolik; Museum of Fine Arts, Boston, 1939.

SELECTED EXHIBITIONS: Boston 1938, no. 100.

SELECTED REFERENCES: Hipkiss 1941, pp. 322–3, no. 253; Prown 1966, II, p. 442, fig. 454; Saunders 1990, p. 14

NOTE

1. Roy Perkinson and Alison Luxner, Department of Conservation, Museum of Fine Arts, Boston, discovered the verso drawing. I thank them for bringing the sketch, unrelated to *The Death of Major Peirson*, to my attention.

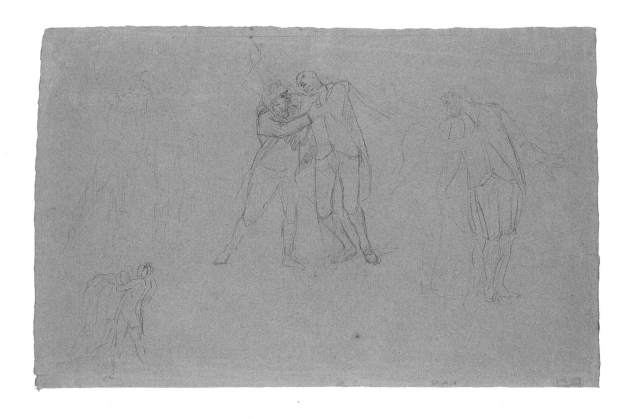

28a.

Study for dead figures in *The Death of Major Peirson* (recto, 60.44.14)

28b.

Study for dying French officer group in *The Death of Major Peirson* (verso, 60.44.14), 1782–83

Recto: black and white chalk on blue-gray paper; verso: pencil; 14¹/₈ × 23 in. (35.9 × 58.4 cm)

Metropolitan Museum of Art, New York, Purchase, Louisa Eldridge McBurney Gift, 1960.44.14

PROVENANCE: The artist, until 1815; his son, John Singleton Copley, Jr., Lord Lyndhurst, until 1863; (Lyndhurst Library sale, 26–7 Feb. 1864, no. 666); to Graves [?]; (Charles D. Childs Gallery, Boston); (The Old Print Shop, New York); to Metropolitan Museum of Art, 1960.

SELECTED EXHIBITIONS: New York 1990–1, nos. 6, 7.

SELECTED REFERENCES: Prown 1966, II, p. 443, figs. 457, 458; Saunders 1990, pp. 14, 30.

29.

Study for dying French officer group and other figures in *The Death of Major Peirson*, 1782-83

Black chalk with white chalk highlights and notations in graphite and brown ink on blue laid paper, 13⁵/₈ × 22³/₈ in. (36.6 × 56.8 cm)

Inscribed upper right: *There were five Regaments Colour of the lappels were White Blew Green Buff & Orange*; upper center: *some of the french were dressed in dirty Read almost Orange, faced with dirty Yellow / so of Militia with round hats with white border & do round y[e] crown & black Feather like the black Short Coats tacked back at the lower Button lined with White*; left: *x green coat* [on dying figure], *O White* [on vest], *Read* [crossed out] *White* [cuff], *Lapels Read* [crossed out] *White, Blew Coats White Do, White Coats Read do ... alet round . . . / colour of the facing*; lower left: *Cockade/Read/ ... White* ; lower center: *French Lapels/Inch to be ...*; lower right: *Scale of feet for the Battle*

Museum of Fine Arts, Boston, M. and M. Karolik Collection, 1939.270

PROVENANCE: The artist, until 1815; his son, John Singleton Copley, Jr., Lord Lyndhurst, until 1863; (Lyndhurst Library sale, 26–7 Feb. 1864, no. 666); to Graves; (Weyhe Galleries, New York, *ca.* 1929); Maxim Karolik; Museum of Fine Arts, Boston, 1939.

SELECTED EXHIBITIONS: Boston 1938, no. 108; Washington, New York, Boston 1965-6, no. 79.

SELECTED REFERENCES: Hipkiss 1941, pp. 322-3, no. 254; Prown 1966, II, pp. 305-6, 442, fig. 455; Saunders 1990, pp. 14, 30.

30a.

Study for the wounded soldier in *The Death of Major Peirson* (recto, 1939.265a)

30b.

Study for the fleeing woman and child in *The Death of Major Peirson* (verso, 1939.265b), 1782–83

Recto: black chalk with white chalk highlights on blue laid paper; verso: black chalk with white chalk highlights and notations in graphite; 13³/₄ × 22¹/₄ in. (34.9 × 56.5 cm)

Museum of Fine Arts, Boston, M. and M. Karolik Collection, 1939.265a,b

PROVENANCE: The artist, until 1815; his son, John Singleton Copley, Jr., Lord Lyndhurst, until 1863; (Lyndhurst Library sale, 26–7 Feb. 1864, no. 666); to Graves; (Weyhe Galleries, New York, *ca.* 1929); to Maxim Karolik; Museum of Fine Arts, Boston, 1939.

SELECTED EXHIBITIONS: Boston 1938, no. 103.

SELECTED REFERENCES: Hipkiss 1941, p. 326, no. 257; Prown 1966, II, p. 442, figs. 456, 462; Saunders 1990, pp. 14, 30.

31.

Study for the fleeing woman and child in *The Death of Major Peirson*, 1782–83

Black chalk with white chalk highlights on blue laid paper, 13³/₄ × 22 in. (34.9 × 55.9 cm)

Museum of Fine Arts, Boston, M. and M. Karolik Collection, 1939.266

PROVENANCE: The artist, until 1815; his son, John Singleton Copley, Jr., Lord Lyndhurst, until 1863; (Lyndhurst Library sale, 26–7 Feb. 1864, no. 666); to Graves; (Weyhe Galleries, New York, *ca.* 1929); to Maxim Karolik; Museum of Fine Arts, Boston, 1939.

SELECTED EXHIBITIONS: Boston 1938, no. 104.

SELECTED REFERENCES: Hipkiss 1941, p. 318, no. 250; Prown 1966, II, p. 443, fig. 460; Saunders 1990, pp. 14, 30.32.

32.
Study for the fleeing woman and
child and boy with hat (J.S.
Copley, Jr.) in *The Death of Major
Peirson*, 1782–83

Black chalk with white chalk highlights and
notations in graphite on blue laid paper,
13⁷/₈ × 22¹/₄ in. (35.2 × 56.5 cm)

Museum of Fine Arts, Boston, M. and M. Karolik
Collection, 1939.264

PROVENANCE: The artist, until 1815; his son,
John Singleton Copley, Jr., Lord Lyndhurst, until
1863; (Lyndhurst Library sale, 26–7 Feb. 1864, no.
666); to Graves; (Weyhe Galleries, New York, *ca.*
1929); to Maxim Karolik; Museum of Fine Arts,
Boston, 1939.

SELECTED EXHIBITIONS: Boston 1938, no.
102; Washington, New York, Boston 1965–6,
no. 78.

SELECTED REFERENCES: Hipkiss 1941, pp.
324–5, no. 256; Prown 1966, II, p. 443, fig. 463;
Saunders 1990, pp. 14, 30.

33.

The Three Youngest Daughters of George III, 1785

Oil on canvas, 104½ × 73¼ in. (265.4 × 185.4 cm)

Signed and dated lower left: *J.S. Copley R.A. 1785*; Phaeton inscribed with the monogram PA (Princess Amelia)

Her Majesty Queen Elizabeth II, 3126

PROVENANCE: Painted for King George III and Queen Charlotte.[1]

SELECTED EXHIBITIONS: London 1785, no. 80; New York 1937, no. 42; London 1946–7, no. 113; Washington D.C., New York, Boston 1965–6, no. 80; London 1992–3, no. 44; Wellington, Canberra, Ottawa 1994–5, no. 25.

SELECTED REFERENCES: Redgrave 1866, I, pp. 229–30; Perkins 1873, pp. 22, 128, 133; Bayley 1915, pp. 16, 31, 202; Sitwell 1936, pp. 76–7, 89; Waterhouse 1953/1969, p. 192; Prown 1966, I, p. 31, II, p. 31, 296n., 312–3n., 313, 315–8, 320, 338n., 344, 345, 365, 387, 416, fig. 468; Millar 1969, I, no. 712, p. 20; II, no.129; Rose 1989, p. 36.

RELATED WORKS:[2] Sketch of Princesses Sophia and Amelia, oil on canvas, 49½ × 39½ in. (125.7 × 100.3 cm), 1785, formerly Max Safran, New York (1966); Study, black and white chalk on blue-gray grounded paper, 8⅝ × 11½ in. (22.2 × 29.2 cm), 1784–5, Museum of Fine Arts, Boston (M. and M. Karolik Collection); Study, black and white chalk on grounded white paper, 17 × 12⅜ in. (43.2 × 31.1 cm), 1784–5, Worcester Art Museum, Worcester, Massachusetts;[3] Study, black chalk on blue-gray paper, 14¼ × 23 in. (36.2 × 58.4 cm), 1784–5, Victoria and Albert Museum, London.

NOTES

1. Presumably Copley was not paid for the portrait until 1798, when he tried to secure payment with the help of Sir William Beechey, portrait painter to Queen Charlotte. According to Prown, no draft on the account has been located, although the diarist Joseph Farington mentions that Copley received payment (Prown 1966, II, pp. 312–3 note 2).
2. In 1796, John Quincy Adams noted in his diary that he saw Copley's "finely finished" painting of *The Three Youngest Daughters of King George III* at his studio. This copy of the larger version probably refers to the painting made for the engraving published in 1792 (Diary of John Quincy Adams, Adams Family Papers, Massachusetts Historical Society, Boston, roll 27, 28 March 1796; see also cat. 39). This copy may be the one listed in Prown 1966, II, p. 416, as belonging to Mrs. Alan Cunningham, Brookline, Massachusetts, oil on canvas, 20½ × 15½ in. Another copy, in pen and gray wash over pencil but not in Copley's hand, 9¾ × 7⅝ in., belongs to Her Majesty Queen Elizabeth II.
3. Oliver Millar believes the Boston and Worcester drawings are not studies for the royal portraits.

Among the most exuberant paintings of Copley's English career, the portrait of the youngest royal princesses was Copley's only successful experience with royal patronage.[4] Following Copley's rousing successes in the field of contemporary history painting, Benjamin West, George III's historical painter, probably encouraged the king to grant Copley permission to paint the royal family, an honor shared by other prominent artists such as West himself, Joshua Reynolds, Thomas Gainsborough, and John Hoppner.[5]

Copley struggled with the composition, making a series of uncertain prepatory studies that suggest his indecision about whom to paint and how to compose them. As the children and the pets became, in the words of West, "equally wearied" during the many sittings Copley required, West had to assure the king "that Copley must be allowed to proceed in his own way, and that any attempt to hurry him might be injurious to the picture, which would be a very fine one when done."[6]

Perhaps thinking of Gainsborough's full-length portraits of the *Three Eldest Princesses*, which were well received when exhibited in 1784, Copley ultimately decided to paint the three youngest princesses frolicking out of doors: Mary (b. 1776, on the left), the infant Amelia (b. 1783), and Sophia (b. 1777, on the right).[7] Copley's characteristic brio spotlights the delicate textures and surfaces of gossamer fabrics, the crisp folds of pink, blue, and yellow flounced dresses, feathery plumes, the satin sheen of well groomed spaniels, blooming flowers, the porcelain skin of young children enlivened by glowing cheeks, and an ethereal pastel-colored sky.

Copley's attention to minute detail does not end with the quality of things. He captures an endearing and affectionate view of childhood: the loving glance of Mary looking over her left shoulder at Amelia; the plump hands of the baby clutching her older sister's thumb and dress; Sophia's expression of concentration as she attempts gracefully to balance herself; and the striking contrast between Amelia's elegant dress and fluffy headgear, and her bare foot as it rests against a cushion. The sensitive portrayal of sisterly bonds of affection combined with the painting's rococo effervescence make this large-scale painting among the most successful of Copley's career.

The picture earned accolades from West, but other critics judged it harshly when Copley exhibited the painting at the Royal Academy exhibition of 1785. Most reviewers found its ebullient spirit unbefitting of royalty and its profusion of details distracting. One critic praised the portraits but found the festoon gave "a heaviness to the whole;" and another lampooned the picture's props, recommending that the "heavy *Exotic Flowers* be made use of to decorate a *May Garland*, the *Vine* be fixt on the poop of the *Vintner's barge*, and the *Birds* sent to *Brook's Repository* in Holborn."[8] (Such was the critical response to these elements that even the advertisement for Bartolozzi's engraving after the painting assured readers that "the *macaws*, *grapes*, *tulips*, and other things in the piece – which share in prominence with the princely portraits themselves – will look better in the Print, than in the Picture.")[9] The most vitriolic of reviews, and the one that probably set the tone for much subsequent criticism, came from John Hoppner, who wrote: "What delightful disorder! Why, you [Copley] have plucked up harmony by the roots, and planted confusion in its stead! Princesses, parrots, dogs, grapes, flowers, leaves, are each striving for preeminence, and opposing, with hostile force, all attempts of our wearied eyes to find repose."[10] Hoppner was hardly an unbiased reviewer, however: he, too, exhibited his portraits of the three youngest royal princesses in the same exhibition and, like Copley, received unfavorable reviews.[11] The disorder and confusion that Hoppner projected onto the painting was, in fact, Copley's masterly effort to depict the royal children as children, the profusion of props conveying an atmosphere of high spirits appropriate to their age. Yet Copley would not overstep the bounds of propriety that deference to royalty required. To convey their social status, Copley depicts the graceful princesses in elaborate clothing surrounded by sumptuous props, with the Round Tower and the Queen's Lodge visible in the background, as keys to their royal identities.

The Three Youngest Daughters, like other light-hearted conversation pieces of the time, participates in the cult of domesticity that emerged in England during the second half of the eighteenth century. New ideals for child-rearing that had been introduced by the English philosopher John Locke and were developed later by the French philosopher and novelist Jean-Jacques Rousseau encouraged more affectionate bonds between parent and child and among siblings.[12] During the

The Worcester drawing is inscribed, however, at upper right, "Daughters of George 3rd," presumably in Copley's hand (Millar 1969, no. 719, p. 20).

4. Copley's later portraits of royalty were unsuccessful. For example, Copley persuaded George IV to sit for his portrait, which resulted in the cumbersome equestrian portrait of George IV (as Prince of Wales), exhibited at the Royal Academy in 1810 (Museum of Fine Arts, Boston).

5. An unsourced, undated notice (*V & A Press Cuttings*, vol. 2, p. 364), presumably written *ca.* 1785, mentions that John Hoppner traveled to Windsor to paint the young princesses, and adds that "*Copley* has also been employed for a short time past, on some of the Royal children." Copley's painting does not appear to have been commissioned by the royal family, and Hoppner's may not have been either. Reynolds's and Gainsborough's royal portraits were commissioned works.

6. The artist C.R. Leslie reported West's account to William Dunlap (Dunlap 1834, I, p. 126). According to Dunlap, Leslie noted that West told him he helped Copley receive the commission.

7. Gainsborough's *The Three Eldest Princesses* (1784, Collection of Her Majesty Queen Elizabeth II) was included in the 1784 Royal Academy exhibition until Gainsborough withdrew it because the Academy refused to hang it according to his specifications. He exhibited it, instead, at Schomberg House. The painting was cut down in 1868 in order to fit in an overdoor. Copley also would have known the background of West's 1779 portrait of Queen Charlotte (fig. 35 on p. 53), which shows the royal children in the background playing quietly, and some children surrounding an infant in a phaeton.

8. *V & A Press Cuttings*, vol. 1, pp. 255, 260.

9. *V & A Press Cuttings*, vol. 2, p. 462. See also *The Morning Chronicle*, 18 May 1785, quoted in Prown 1966, II, p. 316.

10. This sort of criticism continued; in 1796, Anthony Pasquin [John Williams], who rarely reviewed Copley favorably, wrote: "His portrait of The Infant Princesses is all flutter and folly, flowers and ribbands; it seems, at a distance, like a bed of tulips disturbed by the wind; and is certainly more calculated for the meridian of taste at Coventry or Cranbourn-alley than a Royal Palace. When I first saw this picture, I was compelled by its presuming tone of colouring to wink involuntarily; yet what does all this overcharged style of tinnting, this levity of pencilling prove, but a sedulous attempt to make finery overthrow truth? There is a sober loveliness in all nature, which disdains to assign such pert tawdriness, so intolerant a command over the senses" (Pasquin 1796, p. 137). Written more than ten years after the painting was executed, Pasquin's review may suggest a Neoclassical sensibility in vogue at the time.

11. *Princess Mary, Princess Sophia, Princess Amelia* (Collection of Her Royal Majesty Queen Elizabeth II) appeared as nos. 220–2 in the Royal Academy exhibition catalogue. An unsourced, undated

latter decades of the eighteenth century, children were no longer construed as miniature adults but, according to Rousseau's popular analogy, as blooming plants in need of constant attention by a firm but sympathetic hand. Appropriately enough, Rousseau considered outdoor experiences especially conducive to raising a healthy child. Paintings by French Rococo artists, in fact, reflected Rousseau's affectionate views of childhood and the role of nature in forming sturdy children: Jean-Honoré Fragonard and Marguerite Gérard's *The Beloved Child*, for example, painted about the same time as Copley's *Three Youngest Daughters*, includes a similar phaeton, abundant plant and animal life, and an infant artfully arranged to suggest the exuberance of childhood (fig. 77).

In Copley's painting, the artist sets the princesses into a natural environment, linking them together as in a garland – a compositional device appropriate for a family well known for its botanical interests.[13] The circular movement of the figures leads to the vine-wrapped column at upper right, across the top and down to the eldest daughter at left, as if literally staging Rousseau's analogy of the progression of the child from a specimen (seen at right nearest the younger sisters) to a tamed, well pruned plant (seen at left near the eldest sister who leads her siblings forward).

Although Copley's painting is informed by the aristocratic trend of child and nature worship, it also contributed to the cult of royalty that, having elapsed in earlier reigns, was revived during the reign of George III.[14] Engraved images and newspaper accounts of the king as well as Queen Charlotte and the fifteen royal children proliferated during this period, attesting to the popular interest in royal activity and the power of images and the press to shape and mold public perception of the crown. Copley's image of the royal family coincided with George III's carefully

Fig. 77 Jean-Honoré Fragonard and Marguerite Gérard
The Beloved Child, ca. 1785

Oil on canvas, $16^5/8 \times 20^5/8$ in. (44 × 55 cm)
Courtesy of The Fogg Art Museum, Harvard University Art Museums, gift of Charles E. Dunlap

notice from the *V & A Press Cuttings*, vol. 1, p. 256, includes a review of Hoppner's portraits of the princesses: "We cannot complement the artist upon his success in portraying the lovely subjects. He has attempted a tenderness of colouring, and failed in giving that prominence to the features, which is requisite."

12. Locke 1693/1913; Rousseau 1762/1979. See also cats. 1, 3, 13, and 15.

13. In 1784, Lord Bute dedicated his nine-volume *Botanical Tables* to Queen Charlotte, whose botanical hobbies were well known. See Strong 1992, pp. 65–76, and Roberts 1987, pp. 65–7.

14. New Haven 1990, pp. 12–5. As Colley points out, the term 'royal family' came into general use at this time.

15. Colley 1984, pp. 94–129.

16. Hedley 1967, p. 137.

17. For biographical accounts of the three youngest daughters and information about domestic life at Windsor, see Van der Kiste 1992; Hibbert 1964; and Ayling 1972.

constructed transformation into the 'farmer king,' a role assumed in an effort to show his familiarity with and sympathy for rural life and in order to appear unaffected, genial, and accessible.[15] As Dorothy Wordsworth, sister of the poet William, remarked upon seeing the king and his family on their daily public promenades at Windsor, they appeared "as man and women, not as king and princesses."[16] Copley's portrait affirmed the image the royal family wished to portray of congeniality and normalcy; his painting held up a happy fiction of domestic bliss that would last only a few years more, until the king's mental instability made home life at Windsor strained, if not tragic.[17]

34.

Colonel Ernst August von Hugo and Lieutenant Colonel von Schlepegrell, 1787

Oil on canvas, 26 × 22 inches (66 × 55.9 cm)

Fogg Art Museum, Harvard University Art Museums, Gift of Mrs. Gordon Dexter, 1942.180

PROVENANCE: The artist, London, until 1815; his son, John Singleton Copley, Jr., Lord Lyndhurst, London, until 1863; (Lyndhurst sale, Christie's, London, 5 March 1864, no. 66); to Clarke, for the artist's granddaughter, Mrs. Charles Amory (Martha Babcock Greene Amory), Boston, until 1880; her daughter, Mrs. F. Gordon Dexter (Susan Greene Amory), Boston, until 1924; her son, Gordon Dexter, Boston, until 1937; his widow, Mrs. Gordon Dexter (Isabella Hunnewell Dexter), until 1968; Fogg Art Museum, gift of Mrs. Gordon Dexter, 1942.

SELECTED EXHIBITIONS: Washington, New York, Boston 1965–6, no. 86; Cambridge 1972, no. 10; Cambridge 1977; Boston 1976, p. 35; Providence 1991, p. 98, fig. 16a.

SELECTED REFERENCES: Perkins 1873, pp. 128, 132; Bayley 1915, pp. 34, 36, 151, 225; Bolton and Binsse 1930, p. 83; Prown 1966, II, pp. 327, 329n., 402, 423, fig. 498; Shank 1984, p. 140.

A London newspaper reported in 1787: "When Copley reaches Hanover, how will it sound to the German officers whose portraits he is going to take – 'that he is come for their HEADS'."[1] The "heads" the journalist referred to are those of Colonel Ernst August von Hugo, Lieut. Colonel von Schlepegrell, Major General August de la Motte, and Colonel Gustav Friedrich von Dachenhausen, the four German officers who commanded mercenary soldiers during the British defense of Gibraltar in 1782. In that year, Spain sent a flotilla of battering ships to attack the English-held Rock of Gibraltar, which had been under siege by the Spanish and their French allies since 1779. After a continuous barrage of fire, the British troops defeated the Spanish floating batteries, a turning point in the siege, which ended one month later when Admiral Howe broke the last vestiges of the blockade. At a time when England's hold on her empire appeared to be slipping, this monumental victory over neighboring foes boosted British confidence in military affairs, and accorded heroic status to its officers, particularly General George Augustus Eliott (later Lord Heathfield) and Admiral Richard, Earl Howe (cat. 36). To commemorate their success, the City of London awarded Copley in 1783 the largest and most important commission of his career: to commemorate the British victory at Gibraltar in a painting for the Court of Common Council Room at Guildhall, a project that would take the artist eight arduous years to complete (see further pp. 41f. and fig. 19).[2]

Like his other contemporary history paintings, *The Siege of Gibraltar* involved a great deal of research: gathering accounts of the event, making portraits of the officers present at the battle, documenting uniforms, and arranging fortress and ship models in his studio to create the correct positions of the battlements and vessels. Four years into the project, Copley approached the Council Committee for an advance on his commission, admitting that he had already gone to great expense sending artists abroad to sketch the battle site. Six months later, Copley approached the Council again, suggesting that a "request should be made to His Majesty to permit [the four German officers] to come over from Hanover, and that Lord Heathfield had given it as his opinion that they had rendered most essential service in the defence of Gibraltar and that it would be a compliment paid to them to have their portraits in the picture which they well deserved."[3] The Council seems to have ignored his request, although one of its aldermen and Copley's former patron for *The Death of Major Peirson*, John Boydell, joined with Lord Heathfield to contribute to a fund so that Copley could travel to Hanover to take their portraits. Copley's

35.
Major General August de la Motte, 1787

Oil on canvas, 21 × 17 inches (53.3 × 43.2 cm)

Fogg Art Museum, Harvard University Art Museums, Gift of Mrs. Gordon Dexter, 1942.179

PROVENANCE: The artist, London, until 1815; his son, John Singleton Copley, Jr., Lord Lyndhurst, London, until 1863; (Lyndhurst sale, Christie's, London, 5 March 1864, no. 67); to Clarke, for the artist's granddaughter, Mrs. Charles Amory (Martha Babcock Greene Amory), Boston, until 1880; her daughter, Mrs. F. Gordon Dexter (Susan Greene Amory), Boston, until 1924; her son, Gordon Dexter, Boston, until 1937; his widow, Mrs. Gordon Dexter (Isabella Hunnewell Dexter), until 1968; Fogg Art Museum, gift of Mrs. Gordon Dexter, 1942.

SELECTED EXHIBITIONS: Greenwich 1976, p. 208, fig. 561; Providence 1991, p. 98, fig. 16b.

SELECTED REFERENCES: Perkins 1873, p. 132; Bayley 1915, pp. 34, 36, 94, 225; Prown 1966, II, pp. 327, 402, 417, fig. 496; Simon 1987, pp. 20–1, fig. 9.

RELATED WORKS: *Colonel Gustav Friedrich von Dachenhausen*, 1787, oil on canvas, 21 x 17 in. (53.4 x 43.2 cm), Fogg Art Museum, Harvard University, Cambridge, Mass., Gift of Mrs. Gordon Dexter, 1942.178.

NOTES

1. *V & A Press Cuttings*, II, p. 330. The notice is unsourced and undated, but presumably appeared in 1787, when Copley traveled to Hanover.

2. For full accounts of the commission and execution, see Prown 1966, II, pp. 322–36, and Howgego 1958. For an account of Copley's competition with West over the commission and John Trumbull's role in adding to the competitive atmosphere, see Jaffe 1975, pp. 131–8.

3. CRO (Corporation Record Office), MSS 4.16, Committee, 1 August 1787, quoted in Howgego 1958, p. 40.

4. Copley also suggested to the Council Committee that he could commemorate Eliott's army and Howe's naval victory in one, rather than two, compositions, as opposed to West, who proposed two paintings. See Prown 1966, II, p. 324.

5. As a result of numerous delays, the print was not published until 1810, when Copley was seventy-one years old, and the event that it depicted had occurred twenty-seven years before. The exhibition of the painting fared better. Copley constructed an enormous tent in 1791 in Green Park and claimed that 60,000 visitors attended its viewing. If true, this would have represented £3,000 in profits. See Whitley 1928/1968, II, p. 140, and here pp. 64f.

desire to include the four Hanoverian officers indicates a variety of possible motives, including his conscientiousness as a historian and a history painter, and his wish to satisfy the British officers who advised Copley about whom to portray among those present and how they should be depicted. Copley had edged West out of competition for the Guildhall commission because he had, in part, lowered his fee, suspecting that any losses could be recouped through its exhibition and print distribution.[4] It may be that Copley also wished to include the Hanoverian officers in order to broaden his potential market to Germany once the painting was engraved and published.[5]

During the fall of 1787, Copley traveled to Hanover with his wife and daughter Elizabeth on a "pleasurable and professional excursion."[6] Copley probably brought these small canvases to Hanover with the bold outlines of the figures marked before leaving London. Since Copley already knew where the four officers would be depicted within the officer group at right in the final version of the painting, he could have simply sketched the outlines of the composition to scale before he left, and added the portraits once he arrived in Germany.

These deftly handled character studies rank with the *Head of a Negro* (cat. 5) as Copley's most intimate, insightful, and brilliantly painted portraits, in spite of their lack of conventional finish. As in *Death of the Earl of Chatham*, Copley proves a master in arranging portraits in a dramatic sequence that commemorate the sitter's presence in the event without sacrificing the effect of dramatic action – a skill matched only by West and John Trumbull.[7] In the double portrait, Schlepegrell, on the left, conveys a sense of calm alertness in the face of terror, the drama of the situation enhanced by the dramatic play of light that shines on the left side of his face. In von Hugo's face at right, Copley conveys the action and energy of the event through the sitter's raised eyebrows as he strains his head while looking over his left shoulder, a note of agitation and disarray indicated by the wispy tendrils of loosened hair that frame his ear. Intimate details, such as von Hugo's hairy earlobe, a minutia that could never be viewed from a distance in the final version – measuring almost eighteen by twenty-five feet – attest to Copley's lifelong fascination with recording the distinguishing marks of a sitter.[8] Copley would not have needed to finish the details of the officer's uniforms in such a sketch, yet he could not resist fine-tuning the starched effect of von Hugo's crisp collar, or the brilliant highlights of the braid that lines their tricorn hats.

Showing the sitter's slightly wizened features and expressive eyes, the portrait of August de la Motte is the most sensitive of the four sketches. The bushy eyebrows, downturned mouth (perhaps the effect of a stroke), the dark circles and pouchy skin under his eyes offer a poignant portrait of age, which in the finished painting, in the context of the surrounding officers, is transformed into an expression of admiration and respect for the regal Eliott, the focus of his gaze.

6. Copley and his family stopped along the way in Ghent and Antwerp where Copley took special note of the paintings by Peter Paul Rubens and Anthony van Dyck. See Prown 1966, II, p. 327 and note 14.

7. For example, Benjamin West's *The Death of General Wolfe* (here fig. 56 on p. 80) and John Trumbull's *Sortie Made at the Garrison of Gibraltar*, 1789, Metropolitan Museum of Art, New York. Copley was not alone in shaping the public's fascination with the event, and some artists completed and exhibited their canvases years before Copley. Joseph Wright of Derby exhibited *A View of Gibraltar During the Destruction of the Spanish Floating Batteries* at Mr. Robins's Rooms in Covent Garden in April 1785 (unlocated), the same year George

Carter exhibited his version of the event at Pall Mall.

8. Compare, for example, Copley's colonial portrait of Nathaniel Allen, which features two hairy moles (1763, Honolulu Academy of Arts).

36.

Richard, Earl Howe (1726–1799),
Admiral of the Fleet, ca. 1791–94

Oil on canvas, 30 inches diam. (76.2 cm)

National Maritime Museum, Greenwich,
BHC 2790

PROVENANCE: The artist, London, until 1815;
his son, John Singleton Copley, Jr., Lord
Lyndhurst, until 1863; (Lyndhurst sale, Christie's,
London, 5 March 1864, no. 53); to Anthony,
Marquis of Sligo; to the National Maritime
Museum, Greenwich, gift of the Caird Collection.

SELECTED EXHIBITIONS: Washington, New
York, Boston 1965–6, no. 85; Greenwich 1976,
no. 192.

SELECTED REFERENCES: Perkins 1873, pp.
128, 131; Bayley 1915, pp. 34, 149; Prown 1966,
II, pp. 311–2, 323–4, 326–7, 327n., 331, 334, 343,
357–8, 402, fig. 596.

NOTES

1. For accounts of Howe's life and career, see especially Gruber 1972. Gruber implies that Howe
may have received some preferential treatment
from the royal family, as his mother was believed
to the illegitimate daughter of George I. He notes,
however, that he earned high respect from his
peers and superiors as well as loyalty from his seamen because of his conscientiousness and sense of
responsibility.

2. See Howgego 1958, pp. 38–9 and Prown 1966,
II, p. 326, for details surrounding the cancelled
plans for combining both events in one image.

3. Bradford 1971, p. 133.

4. Prown 1966, II, p. 422, lists two copies by
Copley of the Howe portrait. The Greenwich por-
trait may have been used for the engraving by R.
Dunkarton which Copley published in 1794, sure

Thanks to his successful naval leadership at Gibraltar, Richard, Earl Howe entered the pantheon
of British naval heroes that included Augustus, Lord Keppel and later, Horatio, Lord Nelson,
victor of the Battle of the Nile and of Trafalgar. Born in a family of wealth and influence, a
favorite of George III, and possessed of strong leadership abilities, Howe rose quickly through the
ranks of the British Navy, which he had joined at the age of fourteen.[1] Nicknamed "Black Dick"
because of his swarthy complexion, he served in the French and Indian War, and commanded
the British fleet during the American Revolution, eventually becoming First Lord of the
Admiralty, Admiral of the Fleet, and, eventually, a Knight of the Garter.

For three years, the Spanish had besieged the British-held Gibraltar, until Eliott's land forces
successfully defended the fortress in 1782 (see cats. 34, 35). One month after Eliott's success,
Howe penetrated the Franco-Spanish naval blockade, essentially ending the three-year siege of
the Rock. Thus Howe played a significant role in this British victory, which the Corporation of
London determined in 1783 to celebrate by commissioning a monumental painting for the
Guildhall.

Copley had edged West out of the competition for commemorating the Gibraltar victory by
persuading the Council Committee that he could combine in one image the successes of both the
land and the naval forces, whereas West believed the events memorialized should be depicted in
two separate paintings. Copley's overreaching confidence, and his willingness to reduce his commission fee, probably clinched his deal with the Committee. In retrospect, the Committee should
have realized that compressing two events (which had occurred a month apart) into one image
would dissatisfy those participants more interested in a factual record of the event.[2] By 1786–7,
Copley himself recognized that he would have to commemorate Howe's penetration of the
Franco-Spanish blockade in some other manner, as the officer group at right, originally planned
for the background, had been moved to the foreground of the composition at the request of the
army officers. This change altered the moral thrust of the picture, now slanted to convey a message of British triumph in the face of adversity, putting the keen naval strategy of Howe, as it
were, on a lower plane.

To depict the breaking of the blockade, Copley decided upon a long, narrow panel that
would hang beneath *The Siege of Gibraltar* like a Renaissance predella, flanked by medallion portraits of Admiral Richard, Earl Howe and Admiral Samuel Barrington. Copley did not paint the
predella, but subcontracted the marine painter Dominic Serres to paint Howe's relief forces;
Serres's painting appears in Bartolozzi's engraving of the 1791 admission ticket (fig. 49 on p. 71),
as well as in center of the William Sharp engraving Copley published in 1810 (fig. 78). Even the
small-scale Bartolozzi engraving suggests the epic grandeur and complex combination of materials and images that Copley invented to honor the officers and the two events in a dramatic,
swashbuckling celebration of British triumph in a three-year siege in which British forces held

Fig. 78 R. Pollard after Dominic Serres, *The Relief of Gibraltar*, flanked by portraits of Admirals Howe
and Barrington by William Sharp after John Singleton Copley, published by Copley, 22 May 1810

Engraving
British Museum, London

to appeal to a public inspired by Howe's most recent victory against the French on 1 June 1794, known as the Glorious First of June. The flanking medallion of Samuel Barrington is unlocated, although Copley presumably painted a copy for Barrington using a rectangular shaped canvas *ca.* 1794. As Prown notes, *The Relief* by Dominic Serres is unlocated, and known only by the 1810 engraving. *The Relief* and the medallions were detached from the large picture around 1794, when the frame commissioned of James Brewer could not accommodate the entire tableau (Prown 1966, II, pp. 343, 331 note 22, 334 note 28).

5. Caroline Howe to Countess Spencer, 20 June 1780, *Howe-Spencer Letters*, IV, Althorp, quoted in Gruber 1972, p. 45. Gainsborough painted pendant portraits of Richard, Earl Howe (*ca.* 1763–4, The Trustees of the Howe Settled Estates) and his wife, Mary, Countess Howe (*ca.* 1763–4, The Iveagh Bequest, Kenwood, London) that show Howe in the undress uniform of a Commodore.

6. According to object file notes at the National Maritime Museum, Greenwich.

37.

John, 2nd Viscount Dudley and Ward (1725–1788), after 1781/before 1804

Oil on canvas, 56 × 46³⁄₄ in. (142.2 × 118.7 cm)

Inscribed on letter: *The Rt Honbl[e]/Lord Visct Dudley [& Ward?]*

Hirschl and Adler Galleries, New York

PROVENANCE: The Dudley Family, by descent, until 1984; to Hirschl and Adler Galleries, New York

SELECTED EXHIBITIONS: London 1804, no. 96; Birmingham, 1934, no. 443, incorrectly attributed to Thomas Lawrence.

SELECTED REFERENCES: Perkins 1873, p. 129; Bayley 1915, pp. 33, 97; Prown 1966, II, pp. 286n., 361, 373, 388, 418, fig. 630.

NOTES

1. William Murray, Earl of Mansfield, may have sat to Copley again in 1782–3, when Copley painted his full-length portrait. Surviving studies for this are located at Yale University Art Gallery; Bayou Bend Collection and Gardens, Museum of Fine Arts, Houston; Mead Art Museum, Amherst College, Amherst; Cleveland Museum of Art; and the British Museum, London. See Prown 1966, II, pp. 297, 426, figs. 430–5.

2. Copley may have used the figure of Richard Brocklesby in *The Death of the Earl of Chatham* for a later portrait (now possibly destroyed). See Prown

John, 2nd Viscount Dudley and Ward is among four known individual portraits Copley derived from his enormously successful contemporary history painting, *The Death of the Earl of Chatham* (fig. 18 on p. 39). The first artist to paint a contemporary political rather than military history subject, Copley included in that work portraits of fifty-five Members of Parliament. Copley recorded the moment in which William Pitt, the Earl of Chatham, collapsed in the House of Lords after passionately arguing for continuing the British war effort against the rebellious American colonies, which were the source of new English wealth based on trade.

Copley must have felt confident that this novel painting, his first large-scale history painting following the successful *Watson and the Shark* (cat. 4), would further his claim to fame; he also hoped the work would reap financial reward. Encouraged by Benjamin West, he painted the subject on speculation in 1779, and spent almost two years completing it. The process of taking portraits from the life of over fifty lords introduced the artist to the best connected and most influential members of the aristocracy. With the portrait studies for *The Death of the Earl of Chatham* in hand, Copley could offer his patrons a likeness at any time, free from the tedium of additional sittings.[1] Most importantly, the individual portraits, such as that of John, 2nd Viscount Dudley and Ward, of William Murray, 1st Earl of Mansfield (fig. 32 on p. 51), and of William Ponsonby, 2nd Earl of Bessborough (fig. 48 on p. 70), permanently made reference to the larger painting, for the sitters are posed as they appear in *The Death of the Earl of Chatham*.[2] They re-enact the role they play in the history painting, and by virtue of this their portraits convey the civic role of the sitters not only in the fictive space Copley created in the House of Lords, but in real life. By the same token the portraits are elevated into the higher genre of history painting – here, in a new and inventive way, Copley heeds Reynolds's advice on this subject and implements the strategy that Reynolds, the president of the Royal Academy, had devised for an artistic society dominated by 'face painters'.

A reviewer of the 1781 exhibition of *The Death of the Earl of Chatham* found Copley's depiction of John, 2nd Viscount Dudley and Ward within the large painting "capital."[3] The Viscount occupied a distinguished place in the composition (see detail) as the figure slightly left of center who directly faced and pointed to the ailing Chatham (who, in fact, died one month later, and not on Parliament premises as Copley imaginatively indicated). In the single-figure portrait of the Viscount, Copley repeats the profile pose and shows the sitter dressed in his Parliamentary robes of brilliant red fabric trimmed in ermine and gold braid. Beams of light illuminate his powdered

1966, II, pp.298, 413, figs. 405, 618 (engraving).

3. *The Gazetteer*, 5 May 1781, quoted in Prown 1966, II, p. 286 note 23.

4. After completing *The Siege of Gibraltar*, Copley painted a portrait of an officer that he had included in in the larger painting and who had since died: *Colonel George Lewis* (1794, The Detroit Institute of Arts).

5. Prown 1966, II, pp. 361–2, 388, figs. 631–2. John Ward, 2nd Viscount Dudley and Ward succeeded to his father's title in 1774. A Tory and a supporter of Lord North's ministry, he served as a Member of Parliament for Marlborough from 1754 to 1761, and for Worcestershire from 1761 to 1774, before entering the House of Lords at his father's death. His half-brother, William Ward, succeeded in 1788, and was married to Julia Bosville of Guntwaite. See Valentine 1970, pp. 905–6.

6. Copley tried unsuccessfully to sell *The Death of the Earl of Chatham* at auction. It sold by lottery in 1806 to Alexander Davison.

7. Quoted in Prown 1966, II, p. 358; written by Copley's son, John Singleton Copley, Jr.

wig and his back, and cast his face partially in shadow, as in the larger painting. Instead of setting the figure in the House of Lords, Copley surrounds him with the standard props of portraiture: patterned green damask drapery, columns, red roses leading to a brilliant sky, and a table covered with a patterned carpet. Instead of pointing to a figure of the Earl of Chatham, the Viscount points to a table featuring pen and ink, a book, papers, and, most importantly, a letter addressed to the sitter, which identifies him and indicates his role as a civic leader.

The circumstances surrounding the commission of the portrait are unknown. The title inscribed on the letter conforms closely to that listed in the Royal Academy exhibition catalogue of 1804, which notes "no. 96, The Right Honorable Viscount Dudley and Ward," suggesting that this portrait was the painting Copley exhibited that year. Copley may, however, have painted the portrait years earlier, perhaps during the time in which he painted the portraits of the other sitters in the history painting, or as a posthumous portrait after the sitter died in 1788.[4] It is also possible that Copley painted the Viscount's (posthumous) portrait at the same time as he painted John's half-brother, the 3rd Viscount Dudley and Ward, and his wife, whose pendant portraits Copley exhibited to the Royal Academy in 1800.[5] Whether the portrait was painted in the 1780s or around 1800, Copley may have chosen to exhibit it in 1804 in order to keep the idea of *The Death of the Earl of Chatham* in circulation at a time when he was trying, albeit unsuccessfully, to sell it.[6]

Copley's insistence on including portraits in history painting stemmed, in part, from his desire to elevate the popular genre of portraiture into the realm of history painting, and to record, however imaginatively, contemporary nationalist themes. As he had claimed in his brochure for the painting *The Victory of Admiral Duncan* (fig. 40 on p. 63), "The introduction of portraits in works of this nature must infinitely enhance their value, as well to the present age as to posterity. And here, perhaps, posterity may be mentioned without presumption, since, whatever are the merits of the artist, a painting which records so glorious and splendid an event can never be neglected or forgotten."[7] While the single-figure portraits Copley generated following *The Death of the Earl of Chatham* indicate his desire to further the Academy program of elevating portraiture, at the same time they represent another sign of Copley's entrepreneurial spirit on the competitive London scene.

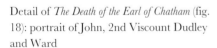

Detail of *The Death of the Earl of Chatham* (fig. 18): portrait of John, 2nd Viscount Dudley and Ward

38.
The Red Cross Knight, 1793

Oil on canvas, 84 × 107¹/₂ in. (213.5 × 273 cm)

Illustration reflects conservation in progress

National Gallery of Art, Washington, D.C., Gift of
Mrs. Gordon Dexter, 1942.4.2

PROVENANCE: The artist, London, until 1815;
his son, John Singleton Copley, Jr., Lord
Lyndhurst, London, until 1863; (Lyndhurst sale,
Christie's, London, 5 March 1864, no. 86); to
Clarke for the artist's granddaughter, Mrs. Charles
Amory (Martha Babcock Greene Amory) and her
husband Charles Amory, Boston; purchased in
1872 by their daughter, Mrs. Franklin Gordon
Dexter (Susan Greene Amory Dexter) and son-in-
law Franklin Gordon Dexter, Boston; their son
Gordon Dexter, Boston; his widow, Mrs. Gordon
Dexter (Isabella Hunnewell Dexter); National
Gallery of Art, Gift of Mrs. Gordon Dexter, 1942.[1]

SELECTED EXHIBITIONS: London 1793, no. 75;
Boston 1871–3, no. 242; Washington, D.C., New
York, Boston 1965–6, no. 90.

SELECTED REFERENCES: Perkins 1873,
pp. 98–9, 133; Amory 1882, pp. 75, 104, 453–5;
Bayley 1910, p. 85; Bayley 1915, pp. 32, 35–6,
170, 205–6; Bolton and Binsse 1930, p. 116;
Prown 1966, II, pp. 342, 350, 388, 403, 445,
fig. 592; Bradley 1980, p. 42; Walker 1984,
p. 390, no. 554.

RELATED WORKS: Study for *The Red Cross
Knight*, *ca.* 1793, oil on canvas, 17 × 21 in.
(43.25 × 53.25 cm), Yale Center for British Art,
Paul Mellon Collection.

NOTES

1. See Miles 1994, pp. 76–80, for an informative
discussion of the painting, including a full exhibition history and references to the painting.

2. Copley was on the exhibition hanging committee and secured one of the four central places in
the Great Room for exhibiting the painting, with
West receiving two and Lawrence one. See Prown
1966, II, p. 342.

3. Spenser 1596/1981, pp. 160–77.

4. *The True Briton*, Wednesday, 1 May 1793, *The
London Chronicle*, 27–30 April 1793, and *The Public
Advertiser*, 30 April 1793. See National Gallery
curatorial files for full typescript for these and
other reviews, and a listing in Miles 1994, p. 81.

5. For example, the portrait of *Lady Caroline
Harbord*, later Lady Suffield (1793, Marquess of
Lothian) by Thomas Lawrence hung prominently
in the same Academy show.

6. *The True Briton*, 1 May 1793. See Bradley 1980,
pp. 31–51, for a discussion of how Spenser's poem
became a rich source for British artists interested in
sublime themes of Gothic subject matter.

Copley exhibited *The Red Cross Knight* at the Royal Academy exhibition in 1793, the year after his
rival Benjamin West was elected president. This was the first time since 1786 that he submitted
his work to the annual Royal Academy show, and the timing was not coincidental: Copley strove
to assert his rank by showing this large painting prominently hung in the Great Room, a visual
reminder to all viewers of his allegiance to the institution and his formidable position within it.[2]

The painting appeared in the Academy exhibition catalogue with the title "*Portraits in the
characters of the Red Cross knight, Fidelia and Speranza*," characters who appear in Book I, canto 10 of
The Faerie Queene (1596) by Edmund Spenser, the Elizabethan poet whose work was enormously
popular during this time. The portraits are of Copley's children, John, Jr. (later Lord Lyndhurst),
age twenty-one, as the Knight on the left; Elizabeth, age twenty-three, as Fidelia in the center;
and Mary, age twenty, as Speranza on the right. The passage Copley chose focuses on the
beleaguered knight, who is brought to Dame Celia's "house of Holinesse,/ Where he is taught
repentance, and the way to heauenly blesse" by several characters including Fidelia (Faith) and
Speranza (Hope).[3]

Copley remains true to the elided text, picturing the knight striding in to see Fidelia in "lilly
white" and Speranza in "blew": "two most goodly virgins come in place,/ Ylinked arme in arme
in louely wise,/ With countenance demure, and modest grace" (stanza 12:13–14). Fidelia, a
heavenly light shining around her, holds a book and a gold cup filled with wine and water and a
serpent coiled within it, while Speranza lovingly grasps her arm, her eyes heavenward in prayer.
In the story, Fidelia taught the knight "celestiall discipline" from her book, while Speranza gave
him "comfort sweet," supportive roles virtuous eighteenth-century women were expected to fulfill (stanzas 18:8, 22:1).

As visually close to the text as Copley is, the painting remains, as Copley titled it, a series of
portraits (of his children) playing the role of virtuous characters in one of the most famous poems
in English literature. An exhibition reviewer recognized the painting as "a Family Picture, which
represents the Son and Daughters of the artist who painted it," and, another, as an "allegorical,
historical, and portraitical picture," as if to spoof the commingling of genres that had become
such a distinguishing feature of eighteenth-century British art.[4] John strides in from left, his silver
shield held aloft, the red cross emblazoned on his armor, and red drapery swirling around him,
but both Elizabeth and Mary are costumed in the latest London fashions, including classically
inspired headwraps not unlike the garments affected by stylish society portraitists.[5] Their modern
dress, graceful gestures, elongated limbs, and the swirling sky that forms their backdrop set them
apart. Copley conceived *The Red Cross Knight* in terms of fashionable portraiture, but with enough
literary associations to qualify it as history painting. As one critic wrote, the painting included
"images of fairy and chivalric history," an indication of how some viewers may have received
Copley's painting in terms of the Gothic revival then sweeping British architecture, literature,
and art.[6]

The Red Cross Knight is an anomaly in Copley's career; never before and never again would he
paint a subject from a literary source. Many English artists from the 1770s onward appropriated
subjects from the works of English poets – particularly Spenser – and Copley was a latecomer in
joining them. This phenomenon derived in part from the relationships among printers, book
publishers, and artists: books such as John Boydell's Shakespeare Gallery (1786–1805) and Thomas
Macklin's *Poets' Gallery* (1788–99) celebrated British authors such as Chaucer, Spenser,
Shakespeare, Pope, and Goldsmith.[7] Such ventures disseminated 'culture' to a broader public
than ever before, and contributed to the democratization of the visual arts that began to occur
during the eighteenth century. Artists and print publishers recognized that subjects taken from
celebrated British authors and poets would appeal to audiences perhaps unfamiliar with erudite
subjects from the classical past. By choosing to illustrate the great works of their literary history,
eighteenth-century British artists could associate themselves with a longer established, already
celebrated tradition.[8] By extension, the sitters would be crowned by the venerated literary association the painter gave them. This element of role-playing flattered the sitters at the same time as
it insinuated them into a distinguished English literary heritage.

Spenserian subjects had no pictorial record at the Royal Academy until the 1770s.[9] Not
surprisingly, many artists borrowed pictorial sources for the new literary themes from venerated

7. Altick 1978, pp. 106–8 and Boase 1963. Other important publishing ventures included Macklin's *Illustrated Bible* (1791–1800) and Robert Bowyer's illustrated *History of England* (1792–1805) by David Hume. Copley appears on the prospectus lists of both Bowyer's *History of England* (presumably for an illustration of his large history painting *Charles I Demanding in the House of Commons the Five Impeached Members*, 1782–95, City of Boston, Boston Public Library) and Boydell's *Shakespeare Gallery*; ultimately, he did not contribute to either. See Prown 1966, II, p. 344 and 306 note 5.

8. John Quincy Adams (cat. 39), when sitting to Copley for his portrait in 1796, penned several lines of poetry celebrating *The Red Cross Knight*, which possibly alludes to this beneficial association between artist and author: "Yet here to rob the poet's store/ (And let the Muse the crime disclose)/ T'is but to gild the golden ore,/ And add new fragrance to the rose" (Copley Family Papers, Acc. 10, 122.1, Library of Congress, dated 24 May 1793).

9. Spenser's characters served as portrait guises for 18th-century sitters and the events of the story served to increase the repertoire of history subjects. For example, Benjamin West exhibited one of the first Spenserian subjects at the Royal Academy in 1772, *Una and the Lion (Mary Hall in the Character of Una)* (fig. 70), followed by others such as *Fidelia and Speranza* (fig. 38) in 1777. John Hamilton Mortimer submitted *Sir Arthegal the Knight of Justice, with Talus the Iron Man* in 1778; Thomas Daniell *The Red Cross Knight and Una* in 1780, the same year as Reynolds's *The Character of Spenser's Una as Mrs. Mary Beauclerc*. The same year Copley submitted *The Red Cross Knight*, Henry Fuseli displayed *Amoret Delivered from the Enchantment of Busirane by Britomart*.

classical, mythological and biblical subjects. Copley was no exception: Speranza's heavenward glance is similar to images of saints and virgins in biblical themes, and the knight's pose is not unlike the Borghese *Gladiator's* (Musée du Louvre, Paris), which features one arm upraised, the other stretched back behind as he strides forward. Copley borrowed Fidelia's pose from the classical past by way of, for example, Joshua Reynolds's portrait of *Miss Mary Meyer in the character of Hebe* (fig. 79), which it closely follows in pose and swirling drapery. Similar to Fidelia, Hebe, whose mythological youth and beauty would be appropriate for images of young sitters, raises her arms to display a ritual vessel as her drapery circles behind her.

While Copley's name appears on prospectus lists for Robert Bowyer's *Hume's History of England* and John Boydell's *Shakespeare Gallery*, he never produced paintings for them. Copley's choice of *The Faerie Queene* may have been an effort to secure a position within the coterie of artists including Reynolds, Gainsborough, Lawrence, and Fuseli commissioned to produce work for Macklin's *Poets' Gallery*. More likely, however, given Copley's demonstrated difficulty working with engravers, publishers, and entrepreneurs, he preferred to maintain his tradition of working virtually alone, painting large history paintings of national or topical interest, displaying them for a fee, publishing an engraving, and reaping most of the profits personally. That Copley painted a portrait in the guise of a literary subject in 1793 marks his versatility as a painter, as well as his desire to remain *au courant* in the London artistic world by contributing to the trend of literary role-playing in fashionable portraiture.

Fig. 79 Joshua Reynolds
Miss Mary Meyer in the Character of Hebe, 1772
Oil on canvas, 51¼ × 39½ in. (130 × 100 cm)
The National Trust – Rothschild Collection, Ascott

39.
John Quincy Adams (1767–1848), 1796

Oil on canvas, 30 × 25 in. (76.2 × 63.5 cm)

Museum of Fine Arts, Boston, Bequest of Charles Francis Adams, 1917.1077

PROVENANCE: Mrs. John Adams (Abigail Smith Adams), Boston, until 1818; her son, John Quincy Adams (the sitter), Washington, D.C., until 1848; his son, Charles Francis Adams, Boston, until 1886; his son, Charles Francis Adams, Washington, D.C.; the Museum of Fine Arts, Boston, Bequest of Charles Francis Adams, 1917.

SELECTED EXHIBITIONS: Boston 1938, no.1; Washington, New York, Boston 1965–6, no. 92; Washington, D.C. 1970, no.3.

SELECTED REFERENCES: Perkins 1873, p. 27; Bayley 1915, p. 39; Bolton and Binsse 1930, p. 116; Bigot [n.d.], p. 53; Prown 1966, II, pp. 300, 343, fig. 598; Oliver 1970a, pp. 37–41; Oliver 1970b, pp. 25, 28.

In early 1797, soon after John Adams was inaugurated in Philadelphia as the second President of the United States, Abigail Smith Adams, who although First Lady was still in Boston, received a crate which she had not been expecting. Upon opening it she found a portrait by Copley of her son John Quincy Adams, to whom she wrote: "It is allowed to be as fine a portrait as ever was taken, and what renders it peculiarly valuable to me is the expression, the animation, the true Character which gives it so pleasing a likeness ... It ... is painted in a masterly manner. No present could have been more acceptable."[1]

Along with Copley's 1782 likeness of Elkanah Watson (cat. 11), *John Quincy Adams* is the only portrait of Copley's career in England for which the circumstances of commission and even the portrait sittings are well documented. In this case, we know that the artist's wife Susannah commissioned the portrait for the sitter's mother, Abigail Smith Adams. Despite their political differences, the elder Adams and Copleys had spent time together when John Adams and his wife visited London in the 1780s, and in 1783 Copley painted a full-length portrait of John Adams surrounded by symbols alluding to the peace treaty with Great Britain (fig. 80).[2] The Copleys were also acquainted with the Adams' son in the mid-1790s, when the young man was serving as Foreign Minister to the Netherlands, and was engaged in London on diplomatic business from October 1795 to May 1796.[3] Mrs. Copley, who, according to the sitter, had desired to send

Fig. 80 John Singleton Copley
John Adams, 1783

Oil on canvas, 93³/₄ × 57¹⁵/₁₆ (238.1 × 147.3 cm)
Courtesy of the Harvard University Art Portrait Collection, Bequest of Ward Nicholas Boyston, 1828, to Harvard College

NOTES

1. Abigail Adams, Quincy, to John Quincy Adams, 23 June 1797 (Adams Family Papers, Massachusetts Historical Society, Boston), quoted in Oliver 1970a, p. 38.
2. See Prown 1966, II, p. 300; also Adams 1840, pp. 199–241. The collection of the Chicago Historical Society includes the plum-colored suit Adams wore for this portrait.
3. In 1794, President Washington appointed Adams Minister Resident to the Netherlands. He received a commission in 1795 to travel to London to exchange ratifications of John Jay's treaty with Great Britain. In 1803, he became a Senator; in 1817, Secretary of State; from 1825 to 1829, President of the United States; and he represented Plymouth in Congress until his death in 1848. See also Adams 1874–77.
4. John Quincy Adams to Abigail Adams, 29 July 1797 (Adams Family Papers, Massachusetts Historical Society, Boston), quoted in Oliver 1970a, p. 40.
5. Bigot [n.d.], p. 53.
6. For information regarding the Copley estate, Mt. Pleasant, on Beacon Hill, and other family affairs, see Prown 1966, II, pp. 340–1.
7. Diary of John Quincy Adams, Adams Family Papers, Massachusetts Historical Society, Boston, roll 27. From 11 February to 4 April, John Quincy Adams sat to Copley seven times (11, 15, 19 February, 4, 5, 28 March, 4 April), and had dinner with him once (23 March 23). On 11 February 1796, he wrote: "At Mr. Copley's to sit for my picture, which Mrs. Copley professes to send to my mother."
8. Ibid., 23 March 1796.
9. Adams's comments regarding Copley's "finely finished" painting of The Three Youngest Daughters of King George III probably refers to the painting made for the engraving published in 1792. See Prown 1966, II. p. 416.
10. Stuart had, in fact, already painted the so called Vaughan portrait of George Washington in the winter of 1795, a painting that created a sensation and affirmed his status as the greatest portraitist living in America.
11. One month after Copley finished Adams's portrait, Adams and Louisa Catherine Johnson, daughter of Joshua Johnson, American consul in London, became engaged.
12. 129 July 1797, Diary of John Quincy Adams (Adams Family Papers, Massachusetts Historical Society, Boston), quoted in Oliver 1970a, p. 40.
13. 15 August 1843, ibid., quoted in Oliver 1970b, pp. 26, 28.
14. Ibid. Adams also praised Stuart's portrait of 1825, Asher B. Durand's portrait of 1836, and a miniature in a bracelet painted for his mother in 1795 (John Quincy Adams to his mother, 29 July 1797, Adams Family Papers, Massachusetts Historical Society, Boston), quoted in Oliver 1970a, p. 40.

Abigail Adams "some token of her remembrance and regard, and thinking a likeness of your [Mrs. Adams's] Son, would answer the purpose," asked John Quincy Adams, aged twenty-eight at the time, to sit to her husband for his portrait.[4] The famous portraitist George P.A. Healy recorded a slightly different, although not incompatible, account of the commission. According to Healy, the sitter said that Copley "took great pains with [the portrait] and sent it as a present to my mother in acknowledgement of some service I had been able to render him."[5] Perhaps the younger Adams had provided introductions or some assistance to John Singleton Copley, Jr., who was then visiting Boston in an attempt to settle long-standing family business affairs.[6]

A conscientious recorder of his life, John Quincy Adams noted the seven dates on which he posed for Copley, beginning on 11 February and ending 4 April 1796.[7] Most diary entries simply mention that he sat at "Mr. Copleys" for his portrait, but two listings provide greater insight into Copley's studio life. On 4 March 1796, Adams wrote: "At Mr. Copley's all the morning sitting for my picture. Conversation with him political, metaphysical, and critical. His opinions not accurate, but well meaning." Adams's comments suggest that sittings with the artist were not a dull affair of silence and frozen gestures, but could be a lively and serious discourse during which the artist could observe the sitter. Adams's condescending tone toward a celebrated artist twenty-five years his senior conveys either his youthful political fervor, or his easy fits of pique; he not only found Copley's opinions inaccurate, he found Copley and the Loyalist "refugees," he wrote, "almost intolerable."[8]

Later, on 28 March, Adams wrote, "At Mr. Copley's all the morning, sitting again for my picture. Stayed there too long gazing at his Charles [Charles I Demanding in the House of Commons the Five Impeached Members], and at a portrait of the 3 youngest princesses [The Three Youngest Daughters of King George III, a version of cat. 33], a finely finished thing."[9] To Adams and probably to other sitters, Copley gave a tour, commenting on the various paintings in his studio. Thus the sitting would include stimulating conversation with the artist, a possible history lesson from the large paintings still in his studio, and a retrospective tour of the artist's work.

Compared with other portraits the artist painted in England, John Quincy Adams is startling in its technique and in its simplicity. More thinly painted and with colors less saturated than in his other portraits, the portrait is truly, in the words of Abigail, "fine," in the delicate, almost ethereal sense of the word. Copley poses Adams slightly at an angle, and shows him staring directly at the viewer. The broadly painted background landscape, the swirls of white paint that indicate his stock, and the wispy threads of loosened hair contrast with the smooth, finely painted facial features of the sitter. He appears gallant yet unpretentious, dignified but accessible. The portrait's delicate wispiness, indeed, seems closer in style to the work of Gilbert Stuart than to Copley's own. Did Copley have Gilbert Stuart in mind when he painted Adams's portrait, a painting he knew was destined for an American audience already completely captivated by the recently returned Stuart?[10] In addition, at the very moment Copley painted his portrait, Adams was courting the woman he was to marry, making the painting's 'romantic' qualities the perfect compliment to the sitter's situation.[11]

John Quincy Adams agreed with his mother that Copley "produced a very excellent picture."[12] Five years before he died, Adams complained to his diary: "This is about the 45th time I have sitten for my pictures, and I question whether another man lives who has been so wofully and so variously bedaubed as I have been."[13] By the end of his life, Adams had served as sixth President of the United States, as Secretary of State, as Representative and Senator to Congress, and as Foreign Minister, and throughout his long career in politics, his image had been recorded dozens of times in paint, marble, and daguerrotype by such well known American artists as John Singleton Copley, Gilbert Stuart, Thomas Sully, Asher B. Durand, Horatio Greenough, and Hiram Powers. Looking back on his life, however, he singled out several portraits that he believed were "the only ones worthy of being preserved," among them the portrait by Copley. It may be that he remembered, half a century later, the gratitude he had felt to the Copleys, as he had written to his mother, "for a present so flattering to me, and in your maternal kindness so acceptable to you."[14]

40.

Baron Graham (Robert Graham, 1744–1836), 1804

Oil on canvas, 57¼ × 46⅞ in. (144.8 × 118.8)

Signed center left on base of column: *J S Copley.R.A.pinx.*

National Gallery of Art, Washington, D.C., Gift of Mrs. Gordon Dexter, 1942.4.1

PROVENANCE: The sitter, Robert Graham, until 1836; to Sir George Henry Smyth, 6th baronet, Berechurch Hall, Colchester, Essex, until 1852; Smyth's grandson, Thomas George Graham White, Wethersfield Manor and Berechurch Hall, Colchester, Essex, until 1878; (sale, Christie's, London, 23 March 1878, no. 25); to Graves; to the artist's granddaughter, Mrs. Charles Amory (Martha Babcock Greene Amory), Boston, until 1880; her husband, Charles Amory, Boston, until 1898; his daughter, Mrs. Franklin Gordon Dexter (Susan Greene Amory Dexter), Boston, until 1924; her son Gordon Dexter, Boston, until 1937; his widow, Mrs. Gordon Dexter (Isabella Hunnewell Dexter), Boston, until 1942; the National Gallery of Art, Washington, D.C., Gift of Mrs. Gordon Dexter, 1942.

SELECTED EXHIBITIONS: London 1804, no. 21; Washington, New York, Boston 1965–6, no. 102; Baltimore 1968, no. 22.

SELECTED REFERENCES: *The Morning Post*, 18 April 1804, p. 3; *The Times*, 28 April 1804, p. 2; *The Daily Advertiser*, 30 April 1804, p. 3; *Oracle*, 30 April 1804, p. 3; *True Briton*, 30 April 1804, p. 3; *The Morning Herald* 1804, p. 3; *The Morning Chronicle*, 30 April 1804, p. 3; *The Daily Advertiser*, 5 May 1804, p. 3; *Oracle*, 5 May 1804, p. 3; *True Briton*, 5 May 1804 p. 3; *The St. James's Chronicle: Or, British Evening-Post*, 12-15 May 1804, p. 4; Cunningham 1831/1837/1868, V, p. 184; Perkins 1873, pp. 18–9, 129; Perkins 1873 Supplement, pp. 18–9; Amory 1882, pp. 239, 241–2, 244; Bayley 1910, p. 43; Bayley 1915, pp. 33, 122; Bolton and Binsse 1930, p. 116; Prown 1966, II, pp. 373–4, 388, 421 and fig. 653; Williams 1981, p. 31, repro. p. 35; Walker 1984, p. 390, no. 555.[1]

NOTES

1. For full bibliographic information, see Miles 1994.
2. See Prown 1966, II, pp. 372–84.
3. Edward L. Morse, ed., *Samuel F.B. Morse: His Letters and Journals* (Boston and New York, 1914), I, p. 47, quoted in Prown 1966, II, p. 381.

Fig. 81 John Singleton Copley

George John, Second Earl Spencer, 1799–1806

Oil on canvas, 104 × 67 in. (264.2 × 170.2 cm)

Reproduced by kind permission of the 9th Earl Spencer

After the turn of the century, Copley encountered controversy in the Academy, the beginnings of ill health, and mounting financial worries.[2] By 1811, the young and promising American artist, Samuel F.B. Morse, noticed signs of infirmity in the aging artist, observing of Copley's late work that "it is really a lamentable thing that a man should outlive his faculties."[3] But as the artist's career began to falter, his son's promising legal career was on the rise, eventually leading to the younger Copley's election to Parliament in 1819, and, beginning in 1827, the same year he was

4. Lord Lyndhurst would eventually become a figure in the kind of contemporary history paintings his father essentially invented as well as popularized. Sir George Hayter's monumental contemporary history painting, *The Trial of Queen Caroline* (1820, The National Portrait Gallery, London), features young Copley in ceremonial robes in a prominent position in a painting similar in composition to his father's *The Death of the Earl of Chatham*.

5. Susanna Copley to Betsy Copley Greene, London, 1 March 1803, as quoted in Miles 1994, p. 88.

6. Miles suggests that this portrait is one of friendship. She suggests that Baron Graham commissioned his painting in memory of his friend Sir Robert Smyth who had died two years before, and to whose family Graham bequeathed his portrait.

7. Miles 1994, p. 88.

8. See *The Times*, 28 April 1804, and *The St. James's Chronicle: Or, British Evening-Post*, 12-15 May 1804, quoted in Miles 1994, p. 88.

9. *The Morning Herald*, 30 April 1804 p. 3, and *The Daily Advertiser*, 30 April 1804, p. 3; *Oracle*, 30 April 1804, p. 3, and *True Briton*, 30 April 1804, p. 3, as quoted in Miles 1994, p. 88. The last reviewer, however, presumably familiar with the sitter, found Graham's portrait "indifferent," noting that the sitter has "more of the milk of human kindness in his visage than the Painter is pleased to allow him."

created Baron Lyndhurst, the first of his three appointments as Lord Chancellor.[4]

In 1803, John Jr. was still a law student, but it was probably through the connections that he had made in his early career that Copley received the commission to paint Judge Graham, the strongest portrait of the older Copley's later career. In March of that year, Susanna Copley wrote to her daughter in Boston that the young Copley would be spending five weeks traveling in England with "Judge Graham as Marshal on the Circuit," a duty he repeated later that year.[5] As Attorney General to the Prince of Wales (1793), Baron of the Exchequer (1799), and a Knight of the Realm (1800), Graham, twenty-seven years young Copley's senior, would have been a distinguished mentor, counting among the early important champions of the young attorney's career.[6] As Miles has suggested, the professional connection between young Copley and Graham, both graduates of Trinity College, Cambridge, likely led Graham to choose his young friend's father to undertake his portrait.[7]

The portrait is vividly colored, with brilliant red robes the complement of bright green patterned drapery, and relieved by the softer rose damask on the gilded armchair, and broad patches of white ermine. The surrounding props – a monochrome background, a single column, the edge of a table featuring a letter addressed to "Baron Graham" – do not vie for the viewer's attention, but provide the elements necessary to the identification of the sitter, and the establishment of his dignified judicial status. The portrait is among the most tightly controlled in Copley's œuvre, vivid proof that even after the turn of the century he could produce exceptional portraits whose tight manner helped him to convey the serious demeanor of sitters devoted to civic duty – as if Copley were still heeding Richardson's dicta on *gravitas* and on brushwork almost a century after they were issued (see cat. 39).

Here, as in other portraits, Copley seems to take special delight in the ceremonial robes of his sitters. In George John, Second Earl Spencer (fig. 81), Copley lavished the kind of attention associated with his colonial career on the elaborate trimmings and accessories of the uniform of the Order of the Garter. The portraits of both Spencer and Graham, in particular, indicate Copley's unparalleled talent in layering different shades of white to create textural variety: the luxurious plumes and cream white stripes of Spencer's costume parallel, in the portrait of Graham, the luxuriant softness of the sitter's ermine-trimmed robe, played off against the crispness of his starched linen collar. The fur trim here is probably the most convincing material that Copley ever painted.

Reviewers at the 1804 Royal Academy exhibition, where the portrait was first exhibited, did not, however, mention Graham's exceptional fur. Instead, they commented on his likeness, calling it "strong," "striking and animated," perhaps responding to the vibrant colors in combination with Graham's ruddy complexion.[8] One critic found it among the most important portraits in the exhibition, a measure of Copley's continuing good reputation despite professional disappointments.[9] The portrait is most remarkable for its evidence of Copley's ability to alter his style at will, for he was just as capable of producing a portrait with a brilliant 'general effect' – as he had in the portrait of John Quincy Adams of 1796 (cat. 39) – rather than one with minute attention to detail and specific parts. Graham's portrait proves that Copley's story in England is not one of gradual development into English and Continental manner – a linear progression from tightly controlled brushwork and composition to broader handling and freer compositions. Copley accommodated his style to the subject at hand, proving himself a master of decorum, expression, and image.

Abrams 1979
Abrams, Ann Uhry, 'Politics, Prints and John Singleton Copley's 'Watson and the Shark,' *Art Bulletin* 61 (June 1979), pp. 265–76

_____1985
The Valiant Hero: Benjamin West and Grand Style History Painting, Washington, D.C.: Smithsonian Institution Press, 1985

Adam 1970
Adam, Frank, *The Clans, Septs, and Regiments of the Scottish Highlands*, 8th edn., rev. Sir Thomas Innes of Learney, Baltimore: Genealogical Publishing, 1970

Adams 1840/1
Letters of Mrs. Adams, the Wife of John Adams, 3rd edn., vol 2, intro. Charles Francis Adams, Boston: Charles C. Little & James Brown, 1841

Adams 1874–77
The Memoirs of John Quincy Adams, Comprising Portions of his Diary from 1795–1848, ed. Charles Francis Adams, 12 vols.

Addison 1924
Addison, Julia de Wolf, *The Boston Museum of Fine Arts*, 2nd edn. Boston, 1924

Ahrens 1978
Ahrens, Kent, 'American Paintings before 1900 at the Wadsworth Atheneum,' *Antiques* 114, no. 3 (September 1978), pp. 508–19

Algarotti 1764
Algarotti, Count Francesco, *An Essay on Painting*, London: Printed for L. Davis & C. Reymers, 1764

Allard 1983
Allard, Joseph, 'West, Copley, and Eighteenth-Century American Provincialism,' *Journal of American Studies* 17, no. 3 (1983), pp. 391–416

Allen 1944
Allen, Josephine L., 'An English Copley,' *Metropolitan Museum Bulletin* 11 (1944), pp. 260–2

Allen 1987
Allen, Brian, *Francis Hayman*, New Haven and London: Yale University Press, in association with English Heritage (The Iveagh Bequest, Kenwood) and the Yale Center for British Art, 1987

Altick 1978
Altick, Richard D., *The Shows of London*, Cambridge and London: The Belknap Press of Harvard University Press, 1978

Amory 1882
Amory, Martha Babcock, *The Domestic and Artistic Life of John Singleton Copley, R.A.*, Boston: Houghton Mifflin, 1882; reprint New York 1969

Analectic 1815
Anonymous, 'Remarks on the Progress and Present State of the Fine Arts in the United States,' *Analectic Magazine* 6 (1815), pp. 363–76

Art Interchange 1889
Art Interchange (23 July 1889), p. 165

Artist 1780
'An Artist,' *A Candid Review of the Exhibition (Being the Twelfth) of the Royal Academy 1780, Dedicated to His Majesty By an Artist*, 2nd edn. London: H. Reynell & T. Evans, 1780

Austin 1806/1966
Austin, Gilbert, *Chironomia or A Treatise on Rhetorical Delivery*, 1806; ed. Mary Margaret Robb and Lester Thonssen, Carbondale and Edwardsville: Southern Illinois University Press, 1966

Ayling 1972
Ayling, Stanley Edward, *George the Third*, New York: Alfred A. Knopf, 1972

Ayres 1993
Picturing History: American Painting, 1770–1930, ed. William S. Ayres, New York: Rizzoli in association with Fraunces Tavern Museum, New York, 1993 (accompanied traveling exhibition of the same title)

Baker 1936
Baker, C.H. Collins, *Catalogue of British Paintings in the Henry E. Huntington Library and Art Gallery*, intro. Sir Charles Holmes, San Marino, California, 1936

Baldini and Casazza 1992
Baldini, Umberto and Casazza, Ornella, *The Brancacci Chapel*, New York: Harry N. Abrams, 1992

Baltimore 1968
From El Greco to Pollock: Early and Late Works by European and American Artists, Baltimore, Baltimore Museum of Art, exhib. cat., 1968

Baretti 1781
Baretti, Giuseppe Marco Antonio, *A Guide Through the Royal Academy*, London: T. Cadell, 1781

Barker 1950a
Barker, Virgil, *American Painting: History and Interpretation*, New York: Macmillan, 1950

Barker 1950b
Barker, Virgil, 'Copley's American Portraits,' *Magazine of Art* 43 (March 1950), pp. 82–88

Barrell 1986
Barrell, John, *The Political Theory of Painting from Reynolds to Hazlitt*, New Haven and London: Yale University Press, 1986

Bayley 1910
Bayley, Frank, *Sketch of the Life and a List of Some of the Works of John Singleton Copley*, Boston 1910

_____1915
The Life and Works of John Singleton Copley, Boston: Taylor Press, 1915

Benjamin 1880
Benjamin, Samuel G.W., *Art in America, A Critical and Historical Sketch*, New York: Harper & Brothers, 1880

Berlin, Zurich 1988–9
Bilder aus der Neuen Welt: Amerikanische Malerei des 18. und 19. Jahrhunderts, Berlin, Orangerie des Schlosses Charlottenburg; Zurich, Kunsthaus, exhib. cat., 1988–9

Bermingham 1986
Bermingham, Ann, *Landscape and Ideology: The English Rustic Tradition, 1740–1860*, Los Angeles, Berkeley, and London: University of California Press, 1986

Bigot [n.d.]
Bigot, Marie Healy, *Life of G.P.A. Healy*, privately printed [n.d.]

Birmingham 1934
Jubilee Commemorative Exhibition of the Treasures of the Gallery, Birmingham (England), City of Birmingham Museum and Art Gallery, exhib. cat., 1934

Birmingham, Sheffield, Bolton, Swansea, Plymouth 1961–2
Diploma and other Pictures from the Collections of the Royal Academy, Birmingham (England), Birmingham City Art Gallery; Sheffield, Graves Art Gallery; Bolton, Art Gallery; Swansea, Glynn Vivian Art Gallery; Plymouth, Plymouth City Art Gallery, cat. for Arts Council touring exhib., 1961–2

Bland 1727/1759
Bland, Humphrey, *A Treatise of Military Discipline: In Which is Laid down and Explained the Duty of the Officer and Soldier; through the Several Branches of the Service*, 1727; 8th edn. London: Printed for R. Baldwin, *et al.*, 1759

Boase 1963
Boase, T.S.R., 'Macklin and Bowyer,' *Journal of the Warburg and Courtauld Institutes* 26 (1963), pp. 148–77

_____1966
'Biblical Illustration in Nineteenth-Century English Art,' *Journal of the Warburg and Courtauld Institutes* 29 (1966), pp. 349–67

Boime 1989
Boime, Albert, 'Blacks in Shark-Infested Waters: Visual Encodings of Racism in Copley and Homer,' *Smithsonian Studies in American Art* 3 (Winter 1989), pp.19–47

_____1990
The Art of Exclusion: Representing Blacks in the Nineteenth Century, Washington, D.C., 1990

Bolton and Binsse 1930
Bolton, Theodore, and Binsse, Harry Lorin, 'John Singleton Copley,' *Antiquarian* 15 (December 1930), pp. 76–83, 116, 188

Boston 1928
Boston Athenaeum Annual Exhibition, Boston, Boston Athenaeum, exhib. cat., 1873

Boston 1873
Boston Athenaeum Annual Exhibition, Boston, Boston Athenaeum, exhib. cat., 1873

_____1874
Boston Athenaeum Annual Exhibition, Boston, Boston Athenaeum, exhib. cat., 1874

_____1938
John Singleton Copley: American Portraits in Oil, Pastel, and Miniature, Boston, Museum of Fine Arts, exhib. cat. by Barbara Neville Parker, 1938

Boston 1970
Masterpieces of Painting in the Metropolitan Museum of Art, Boston, Museum of Fine Arts, exhib. cat. by E.A. Standen and T.M. Folds, 1970

_____1976
John Singleton Copley, Gilbert Stuart, and Benjamin West in America and England, Boston, Museum of Fine Arts, exhib. cat., 1976

_____1980
The Boston Tradition: American Paintings from the Museum of Fine Arts, Boston, Boston, Museum of Fine Arts, exhib. cat. by Carol Troyen, New York: The American Federation of Arts, 1980

Boston, Cleveland, Houston 1992
The Lure of Italy: American Artists and the Italian Experience, 1760–1914, Boston, Museum of Fine Arts; Cleveland Art Museum; Houston, Museum of Fine Arts, exhib. cat. by Theodore E. Stebbins, *et al.*, New York: Harry N. Abrams in association with Museum of Fine Arts, Boston, 1992

Boston, Detroit, Washington 1993
John Singleton Copley's "Watson and the Shark," Boston, Museum of Fine Arts; Detroit Institute of Arts; Washington, D.C., National Gallery of Art, exhib. brochure by Ellen G. Miles, 1993

Bournemouth 1957
Diploma Works from the Royal Academy, Bournemouth (England), Russell-Cotes Art Gallery and Museum, exhib. cat., 1957

Bowron 1983
Ed. Bowron, Edgar Peters, *Introduction to the Collections*, Raleigh: North Carolina Museum of Art, 1983

Boydell Leaflet 1796
Leaflet announcing delivery of the print for *The Death of Major Peirson* on 2 May 1796, published by John Boydell, and including description of the event, copy in the National Art Library, Victoria and Albert Museum, London

Bradford 1971
Bradford, Ernle, *Gibraltar: The History of a Fortress*, New York: Harcourt Brace Jovanovich, 1971

Bradley 1980
Bradley, Laurel, 'Eighteenth-Century Paintings and Illustrations of Spenser's Faerie Queene: A Study in Taste,' *Marsyas: Studies in the History of Art* 20 (1979–80), pp. 31–51

Breen 1988
Breen, T.H., '"Baubles of Britain:" The American and Consumer Revolutions of the Eighteenth Century,' *Past and Present* 119 (1988), pp. 73–104

Breen 1990
Breen, T.H., 'The Meaning of "Likeness:" American Portrait Painting in an Eighteenth Century Consumer Society,' *Word and Image* 6, no. 4 (October-November 1990), pp. 325–50

Browne-Wilkinson 1982
Browne-Wilkinson, Virginia, *Pepperrell Posterity*, Florence (Italy): privately printed, 1982

Bruntjen 1974/1985
Bruntjen, Sven H.A., *John Boydell (1719–1804): A Study of Art Patronage and Publishing in Georgian London*, Ph.D. diss., Stanford University, 1974; New York and London: Garland Publishing, 1985

Bryant 1829
Bryant, William Cullen, 'To Thomas Cole, The Painter, Departing for Europe,' 1829; in *American Art 1700–1960, Sources and Documents*, ed. John W. McCoubrey and H.W. Janson, Englewood Cliffs, New Jersey: Prentice-Hall, 1965

Burke 1757/1958
Burke, Edmund, *A Philosophical Enquiry into the Origin of Our Ideas of the Sublime and Beautiful*, 1757; reprint Notre Dame, Indiana: University of Notre Dame Press, 1958

Caffin 1907
Caffin, Charles H., *The Story of American Painting*, New York: Frederick A. Stokes, 1907

Cambridge 1972
American Art at Harvard, Cambridge, Harvard University Art Museum, exhib. cat., 1972

_____1977
Master Paintings from the Fogg Collections, Cambridge, Fogg Art Museum [no. cat], 1977

Chicago 1933
A Century of Progress, Chicago, Art Institute, exhib. cat., 1933

Cholmondeley 1950
Ed. Cholmondeley, R.H., *The Heber Letters, 1783–1832*, London: Batchworth Press, 1950

Christman 1978
Christman, Margaret C.S., *Fifty American Faces from the Collection of the National Portrait Gallery*, Washington, D.C.: Smithsonian Institution Press, 1978

Colley 1984
Colley, Linda, 'The Apotheosis of George III: Loyalty, Royalty, and the British Nation, 1760–1820,' *Past and Present* 102 (1984), pp. 94–129

Combe 1777
Combe, William, *A Poetical Epistle to Sir Joshua Reynolds, [Knight] and President of the Royal Academy*, London: Printed for Fielding and Walker, 1777

Comstock 1942
Comstock, Helen, 'Drawings by J.S. Copley in the Karolik Collection,' *The Connoisseur* 109, no. 484 (July 1942), pp. 150–3

Connoisseur 1946
Ed. Fell, H. Granville, 'American Paintings Shown in London,' *The Connoisseur* 118, no. 505 (September 1946), p. 57

Council Minutes
Council Minutes of the Royal Academy of Arts, 1768–1950

Cunningham 1831/1837/1868
Cunningham, Allan, *The Lives of the Most Eminent British Painters and Sculptors*, 1831; 2nd edn., 6 vols., London, 1837; reprint, 5 vols., New York: Harper & Brothers, 1868

Curwen 1972
Curwen, Samuel, *The Journal of Samuel Curwen, Loyalist*, ed. Andrew Oliver, 2 vols., Cambridge: Harvard University Press, 1972

Davis 1983
Davis, Lennard J., *Factual Fictions: The Origins of the English Novel*, New York: Columbia University Press, 1983

Detroit 1934
American Portrait Painting, Detroit Institute of Arts [no exhib. cat.; exhib. checklist in Richardson 1934]

_____1991
American Paintings in the Detroit Institute of Arts. Vol. 1. Works by Artists Born Before 1816, New York: Hudson Hills Press in association with the Founders Society Detroit Institute of Arts, 1991

Dinnerstein 1981
Dinnerstein, Lois, 'The Industrious Housewife: Some Images of Labor in American Art,' *Arts Magazine* 55 (April 1981), pp.109–19

Dublin, London, Paris, Liverpool, Cambridge 1976–7
One Hundred American Drawings: Loan Exhibition from the Collection of John Davis Hatch, Dublin, National Gallery of Ireland; London, Heim Gallery; Paris, Galerie Heim; Liverpool, Walker Art Gallery; Cambridge (England), Fitzwilliam Museum, essay by John Wilmerding, entries by Gary Burger, exhib. cat., 1976–7

Duncan 1973
Duncan, Carol, 'Happy Mothers and Other New Ideas in French Art,' *Art Bulletin* 55 (December 1973), pp. 570–83

Dunlap 1834/1969
Dunlap, William, *A History of the Rise and Progress of the Arts of Design in the United States*, 1834; ed. Rita Weiss, reprint, 2 vols. bound as 3, New York: Dover Publications, 1969

Earland 1910
Earland, Ada, *Ruskin and his Circle*, London: Hutchison, 1910

Ear-Wig 1781
The Ear-Wig; or An Old Woman's Remarks on the Present Exhibitions of Pictures at the Royal Academy, London: G. Kearsly, 1781

Farington 1978–
Farington, Joseph, *The Farington Diary*, edd. Kenneth Garlick and Angus MacIntyre, 16 vols., New Haven and London: published for the Paul Mellon Centre for Studies in British Art by Yale University Press, 1978

Flexner 1948
Flexner, James Thomas, *John Singleton Copley*, Boston: Houghton Mifflin, 1948

Fliegelman 1982
Fliegelman, Jay, *Prodigals and Pilgrims: The American Revolution against Patriarchal Authority, 1750–1800*, Cambridge: Cambridge University Press, 1982

Fort and Quick 1991
Fort, Susan, and Quick, Michael, *American Art: A Catalogue of the Los Angeles Museum of Art Collection*, Los Angeles: Los Angeles County Museum of Art, distributed by University of Washington Press, 1991

Frankenstein 1970
Frankenstein, Alfred, *et al.*, *The World of Copley 1738–1815*, New York: Time-Life Books, 1970

Friedman 1976
Friedman, Winifred, *Boydell's Shakespeare Gallery*, New York: Garland Publishing, 1976

Fryd 1995
Fryd, Vivien Green, 'Rereading the Indian in Benjamin West's *The Death of General Wolfe*,' *American Art* 9, no. 1 (Spring 1995), pp. 73–85

Fryer 1984
Fryer, Peter, *Staying Power: The History of Black People in Britain*, London and Sydney 1984

Galt 1820
Galt, John, *The Life and Works of Benjamin West, Esq., President of the Royal Academy of London, Subsequent to his Arrival in this Country: Composed from Materials Furnished by Himself ... Part II*, London 1820

Gilpin 1809
Gilpin, William, *Observations on Several Parts of the Counties of Cambridge, Norfolk, Suffolk, and Essex*, London: T. Cadell & W. Davies, 1809

Grand Rapids 1943
Exhibition, Grand Rapids, Michigan, Art Gallery [no cat.], 1943

Green 1988
Green, Benny, *A History of Cricket*, London: Barrie & Jenkins, 1988

Greenwich 1976
1776: The British Story of the American Revolution, Greenwich, National Maritime Museum, exhib. cat., 1976

Gruber 1972
Gruber, Ira D., *The Howe Brothers and the American Revolution*, New York: Atheneum, for the Institute of Early American History and Culture at Williamsburg, Virginia, 1972

_____1980
'For King and Country: The Limits of Loyalty of British Officers in the War for American Independence,' in *Limits of Loyalty*, ed. Edgar Denton, III, Waterloo, Ontario: Wilfrid Laurier University Press, 1980

Gustafson 1978
Gustafson, Eleanor H., 'Museum Accessions,' *Antiques* 112, no. 6 (June 1978), p. 1256

Hagen 1940
Hagen, Oskar, *The Birth of an American Tradition in Art*, New York: Charles Scribner's Sons, 1940

Harrington 1993
Harrington, Peter, *British Artists and War: The Face of Battle in Paintings and Prints, 1700–1914*, London: Greenhill Books, and Rhode Island: Stackpole Books in association with Brown University, 1993

Harris 1990
Harris, Eileen, 'Robert Adam's Ornaments for Alderman Boydell's Picture Frames,' *Furniture History* 26 (1990), pp. 92–7

Harris 1966
Harris, Neil, *The Artist in American Society: The Formative Years, 1790–1860*, New York: Braziller, 1966

Hartley [ca. 1930]
Hartley, Marsden, 'Copley's Americanism,' in *On Art*, ed. with intro. Gail R. Scott, New York: Horizon Press [ca. 1982]

Hartford 1952
Art of the Bible in Five Centuries, Hartford, Connecticut, Wadsworth Atheneum [no cat.], 1952

Hartmann 1901
Hartmann, Sadakichi, *A History of American Art*, 2 vols., Boston: L.C. Page & Co., 1901

Haskell and Penny 1981
Haskell, Francis, and Penny, Nicholas, *Taste and the Antique*, New Haven and London: Yale University Press, 1981

Hecht 1954
Hecht, J. Jean, *Continental and Colonial Servants in Eighteenth-Century England*, Smith College Studies in History 40, 1954

_____1956
The Domestic Servant Class in Eighteenth-Century England, London: Routledge & Paul, 1956

Hedley 1967
Hedley, Olwen, *Windsor Castle*, London: Robert Hale, 1967

Hibbert 1964
Hibbert, Christopher, *The Court at Windsor: A Domestic History*, London: Longmans Green & Co., 1964

Hipkiss 1941
Hipkiss, Edwin J., *Eighteenth-Century American Arts: The M. and M. Karolik Collection*, with notes on drawings and prints by Henry P. Rossiter, comments on collection by Maxim Karolik, Boston 1941

Hole 1948
Hole, Christina, *English Sports and Pastimes*, London: B.T. Batsford, 1948

Hollander 1978
Hollander, Anne, *Seeing Through Clothes*, New York: Viking Press, 1978

Honour 1989
Honour, Hugh, *The Image of the Black in Western Art*, vol. 4, part 1, Houston: Menil Foundation, distributed by Harvard University Press, 1989

Hoppner 1785
Hoppner, John, in *The Morning Post*, London, 5 May 1785

Howard 1894–5
Howard, Cecil Hampden Cutts, 'The Pepperrell Portraits,' *Historical Collections of the Essex Institute*, vol. 31, Salem, Mass.: printed for the Essex Institute, 1894–5

Howgego 1958
Howgego, James L., 'Copley and the Corporation of London,' *Guildhall Miscellany* 1, no. 9 (July 1958), pp. 34–43

Hull 1976
American Artists in Britain, Hull (England), North Humberside Arts Association Gallery; Leeds, University Art Gallery, exhib. cat., 1976

Hume 1770
Hume, David, *The History of Great Britain, from the Accession of James I to the Revolution in 1688*, 8 vols., London 1770

Hutchison 1968
Hutchison, Sidney C., *The History of the Royal Academy, 1768–1968*, New York: Taplinger Publishing, 1968

Isham 1905/1907/1942
Isham, Samuel, *The History of American Painting*, New York: Macmillan, 1905; reprint 1907, 1942

Jaffe 1975
Jaffe, Irma, *John Trumbull: Patriot-Artist of the American Revolution*, Boston: New York Graphic Society, 1975

_____1977
'John Singleton Copley's *Watson and the Shark*,' *American Art Journal* 9 (May 1977), pp. 15–25

Johnson 1976
Johnson, Edward Mead, *Francis Cotes*, Oxford: Phaidon Press, 1976

Kemp 1989
Leonardo On Painting, ed. and trans. Martin Kemp and Margaret Walker, New Haven and London, Yale University Press, 1989

Knox 1916/1968
The Journal of Captain John Knox, ed. Arthur G. Doughty, 3 vols., Champlain Society X, 1916; facsimile edn. New York: Greenwood Press Publishers, 1968

La Follette 1929
La Follette, Suzanne, *Art in America*, New York and London: Harper & Brothers, 1929

Larkin 1949/1960
Larkin, Oliver W., *Art and Life in America*, revised and enlarged edn. New York: Holt, Rinehart & Winston, 1949; reprint 1960

Le Brun 1698/1734/1980
Le Brun, Charles, *Conférence de M. Le Brun sur l'expression générale et particulière*, Paris, 1698; *Method to Learn to Design the Passions*, trans. John Williams, 1734; reprint Los Angeles: The Augustan Reprint Society, William Andrews Clark Memorial Library, University of California, 1980

Lee 1967
Lee, Rensselaer W., *Ut Pictura poesis: The Humanistic Theory of Painting*, New York and London: W.W. Norton & Co., 1967

Leeds 1868
National Exhibition of Works of Art, Leeds (England), exhib. cat., 1868

LeGates 1976
LeGates, Marlene, 'The Cult of Womanhood in Eighteenth-Century Thought,' *Eighteenth-Century Studies* 10, no. 1 (Fall 1976), pp. 21–39

Letters of Copley and Pelham 1914/1972
Letters and Papers of John Singleton Copley and Henry Pelham, 1739–1776, ed. Guernsey Jones, Boston: Massachusetts Historical Society, 1914; reprint New York: AMS Press, 1972

Lipking 1970
Lipking, Lawrence, *The Ordering of the Arts in Eighteenth Century England*, Princeton, New Jersey: Princeton University Press, 1970

Lippincott 1983
Lippincott, Louise, *Selling Art in Georgian London: The Rise of Arthur Pond*, New Haven and London: Yale University Press for the Paul Mellon Centre for Studies in British Art, 1983

Locke 1693/1913
Locke, John, *Some Thoughts Concerning Education*, London 1693; reprint Cambridge: Cambridge University Press, 1913

London 1777
London, Royal Academy of Arts, exhib. cat., 1777

_____1778
London, Royal Academy of Arts, exhib. cat., 1778

London 1780
London, Royal Academy of Arts, exhib. cat., 1780

_____1783
London, Royal Academy of Arts, exhib. cat., 1783

_____1785
London, Royal Academy of Arts, exhib. cat., 1783

_____1793
London, Royal Academy of Arts, exhib. cat., 1793

_____1804
London, Royal Academy of Arts, exhib. cat., 1804

_____1817
Exhibition of Pictures by Deceased British Artists, London, British Institution, exhib. cat., 1817

_____1862
International Exhibition, London, exhib. cat., 1862

_____1865
London, British Institution, exhib. cat., 1865

_____1868
National Portrait Exhibition, London, South Kensington [Victoria & Albert] Museum, exhib. cat., 1868

_____1934
A Loan Exhibition Depicting Children Throughout the Ages, London, Chesterfield House, exhib. cat., 1934

_____1946
Exhibition of the King's Pictures, London, Royal Academy of Arts, 1946–7

_____1946–7
American Painting from the Eighteenth Century to the Present Day, London, The Tate Gallery, exhib. cat., 1946

_____1951–2
The First Hundred Years of the Royal Academy, 1768–1868, London, Royal Academy of Arts, exhib. cat., 1951–2

_____1963
Treasures of the Royal Academy, London, Royal Academy of Arts, exhib. cat., 1963

_____1968–9
Royal Academy of Arts Bicentenary Exhibition, 1768–1968, London, Royal Academy of Arts, exhib. cat., 1968–9

_____1986
Reynolds, London, Royal Academy of Arts, exhib. cat. ed. Nicholas Penny, London: Weidenfeld and Nicolson, 1986

London 1991
From Reynolds to Lawrence: The First Sixty Years of the Royal Academy of Arts and its Collection, London, Royal Academy of Arts, exhib. cat. by Helen Valentine, 1991

_____1992–3
The Swagger Portrait: Grand Manner Portraiture in Britain from Van Dyck to Augustus John, 1630–1930, London, Tate Gallery, exhib. cat. by Andrew Wilton, 1992

_____1994
Gainsborough and Reynolds: Contrasts in Royal Patronage, London, Buckingham Palace, The Queen's Gallery, exhib. cat., 1994

Longinus
Longinus, *On the Sublime*, trans. A.O. Prickard, Oxford: Clarendon Press, 1906; 1926

Los Angeles 1974
American Narrative Painting, Los Angeles County Museum of Art, exhib. cat., 1974

_____1975
Los Angeles County Museum of Art, exhib. cat., entry by Donelson Hoopes and Nancy D.W. Moure, 1975

_____1981–2
American Portraiture in the Grand Manner, Los Angeles County Museum of Art, exhib. cat. by Michael Quick, 1981–2

Lovell 1987
Lovell, Margaretta, 'Reading Eighteenth-century American Portraits,' *Winterthur Portfolio* 22, no. 4 (Winter 1987), pp. 243–64

_____1991
'To be "Conspecuous in the Croud:" John Singleton Copley's *Sir William Pepperrell and his Family*,' *North Carolina Museum of Art Bulletin* 15 (1991), pp. 29–42

Maarinan 1988
Maarinan, Michael, *Painting Politics for Louis-Philippe: Art and Ideology in Orleanist France, 1830–1848*, New Haven and London: Yale University Press, 1988

MacLean 1900
MacLean, J.P., *An Historical Account of the Settlements of Scotch Highlanders in America Prior to the Peace of 1783*, Cleveland: The Helman-Taylor Company; Glasgow: John Mackay, 1900

Magazine of Art 1879
'Life of John Singleton Copley, R.A.,' *The Magazine of Art*, London, Paris,

and New York: Cassell, Petter, Galpin, 1879

Manchester 1857
Art Treasures Exhibition, Manchester (England), exhib. cat., 1857

Mantz 1862
Mantz, Paul, 'Exposition de Londres: Ecole Anglaise,' *Gazette des Beaux Arts* 13 (July 1862), pp. 97–125

Mason 1879
Mason, George C., *The Life and Works of Gilbert Stuart*, 2 vols., New York: Charles Scribner's Sons, 1879

Mayne 1981
Mayne, Richard, *The Battle of Jersey*, London: Phillimore & Co., 1981

McClenen 1977
Compiler Edward W. McClenen, *Boston Marriages from 1700 to 1809*, vol. 1752–1809, Baltimore: Genealogical Publishing, 1977

McGuyre and Wakefield 1988
Compilers McGuyre, Ruth C., and Wakefield, Robert S., *Mayflower Families in Progress, Edward Winslow of the Mayflower and His Descendants for Five Generations*, Plymouth, Mass.: General Society of Mayflower Descendants, 1988

McLanathan 1986
McLanathan, Richard, *Gilbert Stuart*, New York: Harry N. Abrams in association with The National Museum of American Art, Smithsonian Institution, 1986

Metropolitan Museum of Art 1965
American Paintings. A Catalogue of the Collection of The Metropolitan Museum of Art. Painters Born by 1815, catalogue by Albert TenEyck Gardner and Stuart P. Feld, New York: Metropolitan Museum of Art, 1965

_____1975–6
Metropolitan Museum of Art Bulletin 33, no. 4 (Winter 1975–6): no. 24 [n.p.]

_____1994
American Paintings in the Metropolitan Museum of Art. Vol 1. A Catalogue of Works by Artists Born by 1815, catalogue by John Caldwell and Oswaldo Rodriguez Roque with Dale T. Johnson, ed. Kathleen Luhrs, New York: Metropolitan Museum of Art in association with Princeton University Press, 1994

Mexico City 1980–1
La Pintura de Los Estados Unidos de Museos de la Ciudad de Washington, Mexico City, Museo del Palacio de Bellas Artes, exhib. cat., 1980–1

Miles 1993
Miles, Ellen G., 'Copley's *Watson and the Shark*,' *Antiques* 143 (January 1993), pp. 167–71

_____1994
American Paintings of the Eighteenth Century: The Collection of the National Gallery of Art Systematic Catalogue, Cambridge: Cambridge University Press, National Gallery of Art, 1994

Millar 1969
Millar, Oliver, *The Later Georgian Pictures in the Collection of Her Majesty the Queen*, 2 vols., London: Phaidon, 1969

Minneapolis 1952
Great Portraits by Famous Painters, Minneapolis Institute of Arts, exhib. cat., 1952

Mitchell 1944
Mitchell, Charles, 'Benjamin West's "Death of General Wolfe" and the Popular History Piece,' *Journal of the Warburg and Courtauld Institutes* (1944), pp. 20–33

Montagna 1981
Montagna, Dennis, 'Benjamin West's "The Death of Wolfe": A Nationalist Narrative,' *American Art Journal* 12 (Spring 1981), pp. 72–88

Montreal 1950
The Eighteenth Century Art of France and England, Montreal Museum of Fine Arts, exhib. cat., 1950

_____1967
The Painter and the New World: A Survey of Painting from 1564 to 1867, Marking the Founding of the Canadian Confederation, Montreal Museum of Fine Arts, exhib. cat., 1967

Morris 1966
Morris, John L., *Versions of the Self: Studies in English Autobiography from John Bunyan to John Stuart Mill*, New York and London 1966

Museum of Fine Arts, Boston 1892
Catalogue of Paintings and Drawings, with a Summary of Other Works of Art, Exhibited on the Second Floor, Third Edition, Winter 1891–1892, 1892

_____1895
Catalogue of Paintings and Drawings, with a Summary of Other Works of Art, Exhibited on the Second Floor, Winter 1895–1896, Boston 1895

_____1903
Museum of Fine Arts, Boston Bulletin 18 (1903)

New Haven 1990
Crown Pictorial: Art and the British Monarchy, New Haven, Conn., Yale Center for British Art, exhib. cat. by Linda Colley, *et al.*, 1990

New York 1909
The Hudson-Fulton Celebration, New York, Metropolitan Museum of Art, exhib. cat., 1909

_____1929
Exhibition, New York, Rinehardt Gallery [no cat.], 1929

_____1936
Franklin and His Circle, New York, Metropolitan Museum of Art, exhib. cat., 1936

_____1937
An Exhibition of Paintings by John Singleton Copley, New York, Metropolitan Museum of Art, exhib. cat., 1937

_____1958
Masterpieces from Wadsworth Atheneum, Hartford, Connecticut, New York, Knoedler Galleries, exhib. handbook, 1958

_____1958–9
Fourteen American Masters, New York, Metropolitan Museum of Art [no. cat.], 1958–9

_____1975–7
The Heritage of American Art, New York, Metropolitan Museum of Art; Dallas, Dallas Museum of Fine Arts; Denver, The Denver Art Museum; Des Moines, Des Moines Art Center; Minneapolis, The Minneapolis Institute of Arts, exhib. cat., New York: American Federation of Arts, 1975–7

_____1990–1
Drawings by John Singleton Copley in the Metropolitan Museum of Art, exhib. cat., 1990–91

New York, Boston, Houston, Milwaukee 1995
John Singleton Copley in America, New York, Metropolitan Museum of Art; Boston, Museum of Fine Arts; Houston, Museum of Fine Arts; Milwaukee Art Museum, exhib. cat., New York: Metropolitan Museum of Art, 1995

Nicolson 1968
Nicolson, Benedict, *Joseph Wright of Derby, Painter of Light*, 2 vols., London: Routledge & Kegan Paul; New York: Pantheon Books for The Paul Mellon Foundation for British Art, 1968

Northcote 1818
Northcote, James, *The Life of Sir Joshua Reynolds*, 2nd edn. London 1818

Nottingham 1959
Diploma Work and other Paintings by the Early Members of the Royal Academy, Nottingham (England), Nottingham University Art Gallery, exhib. cat., 1959

Novak 1969
Novak, Barbara, *American Painting of the 19th Century*, New York: Praeger, 1969

Oakland 1969
Art Treasures in California, Oakland, California, Oakland Museum, exhib. cat., 1969

O'Doherty 1965
O' Doherty, Barbara Novak, 'Copley: Eye and Idea,' *Art News* 6, no. 5 (September 1965), pp. 22, 57

Oliver 1970a
Oliver, Andrew, *Portraits of John Quincy Adams and His Wife*, Cambridge: Belknap Press, Harvard University, 1970

_____1970b
'J.Q. Adams was the Nation's Most Indifferent Sitter,' *Smithsonian Magazine* 1, no. 7 (October 1970), pp. 24–33

Painted Word 1991
The Painted Word: British History Painting, 1750–1830, ed. Peter Cannon-Brookes, Woodbridge (England): The Boydell Press for the Heim Gallery, 1991

Paris 1938
Trois Siècles d'Art aux Etats Unis, Paris, Musée du Jeu de Paume, exhib. cat., 1938

Parker and Wheeler 1938
Parker, Barbara Neville, and Wheeler, Ann Bolling, 'John Singleton Copley: American Portraits,' in Boston 1938

Parsons 1855
Parsons, Usher, *The Life of Sir William Pepperrell, Bart.*, Boston: Little, Brown & Co., 1855

Pasquin 1796
Pasquin, Anthony [John Williams], *Memoirs of The Royal Academicians*, London: Cornmarket, 1796

Paul 1906
Ed. Paul, Sir James Balfour, *The Scots Peerage*, vol. 3, Edinburgh: David Douglas, 1906

Peale 1983
The Selected Papers of Charles Willson Peale and His Family, ed. Lillian B. Miller, vol. 1, *Charles Willson Peale: Artist in Revolutionary America, 1735–1791*; vol. 3, *The Belfield Farm*

Years, 1810–1820, New Haven and London: Yale University Press for the National Portrait Gallery, Smithsonian Institution, 1983

Peale 1855
Peale, Rembrandt, 'Reminiscences, Exhibitions and Academies,' *The Crayon* 1 (9 May 1855), p. 19

Peirson 1784
Proposals By Mr. Boydell, For Publishing by Subscription, an Engraved Print, from the Original Picture, Painted by John Singleton Copley, R.A., Representing the Death of the Late Major Peirson, and the Defeat of the French Troops in the Island of Jersey, 1781. To be Engraved by Mr. Heath, London, 22 May 1784 (original at Tate Gallery, London)

Perkins 1873
Perkins, Augustus Thorndike, *A Sketch of the Life and Some of the Works of John Singleton Copley*, Boston: James R. Osgood & Co., 1873 (includes Supplement)

Perkins 1928
Perkins, Mary Hallowell, *The Servant Problem and the Servant in English Literature*, Boston: Richard G. Badger at the Gorham Press, 1928

Pinto 1928
Pinto, V. de Sola, *The Poetical and Dramatic Works of Sir Charles Sedley*, 2 vols., London: Constable & Co., 1928

Pittsburgh 1940
Survey of American Painting, Pittsburgh, Carnegie Institute, exhib. cat., 1940

Plees 1817
Plees, W., *An Account of the Island of Jersey*, Southampton (England): T. Baker, 1817

Pliny
Gaius Plinius Secundus, *Natural History*, Books 33–35, Loeb Classical Library 9, London and Cambridge, Mass., 1952

Pocock 1975
Pocock, J.G.A., *The Machiavellian Moment*, Princeton, New Jersey: Princeton University Press, 1975

Poesch 1988
Poesch, Jessie, 'A British Officer and His "New York" Cottage: An American Vernacular brought to England,' *American Art Journal* 20, no. 4 (1988), pp. 74–97

Pointon 1993
Pointon, Marcia, *Hanging the Head: Portraiture and Social Formation in Eighteenth-Century England*, New Haven and London: Yale University Press for

the Paul Mellon Centre for Studies in British Art, 1993

Potts 1994
Potts, Alex, *Flesh and The Ideal: Winckelmann and the Origins of Art History*, New Haven and London: Yale University Press, 1994

Praz 1971
Praz, Mario, *Conversation Pieces: A Survey of the Informal Group Portrait in Europe and America*, University Park: Pennsylvania State University Press, 1971

Providence 1991
The Martial Face: The Military Portrait in Britain, 1760–1900, Providence, Rhode Island, David Winton Bell Gallery, List Art Center, Brown University, exhib. cat., 1991

Prown 1966
Prown, Jules David, *John Singleton Copley*, 2 vols., Cambridge: Harvard University Press for the National Gallery of Art, 1966

_____1969
American Painting from its Beginnings to the Armory Show, Cleveland: Skira, 1969

_____1986
'Benjamin West's Family Picture: A Nativity in Hammersmith,' in *Essays in Honor of Paul Mellon, Collector and Benefactor*, ed. John Wilmerding, Washington, D.C.: National Gallery of Art, 1986

Quincy 1879
Quincy, Eliza Susan, *List of Pictures and Furniture, etc., in the House Built 1770 in 1879*, private collection; photostat, The Joseph Downs Collection of Manuscripts and Printed Ephemera, Winterthur Library, Wilmington, Delaware

Raleigh 1963
Carolina Charter Tercentenary Exhibition, Raleigh, North Carolina Museum of Art, exhib. cat., 1963

Rather 1993
Rather, Susan, 'Stuart and Reynolds: A Portrait of Challenge,' *Eighteenth Century Studies* 27 (Fall 1993), pp. 61–84

Rebora 1990
Rebora, Carrie, *The American Academy of the Fine Arts, New York, 1802–1842*, 2 vols., Ph.D. diss., City University of New York, 1990

Redgrave 1866
Redgrave, R. and S., *A Century of*

Painters of the English School, vol. 1, London: Smith, Elder & Co., 1866

Reynolds 1826
Reynolds, Frederick, *The Life and Times of Frederick Reynolds*, 2 vols., London: Henry Colburn, 1826

Reynolds 1769–90/1959/1975
Reynolds, Sir Joshua, *Discourses on Art*, ed. Robert R. Wark, Henry E. Huntington Library and Art Gallery, 1959; New Haven and London: Yale University Press for the Paul Mellon Centre for Studies in British Art, 1975

Ribeiro 1984
Ribeiro, Aileen, *Dress in Eighteenth-Century Europe, 1715–1789*, London: Batsford, 1984

Richardson 1934
Richardson, Edgar P., 'American Portrait Painting,' *Detroit Institute of Arts Bulletin* 14, no. 1 (October 1934), pp. 11–14

_____1952–3
'"Head of a Negro" by John Singleton Copley,' *Art Quarterly* 15 (Winter 1952), pp. 351–2, taken from *idem*, in *Detroit Institute of Arts Bulletin* 32 (1952–3)

Richardson 1715/1725/1971
Richardson, Jonathan, *An Essay on the Theory of Painting*, 1715; 1725; reprint Menston (England): Scolar Press, 1971

Richter 1992
Richter, Simon, *Laocoön's Body and the Aesthetics of Pain*, Ph.D. diss., Johns Hopkins University, 1990; Detroit: Wayne State University Press, 1992

Roberts 1985
English Origins of New England Families, selected and introduced by Gary Boyd Roberts, 2nd series in 3 vols., Baltimore: Genealogical Publishing, 1985

Roberts 1987
Roberts, Jane, *Royal Artists*, London: Grafton Books, 1987

Roberts 1993
Roberts, Perri Lee, *Masolino da Panicale*, Oxford: Clarendon Press, 1993

Roche 1989/1994
Roche, Daniel, *The Culture of Clothing: Dress and Fashion in the 'ancien regime,'* 1989; trans. Jean Birrell, Cambridge: Cambridge University Press, 1994

Rolde 1982
Rolde, Neil, *Sir William Pepperrell of Colonial New England*, Brunswick, Maine: Harpswell Press, 1982

Rose 1989
Rose, Clare, *Children's Clothes Since 1750*, London: B.T. Batsford, 1989

Rosenblum and Janson 1984
Rosenblum, Robert, and Janson, H.W., *Nineteenth-Century Art*, Englewood Cliffs, New Jersey and New York, 1984

Rousseau 1762/1979
Rousseau, Jean-Jacques, *Emile, or On Education*, trans. Allan Bloom, New York: Basic Books, 1979

Royal Pictures 1860
'The Royal Pictures,' *The Art-Journal*, 1860

Rutledge 1957
Rutledge, Anna Wells, 'American Loyalists – A Drawing for a Noted Copley Group,' *Art Quarterly* 20 (Summer 1957), pp. 195–203

St. Louis 1947
Forty Masterpieces, St. Louis City Art Museum, exhib. cat., 1947

San Diego 1992
The Great Age of Sail: Treasures from the National Maritime Museum, Greenwich, England, San Diego Museum of Art, exhib. cat. by Peter Kemp, 1992

Saunders 1990
Saunders, Richard, 'Genius and Glory: John Singleton Copley's "The Death of Major Peirson",' *American Art Journal* 22 (1990), pp. 5–39

Schimmelman 1983
Schimmelman, Janice G., 'A Checklist of European Treatises on Art and Essays on Aesthetics Available in America through 1815,' *Proceedings of the American Antiquarian Society* 93 (April 1983), pp. 95–195

_____1984
'Books on Drawing and Painting Techniques Available in Eighteenth-Century American Libraries and Bookstores,' *Winterthur Portfolio* 19 (Summer/Autumn 1984)

Sellers 1976
Sellers, Charles Coleman, *Patience Wright. American Artist and Spy in George III's London*, Middletown, Connecticut: Weslayan University Press, 1976

Shaftesbury 1727
Anthony Ashley Cooper, 3rd Earl of Shaftesbury, 'An Essay on Painting Being a Notion of the Historical Draught or Tablature of the Judgment of Hercules,' in *Characteristicks of Men, Manner, Opinions, Times*, 3 vols., London: J. Darby, 1727

Shank 1984
Shank, J. William, 'John Singleton Copley's Portraits: A Technical Study of Three Representative Examples,' *Journal of the American Institute for Conservation* 23 (1984), pp. 130–52

Shawe-Taylor 1990
Shawe-Taylor, Desmond, *The Georgians: Eighteenth-Century Portraiture and Society*, London: Barrie & Jenkins, 1990

Sherman 1978
Ed. Sherman, Robert M., *Mayflower Families Through Five Generations*, 2 vols., Plymouth, Mass.: General Society of Mayflower Descendents, 1978

Sheriff 1990
Sheriff, Mary, *Fragonard: Art and Eroticism*, Chicago and London: University of Chicago Press, 1990

Shipton 1972
Shipton, Clifford K., *Sibley's Harvard Graduates: Biographical Sketches of Those who Attended Harvard College*, vol. 16 (classes 1764–67), Boston: Massachusetts Historical Society, 1972

Simon 1987
Simon, Robin, *The Portrait in Britain and America*, Oxford: Phaidon; Boston: G.K. Hall, 1987

Sitwell 1936
Sitwell, Sacheverell, *Conversation Pieces*, London: B.T. Batsford, 1936

Slatkin and Shoolman 1947
Slatkin, Charles, and Shoolman, Regina, *Treasury of American Drawings*, New York 1947

Sloan 1982
Sloan, Kim, 'Drawing – A "Polite Recreation" in Eighteenth-Century England,' *Studies in Eighteenth-Century Culture* 11 (1982), pp. 217–40

Smart 1992
Smart, Alistair, *Allan Ramsay: Painter, Essayist, and Man of the Enlightenment*, New Haven and London: Yale University Press for The Paul Mellon Centre for Studies in British Art, 1992

Solkin 1986
Solkin, David H., 'Great Pictures or Great Men?: Reynolds, Male Portraiture, and the Power of Art,' *Oxford Art Journal* 9, no. 2 (1986), pp. 42–9

_____1992
Painting for Money: The Visual Arts and the Public Sphere in Eighteenth-Century England, New Haven and London: Yale University Press for the Paul Mellon Centre for Studies in British Art, 1992

Spenser 1596/1981
Spenser, Edmund, *The Faerie Queene*, ed. Thomas P. Roche, Jr., assisted by C. Patrick O'Donnell, Jr., New Haven and London: Yale University Press, 1981

Starr 1971
Starr, George A., *Defoe and Spiritual Autobiography*, New York 1989

Stein 1976
Stein, Roger, 'Copley's "Watson and the Shark" and Aesthetics in the 1770s,' in *Discoveries and Considerations: Essays on Early American Literature and Aesthetics*, ed. Calvin Israel, Albany: State University of New York Press, 1976

Stephen and Lee 1917
Ed. Stephen, Sir Leslie, and Lee, Sir Sidney, *Dictionary of National Biography*, Oxford: Oxford University Press, since 1917

Strong 1992
Strong, Roy, *Royal Gardens*, New York and London: Pocket Books, 1992

Strutt 1876
Strutt, Joseph, *Sports and Pastimes of the English People*, London: Chatto & Windus, 1876

Sutherland 1992
Ed. Guilland Sutherland, *British Art 1740–1820: Essays in Honor of Robert R. Wark*, San Marino, California: Huntington Library, 1992

Taylor 1979
Taylor, Arthur R., *Pub Games*, London: Mayflower, 1979

Townsend 1966
Townsend, Gertrude, 'Portrait by John Singleton Copley of a Lady "Knotting,"' *Wadsworth Atheneum Bulletin* 2, no. 2 (Fall 1966), pp. 12–23

Tuckerman 1867
Tuckerman, Henry T., *Book of the Artists*, New York: G.P. Putnam & Son, 1867

Turnbull 1740
Turnbull, George, *A Treatise on Ancient Painting*, London: A. Millar, 1740

Valentine 1970
Valentine, Alan, *The British Establishment 1760–1784*, 2 vols., Norman: University of Oklahoma Press, 1970

Van der Kiste 1992
Van der Kiste, John, *George III's Children*, Wolfeboro Falls, N.H.: Alan Sutton Publishing, 1992

V & A Press Cuttings
Press cuttings collected at the National Art Library of the Victoria and Albert Museum, London

Von Erffa and Staley 1986
Von Erffa, Helmut, and Staley, Allen, *The Paintings of Benjamin West*, New Haven and London: Yale University Press, 1986

Walker 1984
Walker, John, *National Gallery of Art*, rev. edn. New York 1984

Washington 1968
Survey of American Art, National Collection of Fine Arts, Washington, D.C., Smithsonian Institution, exhib. cat., 1968

_____1970
The Life Portraits of John Quincy Adams, Washington, D.C., National Portrait Gallery, Smithsonian Institution, exhib. cat. introduced by Marvin Sadik, 1970

_____1970–1
Great American Paintings from the Boston and Metropolitan Museums, Washington, D.C., National Gallery of Art; St. Louis City Art Museum; Seattle Art Museum, exhib. cat., 1970–1

_____1974
American Self-Portraits 1670–1973, Washington, D.C., National Portrait Gallery, Smithsonian Institution, exhib. cat. by Ann C. Van Devanter, 1974

_____1979
Return to Albion: Americans in England 1760–1940, Washington D.C., National Portrait Gallery, Smithsonian Institution, exhib. brochure by Richard Kenin, 1979

_____1987
American Colonial Portraits, 1700–1776, Washington, D.C., National Portrait Gallery, Smithsonian Institution, exhib. cat. by Ellen Miles and Richard Saunders, 1987

Washington, New York, Boston 1965–6
John Singleton Copley 1738–1815, Washington, D.C., National Gallery of Art; New York, Metropolitan Museum of Art; Boston, Museum of Fine Arts, exhib. cat. by Jules David Prown, 1965–6

Washington, New York 1990
Facing History: The Black Image in

American Art, 1710–1940, Washington, D.C., The Corcoran Gallery of Art; New York, The Brooklyn Museum, exhib. cat. by Guy C. McElroy, 1990

Waterhouse 1953/1969
Waterhouse, Ellis, *Painting in Britain 1530–1790*, 1953; Baltimore: Penguin Books, 1969

Watson 1856/1968
Ed. Watson, Winslow C., *Men and Times of the Revolution; or, Memoirs of Elkanah Watson, including Journals and Travels in Europe and America, From 1777 to 1824*, New York: Dana & Co., 1856; reprint Elizabethtown, N.Y.: Crown Point Press, 1968

Webb 1760
Webb, Daniel, *An Inquiry into the Beauties of Painting; and into the Merits of the Most Celebrated Painters, Ancient and Modern*, London: R. & J. Dodsley, 1760

Wellington, Canberra, Ottawa 1994–95
The Queen's Pictures: Old Masters from the Royal Collection, travelling exhibition, cat. by Christopher Lloyd, 1994–5

Whitley 1928/1968
Whitley, William T., *Artists and their Friends in England, 1700–1799*, 2 vols., New York and London: Benjamin Blom, 1928; reissued 1968

_____1932/1969
Gilbert Stuart, 1932; reprint, New York: Kennedy Galleries, Da Capo Press, 1969

Williams 1981
Williams, William James, *A Heritage of American Paintings from the National Gallery of Art*, Maplewood, New Jersey, 1981

Wilmerding 1980
Wilmerding, John, *American Light and the Luminist Movement 1850–1875*, Washington, D.C.: National Gallery of Art, 1980

_____1988
American Masterpieces from the National Gallery, New York: Hudson Hills Press, 1988

Wilson 1989
Wilson, R. Jackson, *Figures of Speech: American Writers and the Literary Marketplace, from Benjamin Franklin to Emily Dickenson*, New York 1989

Winckelmann 1765/1972
Winckelmann, Johann Joachim, *Reflections on the Painting and Sculpture of the Greeks*, trans. Henry Fusseli, 1765; reprint Menston (England): Scolar Press, 1972

Wind 1932/1986
Wind, Edgar, *Hume and the Heroic Portrait: Studies in Eighteenth-Century Imagery*, first given in lecture form at the Bibliothek Warburg, Hamburg, Germany, in 1932; ed. Jaynie Anderson, Oxford: Clarendon Press, 1986

_____1938–9
'The Revolution of History Painting,' *Journal of the Warburg and Courtauld Institutes* 2 (1938–9), pp. 116–27

Wood 1969
Wood, Gordon S., *The Creation of the American Republic, 1776–1787*, Chapel Hill: University of North Carolina Press, 1969

_____1992
The Radicalism of the American Revolution, New York: Alfred A. Knopf, 1992

Wrexham 1876
Art Treasures Exhibition of North Wales and the Border Counties, Wrexham (Wales), exhib. cat., 1876

Index of Paintings by John Singleton Copley